ANCIENT GREECE

FROM THE ARCHAIC PERIOD TO THE DEATH OF ALEXANDER THE GREAT

The Britannica Guide to Ancient Civilizations

ANCIENT GREECE

From the Archaic Period to the Death of Alexander the Great

Edited by Kathleen Kuiper, Manager, Arts and Culture

IN ASSOCIATION WITH

Published in 2011 by Britannica Educational Publishing
(a trademark of Encyclopædia Britannica, Inc.)
in association with Rosen Educational Services, LLC
29 East 21st Street, New York, NY 10010.

Distributed exclusively by Rosen Educational Services.
For a listing of additional Britannica Educational Publishing titles, call toll free (800) 237-9932.

First Edition

Britannica Educational Publishing
Michael I. Levy: Executive Editor
J.E. Luebering: Senior Manager
Marilyn L. Barton: Senior Coordinator, Production Control
Steven Bosco: Director, Editorial Technologies
Lisa S. Braucher: Senior Producer and Data Editor
Yvette Charboneau: Senior Copy Editor
Kathy Nakamura: Manager, Media Acquisition
Kathleen Kuiper: Manager, Arts and Culture

Rosen Educational Services
Alexandra Hanson-Harding: Editor
Nelson Sá: Art Director
Cindy Reiman: Photography Manager
Matthew Cauli: Designer, Cover Design
Introduction by Dan Faust

Library of Congress Cataloging-in-Publication Data

Ancient Greece: from the archaic period to the death of Alexander the Great / edited by Kathleen Kuiper.—1st ed.
p. cm.—(The Britannica guide to ancient civilizations)
"In association with Britannica Educational Publishing, Rosen Educational Services."
Includes bibliographical references and index.
ISBN 978-1-61530-120-1 (library binding)
1. Greece—History—To 146 B.C. 2. Greece—Civilization—To 146 B.C. I. Kuiper, Kathleen.
DF77.A5876 2010
938—dc22

2010000852

Manufactured in the United States of America

On the cover: The magnificent Parthenon, shown here with a broken column in the foreground, was built on the Acropolis in Athens, Greece, to honour the goddess Athena.
Pete Turner/Stone/Getty Images

On page photo credit pp. 17, 65, 81, 101, 118, 136 *Shutterstock.com*

CONTENTS

79

82

86

105

114

125

153

INTRODUCTION

Among the civilizations that preceded that of the Greeks were those of Minos and Mycenae. On the island of Crete, the Minoans established a sophisticated culture, the ruins of which are still visible at Knossos. Later the Myceneans formed a mighty kingdom in the Peloponnese, the hand-shaped peninsula of southernmost mainland Greece. By and large, however, the term ancient Greece—the subject of this book—usually refers to the period between the end of the Mycenaean era—about 1200 BC—and the death of Alexander the Great in 323 BC. Most of the political, philosophical, scientific, and artistic achievements of Greek civilization date to this period.

The period immediately following the collapse of the Mycenaean civilization is frequently described as a "dark age." Like the western European period after the fall of the Roman Empire that is so described, Greece's Dark Age involved a significant decrease in population and literacy. As a result, historical information from this period is scant; even later historians writing during Greece's Classical Age were possessed of information about this period that was inaccurate and sometimes even false. What we do know about the post-Mycenaean period is that it involved a series of migrations into western Greece, the best known of which would later be named the Dorian invasion.

The Dorians were a linguistic subgroup whose migration into the Peloponnese was said to be connected to the legendary return of the "descendants of Heracles [Hercules]." Of course, when Greek historians wrote about the "return of Heracles' descendants" they were simply trying to explain why the civilizations that inhabited the Peloponnese during their time were different from the ones described in the myths and legends of Homer, the epic poet of the *Iliad* and the *Odyssey*. This "invented tradition" is one of the hurdles we face when reading sources from the time period; that is, certain relatively new aspects of Greek society are retroactively tied to previous traditions—whether historical or mythological—as a means of creating legitimacy. Regardless of who the Dorians were, one thing is abundantly clear: the hostility between the Dorians and the Ionians—another of the three main linguistic subgroups in Greece—would shape the social, political, and cultural landscape of Greece for centuries.

Greece's Dark Age was followed by the Archaic period (c. 650–480 BC), during which time the steadily increasing population brought about reurbanization and expansion, leading to the formation of the city-state, or polis. During the Mycenaean period, Greece had been divided into kingdoms that encompassed numerous small towns, as well as larger

Pericles (495–429 BC), who ruled Athens during its Golden Age, is one of the most pivotal figures in the history of ancient Greece. Hulton Archive/Getty Images

estates owned by nobility. With the collapse of Mycenaean civilization, these kingdoms, towns, and estates vanished, only to be replaced by small villages. Over time, the populations in these villages grew, leading to the *synoikismos*, or gathering together, of the population of a given territory into a city-state. This "gathering together" could occur in two ways: either as a physical concentration of a population within one city or as a more abstract political unification of geographically separate groups. Whichever form of *synoikismos* occurred, a Greek city-state typically consisted of a walled city—which acted as the commercial, political, and religious centre—and the surrounding towns and villages. It should be noted that one of the most influential city-states, Sparta, was never consolidated in this manner, remaining a loose coalition of independent villages.

The Archaic period was also characterized by the growth of overseas colonies, some of which, such as Greek settlements in Italy (*c.* 750 BC) and Sicily (*c.* 734 BC) had been established in earlier times. These settlements spread throughout the Mediterranean and along the coast of the Black Sea. Among the several factors that have been suggested as reasons for this flurry of colonization are commercial interests, political rivalries, overpopulation, or simply the need for adventure and exploration.

Even though these new political entities were referred to as city-states, we should not assume that the older Mycenaean notions of class and nobility had vanished entirely. Many of the Greek city-states during the Archaic period were, in fact, aristocratic in organization, with political power resting in the hands of a small number of exclusive families (or clans). Athens, for example, had two such groups: a general class of aristocrats called the Eupatridae (the "People of Good Descent") and the *basileus*, a word frequently translated as "kings," but being more accurately thought of as hereditary nobility. Furthermore, Sparta—Athens's frequent ideological rival—was ruled by two kings of equal authority. However, as the Archaic period drew to a close, opportunistic individuals would rise up and seize power from the aristocratic classes. The Greeks called these individuals tyrants—a term that meant simply "illegitimate ruler" and encompassed the good and the bad alike. The tyrants of ancient Greece were able to wrest control of a city-state from the nobility by securing support of both the growing middle class and the peasants, many of whom were in debt to the wealthy land-owning aristocracy.

The first recorded Greek tyrant was Cypselus, who took control of Corinth in the seventh century BC. Tyrants seized power in other Greek city-states, as well, including Argos, Megara, and Syracuse. The Athenian tyrant Cleisthenes instituted a number of government reforms during his reign, several of which redistributed power from the hands of the few to the hands of the many. One of Cleisthenes' first changes was the restructuring the tribal system in Athens. He replaced the division of four tribes based upon Ionian descent with a reorganization of the entire population into 10 tribes based on geographic location. These new tribes became the basis for the Boule, or Council of Five Hundred, a new administrative body in charge of the daily affairs of the city. The council was formed by 50 members from each of the 10 tribes, thus giving the populous a louder voice in the political process. The reforms of Cleisthenes helped usher in an age of democracy in Athens, helping the city-state prosper well into the Classical period.

Greece's Classical period, which encompassed most of the sixth, fifth, and fourth centuries BC, was a major influence on Western civilization. Modern political, artistic, scientific, and philosophical thought owe a heavy debt to the Classical period. In addition to these lofty achievements, however, the period was marked by military conflict, notably the Persian Wars and the Peloponnesian War.

The origins of the wars between Greece and the Persian Empire go back to Greece's dark age, when several Greek colonies—the Ionian cities—were first established in Asia Minor. One salient feature of the westward spread of the Persian Empire during the sixth century BC, was the Persian conquest of the Ionians. Once subdued, the new Persian territories were governed by tyrants. Between 499 and 493 BC, unhappy with Persian rule, the Ionian cities rebelled, aided by military support from Athens and Eretria. The rebellion failed, and the Persian king, Darius the Great, vowed to punish Athens and Eretria for supporting the revolt. Furthermore, Darius began to perceive that the Greek city-states in general posed a threat to the Persian Empire, and he determined to conquer the whole of Greece. The first Persian invasion of Greece began in 492 BC and, within a year, all Greek city-states but Athens and Sparta had submitted to the Persians. In 490 BC, the Persian fleet landed at the bay of Marathon on the east coast of Attica, about 25 miles (40 kilometres) from Athens. The Persian and Athenian forces met on the plain of Marathon and, despite being outnumbered, the Athenian hoplites (soldiers) were able to defeat the more lightly armed Persian infantry. According to the Greek historian Herodotus, the Persians lost 6,400 men, while the Athenians lost only 192. The Persian king began to raise a larger army in order to once more attack and defeat his foes. This time, however, the Persian forces were deterred by a rebellion in Egypt. During this time, Darius died, and his son Xerxes took his place on the throne of the Persian Empire. After quelling the revolt in Egypt, Xerxes turned his attention to preparing a full-scale invasion of Greece.

About a decade after the Persians were defeated at the Battle of Marathon, Xerxes and the Persian Empire once again entered Greece. As the Persian army marched into northern Greece, an alliance of Greek city-states met in the south to strategize over the best method of defending themselves. The Athenian politician and general Themistocles suggested a two-pronged defense: hoplites commanded by King Leonidas I of Sparta would engage the Persian infantry at the pass of Thermopylae, while Themistocles would lead a blockade of the straits of Artemisium by allied naval forces. After three days, the Greek hoplites at Thermopylae had been either killed or captured and, no longer needing to support the infantry, the badly damaged allied fleet retreated to the island of Salamis.

Despite the losses suffered at both Thermopylae and Artemisium, Themistocles was able to convince the allied forces to once again engage the Persian fleet at Salamis. Unaccustomed to the narrow straits, the Persian fleet became disorganized. Seizing the upper hand, the Greek forces claimed victory. After the Battle of Salamis, Xerxes ordered most of his army back to Asia; the remaining Persian ground and naval forces were defeated at the Battle of Plataea and the Battle of Mycale, respectively. Once the Persians had retreated from mainland Greece, the Athenians and their allies—the newly formed Delian League—launched a counterattack to liberate the rest of the Aegean from Persian control. Once the Persian Empire had been successfully driven out of Greece and the surrounding territories, the Athenians maintained control over their allies. They further expanded their influence and consolidated power into what would become known as the Athenian Empire.

At the close of the Persian Wars, Athens was the dominant naval and commercial power of Greece. Athenian statesmen used tributes paid by members of the Delian League to build the Parthenon and other monuments in Athens. By the mid-fifth century BC, the growing wealthy leisure class became patrons of the arts, attracting talented artisans from all over the Greek world and making Athens the centre of literature, philosophy, the visual arts, and architecture in the Classical period. At this time, Athens was home to some of Western history's greatest cultural and intellectual figures, including the dramatists Aristophanes and Sophocles; philosophers Aristotle, Plato, and Socrates; and the historians Thucydides and Herodotus. The growing prominence of Athens at this time also led to an increase in Athenian imperialism, which would lead to conflict with Sparta and the Peloponnesian League.

The Peloponnesian War (c. 431 to 404 BC) was a reaction to the growing hegemony of the Athenian Empire. Fearing Athenian dominance of Greece, Sparta led its allies, the Peloponnesian League, in a series of invasions of Attica, the ancient region of east-central Greece in which Athens was located. As the war progressed, Sparta received support from Persia, which allowed the Peloponnesian League to undermine Athenian naval superiority. Sparta also supported rebellions in Athenian cities, further weakening the empire. The

Peloponnesian War ended with the destruction of the Athenian fleet at Aegospotami and the surrender of Athens. The defeat of the Athenian Empire reshaped the Classical Greek world: Sparta became the leading power in Greece, while Athens, once the strongest city-state in the region, was completely devastated. The ideological conflict between democracy (as embodied by Athens) and oligarchy (the Spartan political model) led to an increase in civil wars, as well as all-out wars among city-states. The weakened city-states of central Greece, coupled with the rise of Philip II of Macedon, would usher in the close of the Classical period.

Under Philip II—and, later, his son Alexander the Great—Macedon extended its influence from northern Greece all the way to Persia, Egypt, and India. Even though Alexander the Great spread Greek culture throughout most of the known world, it was not the same culture found in Athens or Sparta a century before. Gone were the fiercely independent city-states of the Classical period, replaced with a more homogeneous "Greek" culture, which historians would later label Hellenistic.

CHAPTER 1

The Archaic Period

This book discusses the period following Mycenaean civilization, which ended in about 1200 BC, to the death of Alexander the Great, in 323 BC. This encompasses the Archaic and Classical periods. This was a time of political, philosophical, artistic, and scientific achievements that formed a legacy with unparalleled influence on Western civilization.

The Archaic period represents an era of artistic development in Greece from roughly 650 to 480 BC, the date of the Persian sack of Athens. It was preceded by a period—often called a Dark Age—between the catastrophic end of the Mycenaean civilization and about 900 BC. This era was a time about which Greeks of the Classical Age (roughly 500 to 320 BC) had confused and false notions.

THE POST-MYCENAEAN PERIOD AND LEFKANDI

An example of this lack of understanding of the preceding period can be found in the work of Thucydides (c. 460–c. 404 BC), the great ancient historian of the fifth century BC. Thucydides wrote a sketch of Greek history from the Trojan War to his own day in which he notoriously fails, in the appropriate chapter, to signal any kind of dramatic rupture. (He does, however, speak of Greece "settling down gradually"

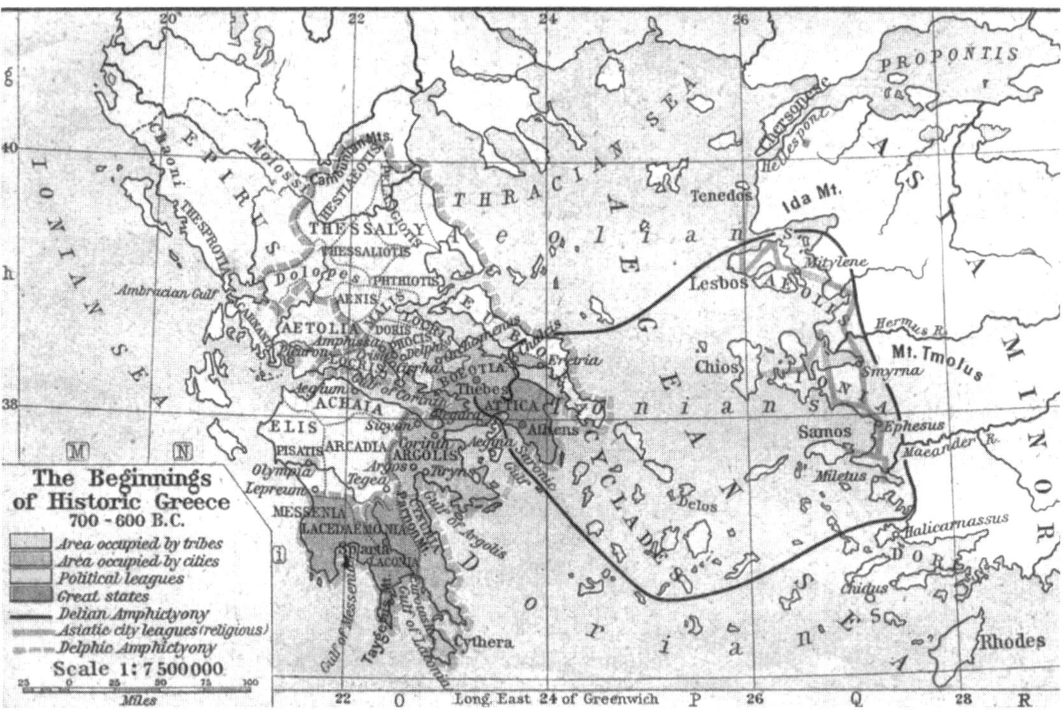

During the Archaic period, Greece comprised not only mainland and islands, but also colonies on the coast of what is now Turkey. Courtesy of the University of Texas Libraries, the University of Texas at Austin

and colonizing Italy, Sicily, and what is now western Turkey. This surely implies that Greece was settling down after something.) Thucydides does indeed display sound knowledge of the series of migrations by which Greece was resettled in the post-Mycenaean period. The most famous of these was the "Dorian invasion," which the Greeks called, or connected with, the legendary "return of the descendants of Heracles." Although much about that invasion is problematic—it left little or no archaeological trace at the point in time where tradition puts it—the problems are of no concern here. Important for the understanding of the Archaic and Classical periods, however, is the powerful belief in Dorianism as a linguistic and religious concept. Thucydides casually but significantly mentions soldiers speaking the "Doric dialect" in a narrative about ordinary military matters in the year 426: this is a surprisingly abstract way of looking at the subdivisions of the Greeks because it would have been more natural for a fifth-century Greek to identify soldiers by cities. Equally important to the understanding of this period is the hostility to Dorians, usually on the part of Ionians, another linguistic and religious subgroup, whose most famous city was Athens. So extreme was this hostility that Dorians were prohibited from entering Ionian sanctuaries. Extant today is a fifth-century example of such a prohibition, an inscription from the island of Paros.

Phenomena such as the tension between Dorians and Ionians that have their origins in the Dark Age are a reminder that Greek civilization did not emerge either unannounced or uncontaminated by what had gone before. The Dark Age itself is beyond the scope of this book. One is bound to notice, however, that archaeological finds tend to call into question the whole concept of a Dark Age by showing that certain features of Greek civilization once thought not to antedate about 800 BC can actually be pushed back by as much as two centuries. One example, chosen for its relevance to the emergence of the Greek city-state, or polis, will suffice. In 1981 archaeology pulled back the curtain on the "darkest" phase of all, the Protogeometric Period (*c.* 1075–900 BC), which takes its name from the geometric shapes painted on pottery. A grave, rich by the standards of any period, was uncovered at a site called Lefkandi on Euboea, the island along the eastern flank of Attica (the territory controlled by Athens). The grave, which dates to about 1000 BC, contains the (probably cremated) remains of a man and a woman. The large bronze vessel in which the man's ashes were deposited came from Cyprus, and the gold items buried with the woman are splendid and sophisticated in their workmanship. Remains of horses were found as well; the animals had been buried with their snaffle bits, mouthpieces that help riders control horses. The grave was within a large collapsed house, whose form anticipates that of the Greek temples two centuries later. Previously it had been thought that these temples were one of the first manifestations of the "monumentalizing" associated with the beginnings of the city-state. Thus this find, and those made in a set of nearby cemeteries in the years before 1980 attesting further contacts between Egypt and Cyprus between 1000 and 800 BC, are important evidence. They show that one corner of one island of Greece, at least, was neither impoverished nor isolated in a period usually thought to have been both. The difficulty is to know just how exceptional Lefkandi was, but in any view it has revised former ideas about what was and what was not possible at the beginning of the first millennium BC.

"COLONIZATION" AND CITY-STATE FORMATION

Thucydides, as was mentioned earlier, wrote about Greek migration and colonization of Italy, Sicily, and modern-day western Turkey. The term *colonization*, although it may be convenient and widely used, is misleading. When applied to Archaic Greece, it should not necessarily be taken to imply the state-sponsored sending out of definite numbers of settlers, as the later Roman origin of the word implies. For one thing, it will be seen that state formation may itself be a product of the "colonizing" movement.

The first "date" in Greek history is 776 BC, the year of the first Olympic Games. It was computed by a fifth-century-BC researcher named Hippias. This man originally came from Elis, a place in the western Peloponnese in whose territory Olympia itself is situated. This date and the list of early victors, transmitted by another literary tradition, are likely to be

Olympic Games

Greek vase showing Olympic athletes in a race. Hulton Archive/Getty Images

The athletic festival known as the Olympic Games originated in ancient Greece and was revived in the late 19th century. Before the 1970s the games were officially limited to competitors with amateur status, but in the 1980s many events were opened to professional athletes. Currently the games are open to all, even the top professional athletes in basketball and football (soccer). The ancient Olympic Games included several of the sports that are now part of the Summer Games program, which at times has included events in as many as 32 different sports. In 1924 the Winter Games were sanctioned for winter sports. The Olympic Games have come to be regarded as the world's foremost sports competition.

Of all the early athletic festivals (including the Olympic Games, held at Olympia; the Pythian Games at Delphi; the Nemean Games at Nemea; and the Isthmian Games, held near Corinth), the Olympic Games were the most famous. Held every four years between August 6 and September 19, they occupied such an important place in Greek history that in late antiquity historians measured time by the interval between them—an Olympiad. The Olympic Games, like almost all Greek games, were an intrinsic part of a religious festival. They were held in honour of Zeus at Olympia by the city-state of Elis in the northwestern Peloponnese. The first Olympic champion listed in the records was Coroebus of Elis, a cook, who won the sprint race in 776 BC. Notions that the Olympics began much earlier than 776 BC are founded on myth, not historical evidence. According to one legend, for example, the games were founded by Heracles, son of Zeus and Alcmene.

reliable, if only because the list is so unassuming in its early reaches. That is to say, local victors predominate, including some Messenians. Messene lost its independence to neighbouring Sparta during the course of the eighth century, and this fact is an additional guarantee of the reliability of the early Olympic victor list: Messenian victors would hardly have been invented at a time when Messene as a political entity had ceased to exist. Clearly, then, record keeping and organized activity involving more than one community and centring on a sanctuary, such as Olympia, go back to the early eighth century. (Such competitive activity is an example of what has been called "peer-polity interaction.") Records imply a degree of literacy, and here too the tradition about the eighth century has been confirmed by finds. A cup, bearing the inscription in Greek in the Euboean script "I am the cup of Nestor," can be securely dated to before 700 BC. It was found at an island site called Pithekoussai (Ischia) on the Bay of Naples.

Overseas Projects

The early overseas activity of the Euboeans has already been remarked upon in connection with the discoveries at Lefkandi. They were the prime movers in the more or less organized—or, at any rate, remembered and recorded—phase of Greek overseas settlement. (Euboean priority can be taken as absolutely certain because archaeology supports the literary tradition of the Roman historian Livy and others: Euboean pottery has been found both at Pithekoussai to the west and at the Turkish site of Al-Mina to the east.) This more organized phase began in Italy *c.* 750 and in Sicily in 734 BC. Its episodes were remembered, perhaps in writing, by the colonies themselves. The word *organized* needs to be stressed because various considerations make it necessary to push back beyond this date the beginning of Greek colonization. First, it is clear from archaeological finds, such as the Lefkandi material, and from other new evidence that the Greeks had already, before 750 or 734, confronted and exchanged goods with the inhabitants of Italy and Sicily. Second, Thucydides says that Dark Age Athens sent colonies to Ionia, and archaeology bears this out—however much one discounts for propagandist exaggeration by the imperial Athens of Thucydides' own time of its prehistoric colonizing role. However, after the founding of Cumae (a mainland Italian offshoot of the island settlement of Pithekoussai) *c.* 750 BC and of Sicilian Naxos and Syracuse in 734 and 733, respectively, there was an explosion of colonies to all points of the compass. The only exceptions were those areas, such as pharaonic Egypt or inner Anatolia, where the inhabitants were too militarily and politically advanced to be easily overrun.

One may ask why the Greeks suddenly began to launch these overseas projects. It seems that commercial interests, greed, and sheer curiosity were the motivating forces. An older view, according to which Archaic Greece exported its surplus population because of an uncontrollable rise in population, must be regarded as largely discredited. In the first place, the earliest well-documented colonial operations were small-scale affairs, too small to make much difference to the situation of the sending community (the "metropolis," or mother city). That is certainly true of the colonization of Cyrene, in North Africa, from the island of Thera (Santorin): on this point an inscription has confirmed the classic account by the fifth-century Greek historian Herodotus. In the second place, population was not uncontrollable in principle: methods such as infanticide and contraception were available. Considerations of this kind much reduce the evidential value of discoveries establishing, for example, that the number of graves in Attica and the Argolid (the area centred on Argos) increased dramatically in the later Dark Age or that there was a serious drought in eighth-century Attica (this is the admitted implication of a number of dried-up wells in the Athenian agora, or civic centre). In fact, no single explanation for the colonizing activity is plausible. Political difficulties at home might sometimes be a factor, as, for instance, at Sparta, which in the eighth century sent out a colony to Taras (Tarentum) in Italy as a way of getting rid of an unwanted half-caste group. Nor can one rule out simple craving for excitement and a desire to see the world. The lyric poetry of the energetic and high-strung poet Archilochus, a seventh-century Parian involved in the colonization of Thasos, shows the kind of lively minded individual who might be involved in the colonizing movement.

So far, the vague term *community* has been used for places that sent out colonies. Such vagueness is historically appropriate because these places themselves were scarcely constituted as united entities, such as a city, or polis. For example, it is a curious fact that Corinth, which in 733 colonized Syracuse in Sicily, was itself scarcely a properly constituted polis in 733. (The formation of Corinth as a united entity is to be put in the second half of the eighth century, with precisely the colonization of Syracuse as its first collective act.)

The Beginnings of the Polis

The name given to polis formation by the Greeks themselves was *synoikismos*, literally a "gathering together." *Synoikismos* could take one or both of two forms—it could be a physical concentration of the population in a single city or an act of purely political unification that allowed the population to continue living in a dispersed way. The classic discussion is by Thucydides, who distinguishes between the two kinds of *synoikismos* more carefully than do some of his modern critics. He makes the correct point that Attica was politically synoecized (gathered into larger units) at an early date but not physically synoecized until 431 BC when Pericles as part of his war policy brought the large rural population behind the city walls of Athens. A more extreme instance of a polis that was never fully synoecized in the physical sense was Sparta, which, as Thucydides elsewhere says, remained "settled by villages in the old Greek way." It was an act of conscious arrogance, a way of claiming to be invulnerable from attack and not to need the walls that Thucydides again and again treats as the sign and guarantee of civilized polis life. The urban history of Sparta makes an interesting case history showing that Mycenaean Sparta was not so physically or psychologically secure as its Greek and Roman successors. The administrative centre of Mycenaean Sparta was probably in the Párnon Mountains at the excavated site of the Menelaion. Then Archaic and Classical Sparta moved down to the plain. Byzantine Sparta, more insecure, moved out of the plain again to perch on the site of Mistra on the opposite western mountain, Taygetos. Finally, modern Sparta is situated, once again peacefully and confidently, on its old site on the plain of the river Eurotas.

The enabling factors behind the beginnings of the Greek polis have been the subject of intense discussion. One approach connects the beginnings of the polis with the first monumental buildings, usually temples like the great early eighth-century temple of Hera on the island of Samos. The concentration of resources and effort required for such constructions presupposes the formation of self-conscious polis units and may actually have accelerated it. As stated above, however, the evidence from Lefkandi makes it hard to see the construction of such monumental buildings as a sufficient cause for the emergence of the polis, a process or event nobody has yet tried to date as early as 1000 BC.

Another related theory argues that the birth of the Greek city was signaled by the placing of rural sanctuaries at the margins of the territory that a community sought to define as its own. This fits admirably a number of Peloponnesian sanctuaries. For instance, the temple complex of Hera staked out a claim, on the part of relatively distant Argos, to the plain stretching between city and sanctuary, and the Corinthian sanctuary on the promontory of Perachora, also dedicated to Hera, performed the same function. Yet there are difficulties. It seems that the Isthmia sanctuary, which at first sight seems a good candidate for another Corinthian rural sanctuary, was already operational as early as 900 BC, in the Protogeometric Period, and this date is surely too early for polis formation. Nor does the theory easily account for the rural temple of the goddess Aphaea in the middle of Aegina. The sanctuary is admittedly a long way from the town of Aegina, but Aegina is an island, and there is no obvious neighbour against whom territorial claims could plausibly have been asserted. Finally, a theory that has to treat the best-known polis, namely Athens, and Attica as in every respect exceptional is not satisfactory: there is no Athenian equivalent of the Argive Heraeum.

A third theory attacks the problem of the beginnings of the polis through burial practice. In the eighth century (it is said) formal burial became more generally available, and this "democratization" of burial is evidence for a fundamentally new attitude toward society. The theory seeks to associate the new attitude with the growth of the polis. There is, however, insufficient archaeological and historical evidence for this view (which involves an implausible hypothesis that the process postulated was discontinuous and actually reversed for a brief period at a date later than the eighth century). Moreover, it is vulnerable to the converse objection as that raised against the second theory: the evidence for the third theory is almost exclusively Attic, and so, even if it were true, it would explain Athens and only Athens.

Fourth, one may consider a theory whose unspoken premise is a kind of "geographic determinism." Perhaps the Greek landscape itself, with its small alluvial plains often surrounded by defensible mountain systems, somehow prompted the formation of small and acrimonious poleis, endlessly going to war over boundaries. This view has its attractions, but the obvious objection is that, when Greeks went to more open areas such as Italy, Sicily, and North Africa, they seem to have taken their animosities with them. This in turn invites speculations of a psychologically determinist sort. One has to ask, without hope of an answer, whether the Greeks were naturally particularist.

A fifth enabling factor that should be borne in mind is the influence of the colonizing movement itself. The political structure of the metropolis, or sending city, may sometimes have been inchoate. The new colony, however, threatened by hostile native neighbours, rapidly had to "get its act together" if it was to be a viable cell of Hellenism on foreign soil. This effort in turn affected the situation in the metropolis because Greek colonies often kept close religious and social links with it. A fourth-century inscription, for instance, attests close ties between Miletus and its daughter city Olbia in the Black Sea region. Here, however, as so often in Greek history, generalization is dangerous. Some mother-daughter relationships, like that between Corinth and Corcyra (Corfu), were bad virtually from the start.

A related factor is Phoenician influence (related, because the early Phoenicians were great colonizers, who must often have met trading Greeks). The Phoenician coast was settled by communities similar in many respects to the early Greek poleis. It is arguable that Phoenician influence, and Semitic influence generally, on early Greece has been seriously underrated.

Theories such as these are stimulating and may each contain a particle of truth. The better position, however, is that generalization itself is as yet premature. In particular, archaeologically based theoretical reconstructions need much more refining. All one can say in summary is that in roughly the same period—namely, the eighth century—a number of areas, such as Corinth and

Megara, began to define their borders, deny autonomy to their constituent villages, and generally act as separate states. Attica's political synoecism, which occurred a little earlier, was complete perhaps around 900. Tempting though it is to seek a single explanatory model for these very roughly contemporaneous processes, one should perhaps allow that different paths of development were followed in different areas, even in areas next door to each other. After all, the Archaic and Classical histories of mighty democratic imperial Athens, of the miserable polis of Megara which nevertheless colonized Byzantium, of wealthy, oligarchic Corinth, and of federal Boeotia were all very different even though Athens, Megara, Corinth, and Boeotia were close neighbours.

One is perhaps on firmer ground when one examines the evidence for prepolis aggregations of larger units, often religious in character. There are a number of such associations whose origins lie in the Dark Age and whose existence surely promoted some feeling of local and particularist identity among the participants. The Ionians in Anatolia formed themselves into a confederation of 12 communities, the Ionian Dodecapolis, with a common meeting place. There were comparable groupings among the Dorian Greeks of Anatolia and even among the Carians (partially Hellenized non-Greeks) in the same part of the world. The central location for such organizations was characteristically small and insignificant. One poorly attested but intriguing early Archaic league was the "Calaurian Amphictyony" (an amphictyony was a religious league of "dwellers round about"). Calauria, the small island now called Póros, was not a place of any consequence in itself, but the league's seven members included Athens and Aegina, two major Greek poleis. The most famous and enduring such amphictyony, however, was the one that, originally from a distance, administered the affairs of the sanctuary of Delphi in central Greece. This sanctuary contained the most famous, though not the oldest, Greek oracle (the oldest was at Dodona). Oracles were a mechanism by which divinely inspired utterances were produced in answer to specific questions. Finally, it is worth noting an adventurous suggestion that Lefkandi itself might have been the centre of some kind of religious amphictyony, but, if so, this would be an exception to the principle that religious centres tended themselves to be insignificant, however mighty their participating members.

EARLY ARCHAIC GREEK CIVILIZATION

Before attempting to characterize Archaic Greece, one must admit candidly that the evidence is unsatisfactory. Only for Athens is anything like a proper political tradition known, and Athens's development toward the democracy of the fifth century was amazingly and untypically rapid by comparison with other states, many of which never became democratic at all.

The Sources

A tiny but salutary scrap of evidence makes this point: Thucydides in Book 2 of his *History of the Peloponnesian War* casually mentions a man named Evarchus as "tyrant" of a small northwestern Greek polis called Astacus in the 420s BC. But for this chance mention, one would never have guessed that tyranny could have existed or persisted in such a place so late or so long. Another difficulty is that, while a fair amount about the social structure of Classical Athens is known, some of it must go back to Archaic times. Precisely how much dates to Archaic times is disputed.

There is a further complication. In both the political and the social spheres, one has to reckon—chiefly at Athens, but elsewhere too—with "invented tradition," a distorting element for which proper allowance is only now beginning to be made. Thus it seems that not just Lycurgus, the famous Spartan lawgiver (whose historicity was doubted even in antiquity), but even a reforming figure like Solon of Athens, who certainly existed in the sixth century and large fragments of whose poetry still survive, was in some respects what anthropologists call a "culture hero." Much was projected onto him anachronistically or just wrongly, and reformers in later generations established their credentials by claiming (if they were reactionaries) that they were trying to "get back to Solon" or (if they were democrats) that Solon was their founding father. Such errors should not induce too much pessimism: at Athens at least, individual aristocratic families preserved oral traditions, which affected the later literary records in ways that can be properly understood with the help of anthropological analogy. That is to say, not all the evidence so preserved is unusable, but it needs handling in special ways.

It has even been argued that social life, too, was creatively manipulated. Later Greek cities contained, alongside such transparent political institutions as the Popular Assembly and the Deliberative ("Probouleutic") Council, a more opaque set of institutions, ostensibly based on kinship groupings. The biggest and most basic of these groupings were the phylae, or "tribes," according to which the citizen body was subdivided. Thus all Dorian states had the same three tribes, and there were four Ionian tribes (although Ionian states were less conservative than Dorian, and one finds among them a greater readiness to innovate. Late sixth-century Athens, for example, switched from a four-tribe hereditary system of citizenship to a 10-tribe one based on simple residence as well as descent). Smaller subdivisions were the phratry, a word connected with a philological root meaning "brother," and the *genos*, a smaller cluster of families (*oikoi*).

The existence of these groupings in historical times is beyond question. One finds them controlling citizen intake (as in the so-called "Demotionidai" inscription from the Attic village of Decelea, datable to as late as the early fourth century BC) and entering into complicated property arrangements. What has become a matter of debate, however, is the question of just how old they actually were. According to the most skeptical view, the whole apparatus of tribe and *genos* was an invention without any Dark Age history to legitimate it. This view, which rests partly on the near absence of the relevant kinship terminology in Homer, is not ultimately convincing in its hypothesis of a kind of complicated collective fraud on posterity. Yet it is right to allow for an element of conscious antiquarianism at certain periods (the 320s in Athens being one), which may well have affected specific traditions.

BACCHIADAE AND EUPATRIDAE

The world of the colonizing states was aristocratic in the sense that a small number of exclusive clans within cities monopolized citizenship and political control. At Corinth, for example, political control was monopolized by the adult males of a single clan, the Bacchiadae. They perhaps numbered no more than a couple of hundred. At Athens there was a general class of Eupatridae, a word that just means "People of Good Descent"—i.e., aristocrats. (The word may have had a simultaneous but narrower application to one single *genos*. This, however, is disputed, and, in any event, that hypothetical family was only one among many privileged *genē*. The case, therefore, is not analogous to that of the Bacchiadae.) It is unlikely that the Eupatridae were as rigidly defined as the Bacchiadae, and the negative tradition that Solon in the early sixth century deprived them of their exclusive claim to political office may just be the excessively formal and precise way in which later ancient commentators described a positive change by which power was made more generally available than it had been before.

With regard to these same early Archaic times one hears, for example, in the poetry of the seventh-century Boeotian Hesiod, of control, sometimes oppressively exercised, by *basileis* (singular *basileus*). This word is usually translated as "kings," and such titles as the Athenian *basileus* (an official, or archon, with a defined religious competence, conveniently but less correctly called the *archon basileus* by modern scholars) are then explained as survivals of an age of monarchy. This account in terms of fossilization certainly eases the awkwardness of explaining why, for instance, the wife of the *basileus* was held to be ritually married to the god Dionysus. The very existence of kingship in Geometric Period (900–700) Greece, however, has been challenged, and a case has been made (though not universally accepted) for seeing most of these Archaic *basileis* not as kings in any sense but as hereditary nobles. In the latter case, there is no great difference between these *basileis* and such aristocrats as the Bacchiadae.

Symposia and Gymnasia

Life inside the Archaic Greek societies ruled by such families can be reconstructed only impressionistically and only at the top of the social scale. The evidence, to an extent unusual even in Greco-Roman antiquity, is essentially elitist in its bias. Aristocratic values were transmitted both vertically, by family oral traditions, and horizontally, by means of a crucial institution known as the symposium, or feast, for which (many literary scholars now believe) much surviving Archaic poetry was originally written. Perhaps much fine painted pottery was also intended for this market, though the social and artistic significance of such pottery is debated. Some scholars insist that the really wealthy would at all times have used gold and silver vessels, which, however, have not survived in any numbers because they have long ago been melted down.

Symposia were eating and dining occasions with a strong ritual element. Their existence is reflected in the marked emphasis, in the Homeric poems, on ostentatious feasting and formal banqueting as assertions of status (what have been called "feasts of merit"). Thus Sarpedon in Homer's *Iliad* reminds Glaucus that both of them are honoured with seats of honour and full cups in Lycia and with land (a sacred precinct, or *temenos*) to finance all the feasting. Symposia were confined to males (a reminder of the military ethos so prevalent in Homer). Although when the institution was introduced, along with the vine, to Etruria—where much of the visual evidence comes from—it changed its character and became open to both sexes. The Greek symposium proper can be seen as an instrument of social control. It is a more tangible unit of social organization, and one with better-attested Homeric antecedents, than the problematic *genē* or phratries discussed above.

In Classical times, strong homosexual attachments were another way in which values were inculcated, passed on by the older man (the *erastes*) to the younger *eromenos*, or beloved. The gymnasium was the venue where such relationships typically developed. As with the symposium, there was an almost ritual element to it all. Certain gifts—such as, for example, the gift of a hare—were thought especially appropriate. The date, however, at which Greek homosexuality became a central cultural institution is problematic. It is notoriously absent from the Homeric poems, a fact that some scholars explain as being the result of poetic reticence. The more plausible view is that homosexuality was in some way connected with the rise of the polis and was part of what has been called the "eighth-century renaissance." If so, Homer's silence is after all significant: he does not mention it because in his time it was not yet important.

Both symposia and gymnasia in different ways mirrored or were preparatory to warfare. Interpolis athletic competitions (such as the Olympic Games) are another reflection of warfare. Epinician poetry of the Classical period (that is, "victory poetry" like that of Pindar, whose epinician odes celebrate the athletic victories of aristocratic individuals) constantly uses the language of war, fighting, and victory. Indeed, one influential view of organized athletic competitions is that they are a restructuring of the instinct to hunt and kill.

Formal Relationships

With the great athletic festivals, which brought Greeks together at set intervals of years to Olympia and later to Delphi, Nemea, and the Isthmus (the four great Panhellenic, or "all-Greek," games), one passes from the internal organization of individual Greek societies to their interrelationships. Two kinds of powerful interrelationship have already been noted—that between colonizing or mother city and daughter city and the shared membership of an amphictyony. Mythical links between one city and another were maintained and exploited throughout all periods by a process that has been felicitously called "kinship diplomacy." The most common such link was that between mother and daughter city and involved the stressing of shared ancestry—that is, common descent from some mythical hero or founder figure. Such kinship diplomacy was taken very seriously by all parties and as late as the Hellenistic period was the basis for alliances or other sorts of common action. Modern historians tend to stress the "particularism" of Greek culture—i.e., the separate development and carefully cultivated local identity of the individual polis. Networks of kinship diplomacy were one means by which this particularism was softened in practice.

At the individual level, the basic institution in intercity relationships was that of "guest-friendship," or *xenia*. This was another area where ritual elements were present to such a marked degree that the whole institution has been called "ritualized friendship." The same aristocrats who drank and heard poetry together inside their own communities naturally expected to find comparable groups inside other states. They cemented their ties, which had perhaps been formed on initially casual or trading visits, with formal relationships of *xenia*. At some point quite early in the Archaic period this institution developed into something still more definite, the *proxenia*. *Proxenoi* were citizens of state A living in state A who looked after the interests of citizens of state B. The status of *proxenos* was surely in origin hereditary, but by Thucydides' time one hears of "voluntary *proxenoi*" (*etheloproxenoi*). The antiquity of the basic institution is not in doubt, however much the fifth-century Athenian empire may have exploited and reshaped it for its own political convenience. A seventh-century inscription from the island of Corcyra mentioning a *proxenos* from Locris is the earliest attestation of the institution.

Another way of institutionalizing relationships between the nationals of different states was *epigamia*, an arrangement by which the offspring of marriage were treated as citizens of the wife's polis if the husband settled there, as was the husband. Athens, for example, granted *epigamia* to Euboea as late as the fifth century, a time when Athenian citizenship was fiercely protected. There are still earlier instances: usually one hears of *epigamia* when for one reason or another it was being suspended or denied. Thus, there was an early arrangement between the islands of Andros and Paros, which, Plutarch says, ended when relations went sour. More interesting is the statement, again by Plutarch, that there was no intermarriage between members of two of the villages, or demes, of Attica, Pallene and Hagnous. Far from being evidence that these places were somehow originally separate states, the prohibition was more like a ban on endogamy: in other words, the two communities were regarded—like members of a family—as being too close to be allowed to intermarry.

Thus, both marriage itself and prohibition of marriage were ways of defining the relations between communities, including communities within a single large state like Attica, and of keeping those relations friendly. One way in which ties of *xenia* and marriage can now be traced in detail is the scientific study of Greek personal names, because patterns of naming reflect social realities. Foreign names enter a city's name pool as a result of both formal connections and less formal ones, such as temporary residence. Such "onomastic" evidence, as it is called, can now be studied in bulk and in depth, thanks to the computer-aided publication of all known Greek personal names, most of them attested from inscriptions.

The chief vehicle of interaction among poleis, however, was through warfare and through the formal suspension or renunciation of warfare by means of heavily ritualized treaties (one of the most common words for such a treaty is *spondai*, which literally means "libations" to the guaranteeing gods). The earliest surviving inscriptional peace treaty "for all time" dates from the sixth century and was found at Olympia. Nonetheless, there were surely agreements to limit warfare over strips of boundary land before that date. Archaeology may offer unexpected help in this matter: it is possible and plausible that some frontier zones were by tacit or explicit agreement left fallow. One such zone seems to have been the remote Skourta plain, which separates part of northern Attica from Boeotia. Preliminary surface survey (i.e., the estimation of settlement patterns by gathering of potsherds) carried out in and after 1985 suggests that it was left—perhaps deliberately—uncultivated in the Archaic period.

The Lelantine War

An important landmark in interstate military relations of the kind considered here was the Lelantine War. It was the earliest Greek war (after the mythical Trojan War) that had any claim to be considered "general," in the sense that it involved distant allies on each side. Fought in perhaps the later eighth century between the two main communities of Euboea, Chalcis and Eretria, it took its name from the fertile Lelantine Plain, which separates the cities and includes the site of Lefkandi. (It is an interesting modern suggestion that Lefkandi itself is the site of Old Eretria, abandoned about 700 BC in favour of the Classical site Eretria at the east end of the plain, perhaps as a consequence of Eretria's defeat in the war. This theory, however, needs to account for Herodotus's statement that at the early sixth-century entertainment of the suitors of Cleisthenes of Sicyon there was one Lysanias from Eretria, "then at the height of its prosperity.")

Other faraway Greek states were somehow involved in the war. On this point Thucydides agrees with his great predecessor Herodotus. Thus Samos supported Chalcis and Miletus, Eretria. Given Euboean priority in overseas settlement, it is natural to suppose that the links implied by the traditions about the Lelantine War were the result of Euboean overseas energy, but that energy would hardly have turned casual contacts into actual alliances without a preliminary network of guest-friendships. Whether the oracle at Delphi took sides in the war, as a modern speculation has it, is less certain, though there is no doubt that, by some means wholly mysterious to the 21st century, Delphi often provided updated information about possible sites for settlement and even (as over Cyrene) gave the original stimulus to the emigration.

One can be more confident in denying the thoroughly anachronistic notion that the Lelantine War shows the existence of "trade leagues" at this early date. Religious amphictyonies are one thing, but trade leagues are quite another. The evidence, such as it is, suggests that early trade was carried on by entrepreneurial aristocratic individuals, who no doubt exploited their guest-friendships and formed more such friendships during their travels. It is true, however, that such individuals tended to come from areas where arable land was restricted, and to this extent it is legitimate to speak in a generic way of those areas as having in a sense a more commercially minded population than others. One example of such an area is the Lelantine Plain, an exceptionally good piece of land on a notably barren and mountainous, though large, island. Herodotus described one such trader from the later Archaic period, Sostratus of Aegina, a man of fabulous wealth. Then in the early 1970s a remarkable inscription was found in Etruria—a dedication to Apollo in the name of Sostratus of Aegina. This discovery revealed that the source of his wealth was trade with Etruria and other parts of Italy. Aegina is an island whose estimated Classical population of about 40,000 was supported by land capable of supporting only about 4,000. One may quarrel with the first figure as too large and the second figure as too pessimistic (it makes insufficient allowance for the possibilities of highly intensive land use). Even after adjustment, however, it is clear that Aegina needed to trade in order to live. It is not surprising to find Sostratus's home city of Aegina included among the Greek communities allowed to trade at Naukratis in pharaonic Egypt. This arrangement is described by Herodotus, and the site has been explored archaeologically. Aegina was the only participating city of Greece proper, as opposed to places in the eastern Aegean.

THE LATER ARCHAIC PERIOD

Dealings with opulent Asian civilizations were bound to produce disparities in wealth, and hence social conflicts, within the aristocracies of Greece. One function of institutions such as guest-friendship was no doubt to ensure the maintenance of the charmed circle of social and economic privilege. This system, however, presupposed a certain stability, whereas the rapid escalation of overseas activity in and after the eighth century was surely disruptive in that it gave a chance, or at least a grievance, to outsiders with the right go-getting skills and motivation. Not that one should imagine concentration of wealth taking place in the form most familiar to the 21st century—namely, coined money. Since 1951 the date of the earliest coinage has been fairly securely fixed at about 600 BC. The crucial discovery was the excavation and scientific examination of the foundation deposit of the Temple of Artemis at Ephesus in Anatolia. The first objects recognizably similar to coined money were found there at levels most scholars (there are a few doubters) accept as securely dated.

Coinage did not arrive in Greece proper until well into the sixth century. There were, however, other ways of accumulating precious metals besides collecting it in coined form. Gold and silver can be worked into cups, plates, and vases or just held as bar or bullion. There is no getting round the clear implication of two poems of Solon (early sixth century) that, first, gold and silver were familiar metals and, second, wealth was now in the hands of arrivistes.

The Decline of the Aristocracy

The first state in which the old aristocratic order began to break up was Corinth. The Bacchiadae had exploited Corinth's geographic position, which was favourable in ways rivaled only by that of the two Euboean cities already discussed. Like Chalcis, which supervised sea traffic between southern Greece and Macedonia but also had close links with Boeotia and Attica, Corinth controlled both a north-south route (the Isthmus of Corinth, in modern times pierced by the Corinth Canal) and an east-west route. This second route was exploited in a special way. Corinth had two ports, Lechaeum to the west on the Gulf of Corinth and Cenchreae to the east on the Saronic Gulf. Between the two seas there was a haulage system, involving a rightly famous engineering feat, the so-called *diolkos*. The *diolkos*, which was excavated in the 1950s, was a line of grooved paving-stones across which goods could be dragged for transshipment (probably not the merchant ships themselves, though there is some evidence that warships, which were lighter, were so moved in emergencies). There is explicit information that the Bacchiadae had profited hugely from the harbour dues. As the Greek world expanded its mental and financial horizons, other Corinthian families grew envious. The result was the first firmly datable and well-authenticated Greek tyranny, or one-man rule by a usurper. This was the tyranny of Cypselus, who was only a partial Bacchiad.

Aristotle, in the fourth century, was to say that tyrannies arise when oligarchies disagree internally, and this analysis makes good sense in the Corinthian context. The evidence of an inscribed Athenian archon list, found in the 1930s and attesting a grandson of Cypselus in the 590s, settled an old debate about the date of Cypselus's coup: it must have happened about 650 (a conclusion for which there is other evidence) rather than at the much later date indicated by an alternative tradition. Cypselus and his son Periander ruled until about 585 BC. Periander's nephew and successor did not last long. Precisely what factor in 650 made possible the success of the partial outsider Cypselus is obscure, as no Bacchiad foreign policy failure can be dated earlier than 650. General detestation for the Bacchiadae, however, is clear from an oracle preserved by Herodotus that "predicts" that Cypselus will bring *dikē*, or justice, to Corinth after the rule of the power-monopolizing Bacchiadae. No doubt this oracle was fabricated after the event, but it is interesting as showing that nobody regretted the passing of the Bacchiadae.

Changes in Warfare

Modern scholars have tried to look for more general factors behind Cypselus's success than a desire in a new world of wealth and opportunity to put an end to Bacchiad oppressiveness and exclusivity. One much-favoured explanation is military, but it must be said straightaway that the specific evidence for support of Cypselus by a newly emergent military class is virtually nonexistent. The background to military change, a change whose reality is undoubted, needs a word.

Aristocratic warfare, as described in the Homeric epics, puts much emphasis on individual prowess. Great warriors used chariots almost as a kind of taxi service to transport themselves to and from the battlefield, where they fought on foot with their social peers. The winner gained absolute power over the person and possessions of the vanquished, including the right to carry out ritual acts of corpse mutilation. This general picture is surely right, though it can be protested that Homer's singling out of individuals may be just literary spotlighting and that the masses played a respectably large part in the fighting described in the epics. There is some force in this objection and in the converse and related objection that in Archaic and Classical hoplite fighting individual duels were more prevalent than is allowed by scholars anxious to stress the collective character of hoplite combat. Still, a change in methods of fighting undoubtedly occurred in the course of the seventh century.

The change was to a block system of fighting, in which infantry soldiers equipped with heavy armour, or *hopla* (including helmet, breastplate, greaves, sword, spear, and a round shield attached to the left arm by a strap), fought, at least during part of an engagement, in something like coherent formation, each man's sword arm being guarded by the shield of the man on his right. This last feature produced a consequence commented on by Thucydides—namely, a tendency of the sword bearer to drift to the right in the direction of the protection offered by his neighbour. For this reason the best troops were posted on the far right to act as anchor-men. The system, whose introduction is not commented on by any literary source, is depicted on vases in the course of the seventh century, though it is not possible to say whether it was a sudden technological revolution or something that evolved over decades. The second view seems preferable since the discovery in the 1950s of a fine bronze suit of heavy armour at Argos in a late eighth-century context.

This statuette of a hoplite shows the kind of armour these ancient Greek foot soldiers wore. Hulton Archive/ Getty Images

Clearly, the change has social and political implications. Even when one acknowledges some continuation of individual skirmishing, much nonetheless depended on neighbours in the battle line standing their ground. An oath sworn by Athenian military recruits (*ephēboi*) in the fourth century includes clauses about not disgracing the sacred weapons, not deserting comrades, and not handing down a diminished fatherland (to posterity). The oath and the word *ephēbe* are fourth-century, but the institutionalizing of hoplite obligations and expectations is surely much older. Early land warfare can, in fact, be thought of as a symbolic expression of the Greek city's identity. This helps to explain the strong ritual elements in a hoplite battle, which typically began with a sacrifice and taking of omens and ended with victory dedications, often of bronze suits of armour, in some appropriate sanctuary. It is above all the heavily armed troops, not the lightly armed or the sailors in the fleet (nor even the cavalry), who were thought of as in a special sense representing the Classical polis. Thus at Classical Athens the 10-tribe citizen system determined the organization of the hoplite army but is much less important in the manning of the fleet.

The influential "hoplite theory" of the origin of tyranny seeks to explain one general phenomenon of the seventh century, namely, the beginning of tyranny, by reference to another, the introduction of hoplite weapons and tactics with their greater emphasis on a collective and corporatist ethos. Insofar as both phenomena represent reactions against aristocratic rule, it is reasonable loosely to associate the two, but it is important to realize that the theory, however seductive, is in its strict form a modern construction.

In the first place, the connection is never made by intelligent ancient writers interested both in the mechanics and psychology of hoplite warfare on the one hand and in tyranny on the other. Thucydides, for instance, a military historian if ever there was one, saw tyranny primarily in economic terms. Aristotle does indeed say that the extension of the military base of a state is liable to produce a widening of the political franchise, but this comment has nothing specifically to do with tyranny. He explains tyranny elsewhere either as resulting from splits within oligarchies or by an anachronistic fourth-century reference to demagogic leadership, which, when combined with generalship, is liable to turn into tyranny (here he is surely thinking above all of Dionysius I of Syracuse).

In the second place, it is discouraging for the hoplite theory that there is so little support for it in the best-attested case, that of Cypselid Corinth. Attempts have indeed been made to get around the natural implication of the evidence, but they are not convincing. For instance, the ancient statement that Cypselus had no bodyguard ought to be given its natural meaning, which is a denial of the military factor. It ought not to be twisted so as to imply that he did not need a bodyguard because (it is argued) he had the support of identifiable army groups. Furthermore, although it is true that Cypselus is called polemarch (which ought to mean a "leader in war"), it is suspicious that his activities in this capacity were entirely civil and judicial. Suspicion increases when one notes that polemarch was indeed the title of a magistrate in Classical Athens.

The Early Tyrannies

Other tyrannies are equally resistant to general explanations, except by circularity of reasoning. The Corinthian tyranny has been treated first in the present section because its dates are secure. There is, however, a more shadowy figure, Pheidon of Argos, who may have a claim to be earlier still and who has also been invoked as an exemplification of the military factor in the earliest tyrannies. Unfortunately, one ancient writer, Pausanias, puts him in the eighth century, while Herodotus puts him in the sixth. Most modern scholars emend the text of Pausanias and reidentify Herodotus's Pheidon as the grandson of the great man. This allows them to put Pheidon the tyrant in the seventh century and to associate him with a spectacular Argive defeat of Sparta at Hysiae in 669 BC. His success is then explained as the product of the newly available hoplite method of fighting. (The eighth-century suit of armour from Argos would in fact allow the connection between Pheidon and hoplites even without discarding Pausanias.)

This construction assumes much that needs to be proved, and the hoplite theory is in fact being invoked in order to give substance to Pheidon rather than Pheidon lending independent support to the theory. It is a further cause for disquiet that some of the detail in the literary tradition about Pheidon is suspiciously suggestive of the fourth century. Thus, Aristotle's statement that Pheidon was a king who became a tyrant is strikingly appropriate for Philip II of Macedon, who built up his military autocracy from a hereditary base of a traditional sort and whose dynasty did in fact interestingly claim Argive origins and thus regarded Pheidon as an ancestor.

Two other tyrannies date securely from the seventh century and perhaps happened in imitation of Cypselus. Both arose in states immediately adjoining Corinth. Theagenes of Megara makes an appearance in history for three reasons: he slaughtered the flocks of the rich (an action incomprehensible without more background information than is available); he tried about 630 to help his son-in-law Cylon to power at Athens; and he built a fountain house that can still be seen off the "Road of the Spring-House" in modern Megara. The last two items reveal something interesting about the social and cultural character of established tyrannies, but none of the three offers much support for the military or any other general theory of the cause of tyranny.

At Sicyon the Orthagorid tyranny, whose most splendid member was the early sixth-century Cleisthenes, may have exploited the anti-Dorianism already noted as a permanent constituent of the mentality of some Greeks. However, since the relevant action—a renaming of tribes—falls in the time of Cleisthenes himself, it is no help with the problem of why the first Sicyonian tyrant came to power at all. In any case, the main object of Cleisthenes' dislike seems to have been not Dorians in general but Argos in particular: the renaming is said to have been done to spite the Argives.

Notwithstanding the skepticism of what has been said above, some solid general points can be made about the tyrannies mentioned (Athens and Sparta followed peculiar paths of development and must be treated separately). First, these tyrannies have more in common than their roughly seventh-century dates: several of the most famous are situated around or near the Isthmus of Corinth. This surely suggests a partly geographic explanation. That is, there was an influx of new and subversive notions alongside the purely material goods that arrived at this central zone. Places with a more stagnant economic and social life, such as Boeotia and Thessaly, neither colonized nor experienced tyrannies. In fact, some version of Thucydides' economic account of the rise of tyranny may be right, though here too (as with the origins of the city-state or the motives behind acts of colonization) one must be prepared to accept that different causes work for different states and to allow for the simple influence of fashion and contagion.

Reflection on the places that avoided tyrannies leads to the second general point. Another way of looking at tyranny is to concentrate on its rarity and seek explanations for that. After all, there were hundreds of Greek states, many of them extremely small, which, as far as is known, never had tyrannies. The suggested explanation is that in places with small populations there was enough scope for office holding by most of the city's ambitious men to make it unnecessary for any of them to aspire to a tyranny. (One can add that certain places are known to have taken positive steps to ensure that regular office did not become a stepping-stone to tyranny. For example, a very early constitutional inscription shows that seventh-century Drerus on Crete prohibited tenure of the office of *kosmos*—a local magistracy—until 10 years had elapsed since a man's last tenure.) This is a refreshing approach and surely contains some truth. Nonetheless, the qualification "as far as is known" is important: with regard to many places there is no better reason for saying that they avoided tyranny than for saying that they had it. Moreover, the view that tyranny was widespread may indeed be a misconception, although, if so, it was an ancient one: Thucydides himself says that tyrannies were established in many places. Finally, the psychological argument from satisfaction of ambition is only partly compelling: it was surely more rewarding in every way to be a tyrant than to be a Dreran *kosmos*.

SPARTA

One of the foundations of ancient Sparta's political institutions, indeed of Greek political thought as a whole, was the Rhetra, an alleged response by the Delphic oracle to the lawgiver Lycurgus in about the ninth or eighth century BC.

Lycurgus. Hulton Archive/Getty Images

tribes and obes must be the units of civic organization. The Rhetra demands the setting up of a council with the kings and stipulates regular meetings for the Assembly (something not attested at Athens until far later). A crucial final clause seems to say firmly that the people, or *damos*, shall have the power. Yet a rider to the Rhetra, associated with the late eighth-century kings Theopompus and Polydorus, says that, if the people choose crookedly, the elders and kings shall be dissolvers. A poem of Tyrtaeus's has traditionally been thought to echo both parts of this document, rider as well as Rhetra, but this relationship has been challenged. Certainly there is some circularity in the usual reconstructions of one crucial corrupt line of the relevant poem.

The Rhetra is a precocious constitutional document, if it really dates to the ninth or early eighth century, and for this and other reasons (Delphi was not active and writing was not common much before the middle of the eighth century) it is common practice to date the whole document or pair of documents a century or two later. On this view, which is not here followed, the Rhetra itself, with its stipulation of powers for the (hoplite) *damos*, is a seventh-century manifestation of hoplite assertiveness: in fact, it represents a kind of Spartan alternative to tyranny. The references to tribes and obes are then seen as part of a reform of the citizen

The Rhetra

The Rhetra purports to define the powers of the various Spartan groups and individuals just mentioned. It begins, however, by saying that the tribes must be "tribed" (or "retained"; the Greek is a kind of pun) and the obes (a word for a locality) must be "obed." This is desperately obscure, but in an eighth-century context it ought to refer to some kind of political synoecism (Sparta, as stated, was never physically synoecized). The body and of the army, comparable to and not much earlier than tribal changes elsewhere (see The Reforms of Cleisthenes section below). The rider then dates from an even later period, when Spartan military reverses called for a reactionary readjustment of the balance of power.

This view, which involves downdating Theopompus and Polydorus to the seventh century from the eighth and still more arbitrarily attributing to them the activity presupposed by the Rhetra rather than the rider, does too much violence to the best chronological evidence (that of Thucydides and Herodotus), and a view in terms of eighth-century political synoecism should be preferred. As for the alleged army reform, nothing can be said about it in detail. The best reconstruction is hardly more than a creative fabrication from Hellenistic evidence that dealt with a Spartan religious festival but had nothing straightforwardly to do with the army at all.

THE HELOT FACTOR

It was definitely in the eighth century that Sparta took the step that was to make it unique among Greek states. It had already, in the Dark Age, coerced into semisubject, or "perioikic," status a number of its more immediate neighbours. Then, in the second half of the eighth century, it undertook the wholesale conquest of Messenia (c. 735–715). One consequence, already noted, was the export of an unwanted group, the Partheniai, to Taras. These were sons of Spartan mothers and non-Spartan fathers, procreated during the absence in Messenia of the Spartan warrior elite. A still more important consequence of the conquest of Messenia, "good to plow and good to hoe" as Tyrtaeus put it, was the acquisition of a large tract of fertile land and the creation of a permanently servile labour force, the "helots," as the conquered Messenians were now called.

The helots were state slaves, held down by force and fear. A seventh-century revolt by the Messenians (the "Second Messenian War") was put down only after decades of fighting and with the help (surely) of the new hoplite tactics. The relationship of hatred and exploitation (the helots handed over half of their produce to Sparta) was the determining feature in Spartan internal life. Spartan warrior peers (*homoioi*) were henceforth subjected to a rigorous military training, the *agoge*, to enable them to deal with the Messenian helots, whose agricultural labours provided the Spartans with the leisure for their military training and life-style—a notoriously vicious circle.

The *agoge* and the Sparta that it produced can best be understood comparatively by reference to the kind of male initiation ceremonies and rituals found in other warrior societies. Up to the Second Messenian War, Sparta's political institutions and cultural life had been similar to those in other states. It had an artistic tradition of its own and produced or gave hospitality to such poets as Alcman, Terpander, and Tyrtaeus. But now Spartan institutions received a new, bleak, military orientation. Social sanctions like loss of citizen status were the consequence of cowardice in battle, while a system of homosexual pair-bonding maintained the normal hoplite bonds at a level of ferocious intensity. In addition, the economic surplus provided by the lots of land worked by the helots was used to finance the elite institution of the *syssitia*, with loss of full citizen status for men who could not meet their "mess bill." The *agoge*, however, transformed Sparta and set it apart from other states. The difficulties of reconstructing the details of the agoge are acute: "invented tradition" has been unusually busy in this area.

The helot factor affected more than Sparta's internal life. Again and again modifications were forced on Sparta in the sphere of foreign policy. The Spartans could not risk frequent military activity far from home, because this would entail leaving behind a large population of discontented helots (who outnumbered Spartans by seven to one). A solution, occasionally tried by adventurous Spartan commanders, was selective enfranchisement of helots. Yet this called for nerve that even the Spartans did not have: on one occasion 2,000 helots, who were promised freedom and were led garlanded round the temples, disappeared, and nobody ever found out what had happened to them. Some person or persons evidently had second thoughts. Xenophon, who was no enemy to Sparta, illuminated helot attitudes in his description of an episode called the "Kinadon affair," which happened at the very beginning of the fourth century; it was suppressed with ruthless and effective speed. The leader Kinadon, according to Xenophon, said that the rebel groups, among whom helots are listed in first place, would have liked to eat the Spartans raw, and incidents such as this one explain why.

Attempts to minimize the importance of this episode as evidence for helot discontent should be firmly resisted. It is a question whether the tension should be seen as Messenian nationalism or as the expression of class struggle, but nationalism cannot be the whole story. One effect of the helot phenomenon was the brutalization of the Spartan elite itself. Spartan violence toward other Greeks, particularly taking the form of threats with or actual use of sticks (*bakteriai*), is attested with remarkable frequency in the sources, as is the resentment of such treatment by other Greeks. It seems that Spartans of the officer class had a habit of treating other Greeks like the helots by whom they were outnumbered and surrounded at home, and this implied insult and humiliation was deeply resented. The arrogant use of a nonmilitary weapon such as a stick actually added to the degradation.

The Peloponnesian League

After the suppression of the Messenian revolt (perhaps not before 600), Sparta controlled much of the Peloponnese. In the sixth century it extended that control further, into Arcadia to the north, by diplomatic as well as by purely military means. On the diplomatic level, Sparta, the greatest of the Dorian states, deliberately played the anti-Dorian card in the mid-sixth century in an attempt to win more allies. Sparta's Dorianism was unacceptable to some of its still-independent neighbours, whose mythology remembered a time when the Peloponnese had been ruled by Achaean kings such as Atreus, Agamemnon, and his son Orestes (in a period modern scholars would call Mycenaean).

The central symbolic act recorded by tradition was the talismanic bringing home to Sparta of the bones of Orestes himself—a way for Sparta to claim that it was the successor of the old line of Atreus. The result was an alliance with Arcadian Tegea, which in turn inaugurated a network of such alliances, to which has been given the modern name of the Peloponnesian League. A valuable fifth-century inscription found in the 1970s concerning a community in Aetolia (north-central Greece) illuminated the obligations imposed by Sparta on its allies: above all, full military reciprocity—i.e., the requirement to defend Sparta when it was attacked, with similar guarantees offered by Sparta in return. Another, more obviously pragmatic, reason why Sparta attracted to itself allies in areas like Arcadia was surely fear of Argos. Archaic and Classical Argos never forgot the great age of Pheidon, and from time to time the Argives tried to reassert a claim to hegemony in mythical terms of their own. One way of doing so was to back the claim of the Pisatans (rather than the Eleans) to run the Olympic Games.

In the same period (the middle of the sixth century), Sparta drew on its enhanced prestige and popularity in the Peloponnese to take its antipathy to tyranny a stage further: a papyrus fragment of what looks like a lost history supports Plutarch's statement that Sparta systematically deposed tyrants elsewhere in Greece—the tyrannies in Sicyon, Naxos, and perhaps even the Cypselid at Corinth (though this may be a confusion for a similarly named community called Cerinthus on Euboea).

The most famous deposition was Sparta's forcible ending of the tyranny at Athens. Finally one must ask, however, what were Sparta's motives for this and other interventions. Perhaps part of the motive was genuine ideological dislike of tyranny. Sparta was to exploit this role as late as 431, when it entered the great Peloponnesian War as would-be liberator of Greece from the new "tyranny" in Greece—namely, the Athenian empire. But this theory can be turned on its head: perhaps the Spartans retrojected their antipathy to tyranny into the Archaic period as a way of justifying their moral stance in the late 430s. Or Sparta may have been worried about the ambitions of Argos, with which certain tyrants, like the Athenian, had close connections. Or it may have longsightedly detected sympathy on the part of certain tyrants toward the growing power of Persia. It is true that Sparta made some kind of diplomatic arrangement with the threatened

Lydian power of the Anatolian ruler Croesus not long before his defeat by Persia in 546.

If suspicion of Persia was behind the deposition of the tyrants, Sparta was inconsistent in carrying out its anti-Persian policy. It did not help Croesus in his final showdown with Persia, nor did it help anti-Persian elements on Samos, nor did it do much in the years immediately before the great Greek-Persian collision of 480–479 called the Persian War (it sent no help to the general rising of Ionia against Persia in 499 nor to Athens at the preliminary campaign of Marathon in 490). Inconsistency of diplomatic decision making on the part of Sparta is, however, always explicable for a reason already noticed—its helot problem.

ATHENS

Athens was also highly untypical in many respects, though perhaps what is most untypical about it is the relatively large amount of evidence available both about Athens as a city and imperial centre and about Attica, the territory surrounding and controlled by Athens. (This is a difficulty when one attempts to pass judgment on the issue of typicality versus untypicality in ancient and especially Archaic Greek history. It often is not known whether a given phenomenon is frequent or merely frequently attested. This kind of thing creates difficulties for what students of modern history call "exceptionalist" theories about particular states.) Even at Athens there is much that is not yet known; for instance, of the 139 villages, or demes, given a political definition by Cleisthenes in 508, only a handful have been properly excavated.

First, it is safe to say that Attica's huge size and favourable configuration made it unusual by any standards among Greek poleis. Its territory was far larger than that of Corinth or Megara. While Boeotia, though in control of a comparable area, resorted to the federal principle as a way of imposing unity. Like Corinth but unlike Thebes (the greatest city of Classical Boeotia), Athens had a splendid acropolis (citadel) that had its own water supply, a natural advantage making for early political centralization. And Athens was protected by four mountain systems offering a first line of defense.

Second, Attica has a very long coastline jutting into the Aegean, a feature that invited it to become a maritime power (one may contrast it with Sparta, whose port of Gythion is far away to the south). This in turn was to compel Athens to import quantities of the ship-building timber it lacked, a major factor in Athenian imperial thinking. (It helps to explain its fifth-century interest in timber-rich Italy, Sicily, and Macedon.)

Third, although Attica was rich in certain natural resources, such as precious metal for coinage—the silver of the Laurium mines in the east of Attica—and marble for building, its soil, suitable though it is for olive growing, is thin by comparison with that of Thessaly or Boeotia. This meant that when Athens's territory became more densely populated after the post-Mycenaean depopulation, which had affected all Greece, it had to look for outside sources of grain, and, to secure those sources, it had to act imperialistically. Some scholars have attempted to minimize Athens's dependence on or need for outside sources of grain and to bring down the date at which it began to draw on the granaries of southern Russia via the Black Sea (as it definitely did in the fourth century). Certainly, there were fertile areas of Attica proper, for instance near Marathon, and at many periods Athens directly controlled some politically marginal but economically productive areas such as the Oropus district to the north or the island of Lemnos. A case can also be made for saying that if Athenians had been prepared to eat less wheat and more barley, Athens could have fed itself. Real needs, however, are sometimes less important than perceived needs, and for the understanding of Athenian imperial actions it is more important that its politicians believed (even if modern statisticians would say they were wrong) that internal sources of grain must be endlessly supplemented from abroad. Nor is it entirely plausible to dissociate Athens's seventh-century acquisition of Sigeum from the provisioning possibilities of the Black Sea region.

Unlike the Peloponnese, with its tradition of Dorian invasion from the north, Athens claimed to be "autochthonous"—that is, its inhabitants had occupied the same land forever. Like any such claim, it was largely fiction, but it helped to make up for Athens's relative poverty in religion and myth: it has nothing to compare with the great legends of Thebes (the Oedipus story) or the Peloponnese (Heracles; the house of Atreus). There was one hero, however, who could be regarded as specially Athenian, and that was Theseus, to whom the original political synoecism of Attica was attributed even by a hardheaded writer like Thucydides.

At whatever date one puts this "Thesean" synoecism, or centralization (perhaps 900 would be safe), it seems that the late Dark Age in Attica saw the opposite process taking place at the physical level. That is, the villages and countryside of Attica were in effect "colonized" from the centre in the course of the eighth century. The process may not have been complete until even later. This explains why Athens was not one of the earliest colonizing powers: the possibility of "internal colonization" within Attica itself was (like Sparta's expansion into Messenia) an insurance against the kind of short-term food shortages that forced such places as Corinth and Thera to siphon off part of their male population.

In fact, Athens did acquire one notable overseas possession as early as 610 BC, the city of Sigeum on the way to the Black Sea. Yet as long as its neighbour Megara controlled Salamis, a large and strategically important island in the Saronic Gulf, the scope for long-distance Athenian naval operations was restricted. The excellent tripartite natural harbour of Piraeus was not safe for use until Salamis was firmly Athenian. Until then,

Theseus

A great hero of Attic legend, Theseus was the son of either Aegeus, king of Athens, and Aethra, daughter of Pittheus, king of Troezen (in Argolis), or the sea god, Poseidon, and Aethra. Legend relates that Aegeus, being childless, was allowed by Pittheus to have a child (Theseus) by Aethra. When Theseus reached manhood, Aethra sent him to Athens. On the journey he encountered many adventures. At the Isthmus of Corinth he killed Sinis, called the Pine Bender because he killed his victims by tearing them apart between two pine trees. Next Theseus dispatched the Crommyonian sow (or boar). Then from a cliff he flung the wicked Sciron, who had kicked his guests into the sea while they were washing his feet. Later he slew Procrustes, who fitted all comers to his iron bed by hacking or racking them to the right length. In Megara Theseus killed Cercyon, who forced strangers to wrestle with him.

On his arrival in Athens, Theseus found his father married to the sorceress Medea, who recognized Theseus before his father did and tried to persuade Aegeus to poison him. Aegeus, however, finally recognized Theseus and declared him heir to the throne. After crushing a conspiracy by the Pallantids, sons of Pallas (Aegeus's brother), Theseus successfully attacked the fire-breathing bull of Marathon. Next came the adventure of the Cretan Minotaur, half man and half bull, shut up in the legendary Cretan Labyrinth.

Theseus had promised Aegeus that if he returned successful from Crete, he would hoist a white sail in place of the black sail with which the fatal ship bearing the sacrificial victims to the Minotaur always put to sea. But he forgot his promise; and when Aegeus saw the black sail, he flung himself from the Acropolis and died.

Theseus killing the Minotaur, detail of a vase painting by the Kleophrades Painter, sixth century BC; in the British Museum. Courtesy of the trustees of the British Museum

Theseus then united the various Attic communities into a single state and extended the territory of Attica as far as the Isthmus of Corinth. To the Isthmian Games in honour of Melicertes, he added games in honour of Poseidon. Alone or with Heracles he captured the Amazon princess Antiope (or Hippolyte). As a result the Amazons attacked Athens, and Hippolyte fell fighting on the side of Theseus. By her he had a son, Hippolytus, beloved of Theseus's wife, Phaedra. Theseus is also said to have taken part in the Argonautic expedition and the Calydonian boar hunt.

The famous friendship between Theseus and Pirithous, one of the Lapiths, originated when Pirithous drove away some of Theseus's cows. Theseus pursued, but when he caught up

with him the two heroes were so filled with admiration for each other that they swore brotherhood. Pirithous later helped Theseus to carry off Helen. In exchange, Theseus descended to the lower world with Pirithous to help his friend rescue Persephone, daughter of the goddess Demeter. But they were caught and confined in Hades until Heracles came and released Theseus.

When Theseus returned to Athens, he faced an uprising led by Menestheus, a descendant of Erechtheus, one of the old kings of Athens. Failing to quell the outbreak, Theseus sent his children to Euboea, and after solemnly cursing the Athenians he sailed away to the island of Scyros. But Lycomedes, king of Scyros, killed Theseus by casting him into the sea from the top of a cliff. Later, according to the command of the Delphic oracle, the Athenian general Cimon fetched the bones of Theseus from Scyros and laid them in Attic earth.

Theseus's chief festival, called Theseia, was on the eighth of the month Pyanopsion (October), but the eighth day of every month was also sacred to him.

Athens had to make do with the more open and less satisfactory port facilities of Phalerum, roughly in the region of the modern airport. Thus there was an obvious brake on naval expansion.

By the later seventh century then, Athens was looking abroad, and it is not surprising to find it experiencing some of the strains that in the eighth century had led to tyrannies elsewhere. Indeed, it narrowly escaped a first attempt at tyranny itself, that of Cylon, the Olympic victor (630s). The close connection between athletic success and military values has been noted. There was an equally close connection between athletic and political achievement, and not just in the Archaic age. Cylon was helped by his father-in-law Theagenes of Megara, a fact that underlines, as does Megarian possession of Salamis until the sixth century, the lateness of Athens's growth to great power status: Classical Megara was a place of small consequence. That Cylon's attempt was a failure is interesting, but too little is known about his potential following to prove either that Athenian tyranny was an idea whose time had not yet come or that there is social and economic significance merely in the fact of his having made the attempt.

Cylon's attempt had two consequences for Athenian history. The first is certain but fortuitous: Cylon's followers were put to death in a treacherous and sacrilegious way, which was held to have incriminated his killers, notably Megacles, a member of the Alcmaeonid *genos*. Pollution attracted in this way is a slippery conception; it could wake or sleep, as Aeschylus put it. This particular pollution adhered even to persons who were not on their father's side members of the Alcmaeonid *genos*, such as the great fifth-century leader Pericles, and was usually "woken up" for deliberate and political ends.

The other consequence may not be a consequence at all but a coincidence in time. It was not many years after the Cylon affair that the Athenian lawgiver

Draco gave the city its first comprehensive law code (perhaps 621). Because of the code's extreme harshness, Draco's name has become a synonym for legal savagery. But the code (the purely political features of which are irrecoverably lost to the present short of some lucky inscriptional find) was surely intended to define and so ameliorate conditions. The Athenian equivalents of the "bribe-eating *basileis*" of the Boeotian Hesiod's poem could still dispense a rough, but no longer arbitrary, justice. Further than that it is not safe to go; Draco's code, like that of the statesman and poet Solon (*c.* 630–560), was destroyed by antidemocrats in the late fifth century. A detailed constitution foisted on Draco has survived in the treatise called the *Constitution of Athens*, attributed to Aristotle and found on papyrus in 1890. This says much about the psychology of 411 BC and little about the situation in 621.

Solon

Whatever the connection between Cylon and Draco—and one must beware the trap of bringing all the meagre facts about the Archaic period into relation with each other—firmer grounds for postulating economic and social unrest in late seventh-century Attica are to be found in the poetry of Solon. Solon is the first European politician who speaks to the 21st century in a personal voice (Tyrtaeus reflects an ethos and an age). Like the other Archaic poets mentioned, Solon wrote for symposia, and his more frivolous poetry should not be lost sight of in preoccupation with what he wrote in self-justification. He was a man who enjoyed life and wanted to preserve rather than destroy.

Solon's laws, passed in 594, were an answer to a crisis that has to be reconstructed largely from his response to it. Most scholars believe that Solon's laws continued to be available for consultation in the fifth and fourth centuries. This (as noted above) did not prevent distortion and manipulation. In any case, by the fourth century, the age of treatises like the *Constitution of Athens* and other works by local historians of Attica ("Atthidographers"), much about early Attica had been forgotten or was misunderstood. Above all, there was a crucial failure to understand the dependent status of those who worked on the land of Attica before Solon abolished that status, which was conceived of as a kind of obligation or debt. This abolition, or "shaking off of burdens," was the single most important thing Solon did. When one divides Solon's work, as will be done here for convenience, into economic, political, and social components, one may fail to grasp the possibility that there was a unified vision organizing it all and that in this sense no one reform was paramount. Perhaps the poem of Solon's that sums up best what he stood for is a relatively neglected and not easily elucidated one, but an important one nonetheless, in which he seems to claim that nobody else could have done what he did and still have "kept the cream on the milk." That is

to say, his was, in intention at least, a more just though still a stratified society that sought to retain the cooperation of its elite.

Solon canceled all "debt" (as stated, this cannot yet have been debt incurred in a monetary form). He also abolished enslavement for debt, pulling up the boundary markers, or *horoi*, which indicated some sort of obligation. This act of pulling up the *horoi* was a sign that he had "freed the black earth." The men whose land was designated by these *horoi* were called "sixth-parters" (*hektēmoroi*) because they had to hand over one-sixth of their produce to the "few" or "the rich" to whom they were in some sense indebted. Solon's change was retrospective as well as prospective: he brought back people from overseas slavery who no longer spoke the Attic language (this is the evidence, hinted at above, for thinking that the problems facing Solon went back at least a generation, into the period of Draco or even Cylon).

Enslavement for debt was not an everyday occurrence in the world of Aristotle or Plutarch (although the concept never entirely disappeared in antiquity), and they seem to have misunderstood the nature of the debt or obligation that the *horoi* indicated. It is not only Aristotle and Plutarch who found the situation bewildering. It has seemed odd to modern scholars that mere defaulting on a conventional debt should result in loss of personal freedom. Hence they have been driven to the hypothesis that land in Archaic Greece was in a strong sense inalienable and thus not available as security for a loan (of perhaps seed-corn or other goods in kind). Only the person of the "debtor" and members of his family could be put up as a kind of security. Incurable damage has, however, been done to this general theory by the independent dismantling of any idea that land in Archaic Greece was in fact inalienable (such Greek prohibitions on alienation as one hears of tend to date from late and semimythical contexts such as the fourth-century literary reworking of tradition about Sparta or from post-Archaic colonial contexts where the object of equal and indivisible land-portions was precisely to avoid the injustices and agricultural buying-up and asset stripping left behind at home).

Evidently then, some new approach is needed, and it can be found in the plausible idea that what Solon got rid of was something fundamentally different from ordinary debt. In fact, *hektemorage* was a kind of originally voluntary contractual arrangement whereby the small man gave his labour to the great man of the area, forfeiting a sixth of his produce and symbolically recognizing this subordination by accepting the installation of a *horos* on the land. In return the other perhaps provided physical protection. This would go back historically to the violent and uncertain Dark Age when Attica was being resettled and there was danger from cattle rustlers, pirates (nowhere in Attica is far from the sea), or just greedy neighbours.

Alternatively, hektemorage may simply have been the contractual basis on which powerful men assigned land to cultivators in the ninth and eighth centuries, when Attica was being reclaimed after the previous impoverished period. As the seventh century wore on, however, there was scope in Attica for enrichment of an entirely new sort, involving concentration of precious metal in marketable or at least exchangeable form as a result of contacts with elegant, rich, and sophisticated new worlds across the sea. This produced more violent disparities of wealth and a motive for "cashing" the value of a defaulting labourer. On his part, the labourer may have felt that his low social status, once acceptable or inevitable, was no longer commensurate with his military value in the new hoplite age. So Solon's abolition of hektemorage was as much a social and political as an economic change.

This theory of the origin of hektemorage is attractive and explains much. It is disconcerting, however, that the best analogies that can be offered for such semi-contractual "servitude for debt" are from older hierarchical civilizations dependent on highly organized exploitation of man-made irrigation systems (so-called "hydraulic economies"). It is hard to see who or what institution, in Geometric Attica, had the authority—in the absence of any kind of priest-king—to impose the hektemorage system generally throughout the large area of Attica. Nonetheless, one can accept that hektemorage was as much a matter of status as of economic obligation.

Solon's main political changes were first to introduce a Council of 400 members alongside the old "Thesean" council of elders known as the Areopagus, from the Hill of Ares next to the Acropolis, where it met. The functions of this new Council of Solon are uncertain, but that is no reason to doubt its historicity. Solon's Council is perhaps important not so much for itself as for what it anticipated—the replacement Council of Five Hundred, introduced by Cleisthenes at the end of the sixth century.

Second, Solon allowed appeal to the *hēliaia*, or popular law court. The composition of this body is the subject of fierce scholarly dispute. One view sees it as a new and wholly separate body of sworn jurors, enjoying even at this date a kind of sovereignty within the state. The more usual view is that the *hēliaia* was the Assembly in its judicial capacity. This view is preferable: neither in Solon's time nor later is it plausible to posit large juries whose makeup or psychology was distinct from that of the political Assembly. In later times, such appeal to the people was regarded as particularly democratic. But this is just the kind of anachronism one must be careful of when estimating Solon: until pay for juries was introduced in the 460s, such juries could not be a buttress of democracy. Moreover, it would take a courageous peasant (there were no professional lawyers or speech writers as yet) to get up and articulately denounce a bribe-swallowing *basileus*, especially if—as seems possible—unsuccessful appeal could actually result in increase of sentence.

Third, Solon admitted to the Assembly the lowest economic "class" in the Athenian state, the *thētes*, whose status was henceforth defined in terms of agricultural produce. The quotes are necessary because investing such fixed economic statuses, or *tele*, with political significance was an innovation of Solon himself. That is, his fourth political reform was to make eligibility for all political office (not just the bare right of attending the Assembly) dependent on wealth and no longer exclusively on birth (a "timocratic" rather than an "aristocratic" system). Solon's four classes were the "five-hundred-bushel men," or *pentakosiomedimnoi*; the *hippeis*, or cavalry class; the *zeugitai*, or hoplites; and the *thētes*, the class that later provided most of the rowers for the fleet.

Again, the immediate impact of the change need not have been cataclysmic: many of the older aristocracy (whether or not one should think of them as a closely defined group of "eupatridae"—that is, "people of good descent") would still have been eligible for office even after the change. But there was also a need to cater to men who were outsiders in the technical sense of not belonging to the older *genē*: the name of one such excluded but high-status category of families has perhaps come down to the present, the so-called *orgeones*. Nor were Solon's four classes themselves entirely new (as indeed the *Constitution of Athens* actually admits in an aside). Thus there were horsemen and even hoplites before Solon, and *thētes* are mentioned in Homer. The phrase five-hundred-bushel men, which at first sight looks like a prosaic and unimaginative new coinage, acquired in 1968 a ninth-century archaeological analogue: a set of five model granaries was found in a female grave excavated in the Agora. It clearly was a pre-Solonian status symbol ("I was the daughter of a *pentakosiomedimnos*"). An interesting suggestion sees the four classes as originally religious in character: their members may have had allocated functions in the festivals of the synoecized Athenian state. This is not strictly provable but is plausible because the political and military life of Athens and Attica was at all times seen in religious terms.

Solon's social legislation seems generally designed to reduce the primacy of the family and increase that of the community, or polis. To that extent it can be regarded as embryonically democratic. For instance, his laws on inheritance made it easier to leave property away from the family. He also legislated to restrict ostentatious mourning at funerals and to prevent spectacular burials, which were potentially a way for aristocratic families to assert their prestige. (And not just a potential way, either: a great noble named Cimon was buried later in the sixth century in true "Lefkandi style"—that is, close to the horses with which he had won three times at the Olympic games. This burial was surely in defiance of the Solonian rules.) As can be seen from the *Antigone* of the fifth-century tragic poet Sophocles, death and funerary ritual were always an area in which the family, and especially the women, had traditional functions. For the state to seek to regulate them was a major shift of emphasis.

The whole thrust of Solon's reforms was to define and enlarge the sphere of activity of the polis. He was concerned to recognize and increase the power of the ordinary Athenian *thēte* and hoplite, while containing without destroying the privileges of the aristocratic "cream." By uprooting the *horoi*, symbols of a kind of slavery, he created the Attica of independent smallholders one encounters as late as the fourth century. And he gave them political rights to match, "as much as was sufficient," as a poem of his puts it.

One result of Solon's reforms cannot have been intentional: the abolition of hektemorage created, in modern terms, a "gap in the work force." From then on it was beneath the dignity of the emancipated Athenian to work for a master. Some other source of labour had to be found, and it was found in the form of chattel slaves from outside. That means that the whole edifice of culture and politics rested on the labour of men and women who by "right" of purchase or conquest had become mere things, mere domestic, agricultural, or mining equipment, and whose presence in Classical Attica rose into the tens of thousands. For by the fifth century, slave owning was not confined to the aristocratic few but had been extended to the descendants of that very class Solon had liberated from another kind of slavery.

Initially the Solonian solution was an economic failure, however true it is to attribute to him the economic shape of Classical Attica. Solon himself was almost, but not quite, a tyrant. The orthodox Greek tyrant was associated with redistribution of land and cancellation of debts, though this association was to a large extent a mere matter of popular perception because wholesale redistribution of land is extraordinarily rare in Greek history.

Solon did cancel debts. He also redistributed the land in the sense that the former *hektēmoroi* now had control without encumbrance of the land they had previously worked with strings attached. He did not, however, redistribute all the land, because he left the rich in possession of the land the *hektēmoroi* had previously worked for them. In this respect Solon's rule differed from tyranny. It also differed in his simple avoidance of the word; after his year of legislative activity he simply disappeared instead of supervising the implementation of that legislation. This was unfortunate for the former *hektēmoroi*, who needed to be supported in the early years. Growing olive trees, which were a staple of Attica, was an obvious recourse for the farmer in new possession of his own plot, but it takes 20 years for olive trees to reach maturity. Such farmers could hardly look

Solon the Lawgiver. Archive Photos/Getty Images

for charity to their former masters, whose wealth and privilege Solon had curtailed. Instead they looked to a real tyrant, Peisistratus.

The Peisistratid Tyranny

It took more than one attempt to establish the Peisistratid tyranny, but in its long final phase it lasted from 546 to 510. After the death of Peisistratus, the tyrant's son Hippias ruled from 527 to 510 with the assistance if not co-rule of his brother Hipparchus, who was assassinated in 514.

Hostility to the tyrants on the part of fifth-century informants like Herodotus makes it difficult to ascertain the truth about them. That they ruled with the acquiescence of the great nobles of Attica is suggested by a fifth-century archon list discovered in the 1930s, which shows that even the post-Peisistratid reformer Cleisthenes, a member on his father's side of what Herodotus calls the "tyrant-hating" Alcmaeonid *genos*, was archon in the 520s. It is also suggested by the fact that Miltiades, a relative of the gorgeously buried Cimon, went out to govern an outpost in the Thracian Chersonese, hardly against the wishes of the tyrants. Furthermore, even the Peisistratids did not confiscate property indiscriminately, though they did levy a tax of 5 percent. This enabled them to redistribute wealth to those who now needed it—that is, those who "had joined him through poverty after having their debts removed (by Solon)." Although a formally ambiguous expression, it must in common sense apply to pre-Solonian debtors, not creditors.

How far Peisistratus, who seems to have started as a leader of one geographic faction, specifically mobilized hoplite support at the outset is uncertain, but such military backing is a little more plausible in his century than in the mid-seventh century when the "Isthmus tyrants" were seizing power. (Peisistratus's position was, however, buttressed by bodyguards. Here, for once, is a tyrant who in some ways fits Aristotle's otherwise excessively fourth-century model.) In any case, Peisistratus's introduction of "deme judges"—that is, judges who traveled round the villages of Attica dispensing something like uniform justice—was an important leveling step, both socially and geographically, and one should imagine this as an appeal to the goodwill of the hoplite and thetic classes. It also, in the longer term, anticipated (as did the well-attested road-building activity of the Peisistratids) the unification of Attica, which Cleisthenes was to carry much further.

Whether or not Peisistratus climbed to power with hoplite help, he surely strengthened Athens militarily in a way that must have involved hoplites. Indeed, the Peisistratid period ought to count as one of unequivocal military and diplomatic success, and literary suggestions otherwise should be discounted as products of aristocratic malice. In this period should be put the first firm evidence of the tension between Athens and Sparta that was to determine much of Classical Greek history—namely, Athenian alliances not just with Sparta's enemy Argos but in 519 with Boeotian Plataea. (The Plataeans, faced with coercion from their bigger neighbour Thebes, sued for this alliance at the prompting of Sparta itself. This, however, is evidence of among other things Spartan-Athenian hostility because Sparta's motive, it was said, was to stir up trouble between Thebes and Athens.) Moreover, it may have been in the Peisistratid period that the sanctuary of Eleusis, near Athens's western border and always important for defensive and offensive as well as for purely religious reasons, was fortified. But this is controversial.

This is also the period in which Athens began to be an organized naval power: Salamis became definitively Athenian in the course of the sixth century (tradition credits its annexation to both Solon and Peisistratus), with consequences already noted. The island was secured by the installation of what was probably Athens's first cleruchy, a settlement of Athenians with defense functions. Again, it is now that one finds definite mention of the first Athenian triremes, which formed a small private fleet in possession of Miltiades.

The trireme, a late Archaic invention (the first Greek ones are said to have been built at Corinth), was a formidable weapon of war pulled by 170 rowers and carrying 30 other effectives. A full-sized working trireme, first launched in Greece in 1987 and demonstrated in 1993 on the River Thames in London, proved beyond any further debate that triremes were operated by three banks of oars (rather than by three men to an oar). More generally, its size, technological sophistication, and visual impact make it possible to understand Classical Athens's psychological and actual domination of the seas.

A proper Peisistratid navy is implied by the tradition that Peisistratus intervened on Naxos and "purified" the small but symbolically important island of Delos, a great Ionian centre. This purification involved ritual cleansing ceremonies and the digging up of graves. As with Eleusis, however, this was deliberate exploitation of religion for the purposes of political assertion.

Elsewhere in Attica also, the Peisistratids interested themselves in organized religion. A literary text first published in 1982 states explicitly what was always probable, that Peisistratus actively supported the local cult of Artemis Brauronia in eastern Attica (the locality from which Peisistratus himself came) and so helped to make it the fully civic cult it is in Aristophanes' play of 411, *Lysistrata*. Too much, however, should not be credited to Peisistratus. It has been protested that the relationship between local and city cults in Attica was always one of reciprocity and dialogue. Nevertheless, the explicit evidence about Peisistratus's care for his home cult of Brauron, and the permanent military importance of Eleusis on the way to Peisistratus's enemies in the Peloponnese, make it plausible to suppose a heightening of interest in these two particular sanctuaries precisely in the tyrannical period.

Peisistratid religious and artistic propaganda, and in particular the extent to which the evidence of painted pottery can be used by the political historian, is a modern scholarly battlefield. It has been suggested, on the basis of this sort of evidence, that Peisistratus deliberately identified himself with Heracles, the legendary son of Zeus and Alcmene, and that this is reflected on vase paintings. Yet there are problems. It may be wrong, for reasons already noted, to accord to painted pottery the importance required for the theory. Certainly it needs to be proved that potters, not a numerous or powerful group at any time, had the kind of social standing that would give weight to their "views" as represented on vases, which price lists show were dirt-cheap. In addition, there are particular difficulties about supposing that any man, tyrant or not, could at this early date get away with posing as a god.

One is on firmer ground with the Peisistratid building program reflecting not only the tyrant's concern for the water supply (comparable to that shown by the Megarian tyrant) but including the construction of a colossal temple to Olympian Zeus (completed at the time of Hadrian). This and more conjectural buildings on the Acropolis were a direct anticipation of the fifth-century building program of imperial Athens. Unlike painted pottery, they could be commissioned only as a deliberate act by men with plentiful command of money and muscle.

The tyrant Hippias was expelled from Athens by the Spartans in 510. They no doubt hoped to replace him with a more compliant regime, true to their general policy, as described by Thucydides, of supporting oligarchies congenial to themselves. Oligarchy, or rule by the relatively wealthy few, however defined, and tyranny were in 510 the basic alternatives for a Greek state. The newly emancipated Athens of the last decade of the sixth century, however, reacted against its Spartan liberators and added a third member to the list of the political possibilities—democracy. Spartan disappointment at this turn of events expressed itself not merely in unsuccessful armed interventions intended to install a prominent Athenian, Isagoras, as tyrant (506) and even to reinstate Hippias (*c.* 504) but also in attempts to persuade the world, and possibly themselves, that their relations with the Peisistratids had actually been good (hence another source of distortion in the tradition about the tyrants, who on this account emerged as friends, not enemies, of Sparta).

The Reforms of Cleisthenes

In 508, after a short period of old-fashioned aristocratic party struggles, the Athenian state was comprehensively reformed by Cleisthenes, whom Herodotus calls "the man who introduced the tribes and the democracy," in that order. The order is important. Cleisthenes' basic reform was to reorganize the entire citizen body into 10 new tribes, each of which was to contain elements drawn from the whole of Attica. These tribes, organized initially on nothing more than residence and not on the old four Ionian tribes based purely on descent, would from then on determine whether or not a man was Athenian and so fix his eligibility for military service.

The tribes were also the key part of the mechanism for choosing the members of a new political and administrative Council of Five Hundred, whose function it was to prepare business for the Assembly. This Council, or Boule, insofar as it was drawn roughly equally from each tribe, could be said to involve all Attica for the first time in the political process: all 140 villages, or demes, were given a quota of councillors—as many as 22 supplied by one superdeme and as few as 1 or 2 by some tiny ones. An interesting case has been made for saying that this political aspect was secondary and that the Cleisthenic changes were in essence and intention a military reform. Herodotus, for example, remarks on the military effectiveness of the infant Cleisthenic state, which had to deal immediately and successfully with Boeotian and Euboean invasions. And there were arguably attempts, within the Cleisthenic system, to align demes from different *trittyes* (tribal thirds) but the same tribe along the arterial roads leading to the city, perhaps with a view to easy tribal mobilization in the city centre. It is right that the political aspects of Cleisthenes (who was in fact far from producing democracy in the full sense) can too easily be overemphasized at the expense of the military. However, the better view is that the new system had advantages on more than one level simultaneously.

One military result of Cleisthenes' changes is not in dispute: from 501 on, military command was vested in 10 *stratēgoi*, or commanders (the usual translation "generals" obscures the important point that they were expected to command by sea as well as by land). Normally, each of the 10 tribes supplied one of these generals. They were always directly elected. Direct election for the *stratēgia* remained untouched by the tendency in subsequent decades to move in the general direction of appointment by lot. (Appointment by lot was more democratic than direct election because the outcome was less likely to be the result of manipulation, pressure, or a tendency to "deferential voting.")

Even the Athenians were not prepared to sacrifice efficiency to democratic principle in this most crucial of areas. The number 10 remained sacrosanct and so (probably) did the "one tribe, one general" principle, though later in the fifth century, and in the fourth, it was possible for one tribe to supply two generals, one of whom was elected at the expense of the tribe whose candidate had polled the fewest votes. Again, the object was to ensure maximum efficiency: there might be two outstanding men in one tribe. Another peculiarity of the *stratēgia*, to be explained in the same way, was that reelection, or "iteration," was possible. (Actually it is not quite certain that the *stratēgia* was unique in this respect. It is possible that iteration was possible for the archonship as well.)

The Cleisthenic system was based on the *trittys*, or tribal "third" mentioned above. There were three kinds of *trittys* to each of the 10 tribes, the kinds being called "inland," "coastal," and "city." There were therefore 30 *trittyes* in all, and each of the 139 demes belonged to a *trittys* and a tribe. The numbers of demes in a tribe could and did vary greatly, but the tribes were kept roughly equal in population as far as one can see. (The last words represent an important qualification: it is just possible that the whole system was overhauled in 403 to take account of changes in settlement patterns effected by the great Peloponnesian War. In that case the evidence for deme quotas—evidence that is mostly derived from fourth-century or Hellenistic inscriptions—would not be strictly usable for the sixth or fifth centuries. But in fact there is just enough evidence from the fifth century to make the assumption of continuity plausible.)

Each of the 10 tribes supplied 50 councillors to the new Council. In this way, even the remotest deme was involved in what happened in the city. Cleisthenes' solution can thus be seen in its political aspect as an attempt to deal with a characteristic problem of ancient states, which were mostly agriculturally based. That problem was to avoid the domination of city assemblies by the urban population. Cleisthenes' system gave an identity to the deme that it had not had before, even though the word *dēmos* just means "the people," hence "where the people live," hence "village" (the word and concept certainly predate Cleisthenes). Now it had a more precise sense: it was an entity with an identifiable body of demesmen and a right to representation in the Council.

The Cleisthenic deme was the primary unit for virtually all purposes. It was a social unit: to have been introduced to one's demesmen in an appropriate context was good evidence that one was a citizen. It was the primary agricultural unit—though it is disputed whether all settlement in Attica was "nucleated" (that is, whether all farms were clustered together around demes), as one view holds. In fact, there is much evidence for nonnucleated (i.e., isolated) settlement. It was, as stated, a legal unit—although deme judges were suspended from 510 to the 450s. It was a financial unit: temple accounts from the distant deme of Rhamnus date from well back in the fifth century. It was a political unit: as shown, it supplied councillors to the new Council and enjoyed a vigorous deme life of its own (though it seems that there was little overlap between deme careers and city careers). It was a military unit: not only did tribes train together, but a dedication by the demesmen of Rhamnus may show that they participated as a group in the conquest of Lemnos by Miltiades about 500 BC. (Another view puts this inscription in the years 475–450 and sees it as a dedication by cleruchs or a garrison.) Above all it was a religious unit: deme religious calendars, some of the most informative of them published in the 1960s and 1970s, show a rich festival life integrated with that of the polis in a careful way so as to avoid overlap of dates. It has been suggested that the worship of Artemis of Brauron, a predominantly female concern, was somehow organized according to the 10-tribe system. Finally, and related to the last, it was a cultural unit: at the deme festival for Dionysus (the "Rural Dionysia") there were dramatic festivals, subsidized, as inscriptions show, by wealthy demesmen and sometimes even by foreigners (one wealthy Theban is attested).

Cleisthenes seems also to have addressed himself to the definition of the Assembly, or Ecclesia. As seen, Solon admitted *thētes* to the Assembly, but Cleisthenes fixed the notional number of eligible Athenians (adult free male Athenians, that is) at 30,000. One-fifth of this total, 6,000, was a quorum for certain important purposes, such as grants of citizenship.

Cleisthenes' ulterior motive in all this must remain obscure in the absence of any corpus of poetry by the man himself, of any biographical tradition, and even of good documentary or historiographic evidence from anywhere near Cleisthenes' own time (the *Constitution of Athens* is reasonably full, but it was written nearly 200 years later).

That the tribal aspect of Cleisthenes' changes was central was recognized even in antiquity, but Herodotus's explanation, that he was imitating his maternal grandfather, Cleisthenes of Sicyon, does not suffice as an explanation on its own. The question is why he should have been anxious that each Athenian tribe should be a kind of microcosm of all Attica. Politically, the tribe does feature in Athenian public life (for instance, tribal support in lawsuits was valuable, and each of the 10 tribes presided by rotation over the Council for one-tenth of the year. This is the so-called prytany system). But the tribe was not a voting unit like the Roman tribe—Athenian votes were recorded as expressions of individual opinion, not submerged in some larger electoral or legislative bloc—and the later political functions of tribes were not quite numerous enough to explain why Cleisthenes felt it necessary to subdivide them into "thirds" in the way he did.

Cleisthenes' changes should be seen in their context. First, the Attica he inherited had a relatively small number of militarily experienced fighters, many of them former Peisistratid mercenaries. It was essential that these be distributed among the tribes if the latter were to be militarily effective. (It is a corollary of this that one accepts that at some preliminary stage in Cleisthenes' reforms there was widespread granting of citizenship to residents of Attica whose status was precarious. There was surely plenty of immigration into prosperous Peisistratid Attica, not all of it military in character.)

Second, in the late Archaic period tribal reform took place in other communities, some far removed from Attica in both character and geography. Cleisthenes' system looks subtle, theoretical, and innovatory in its decimal approach to political reform and its reorganization of "civic space," but there were precedents and parallels. For example, at Cyrene, three-quarters of a century after its colonization by Thera, there was *stasis* (political strife), which Demonax, a reformer who was called in from Mantinea on the mainland, settled by reorganizing Cyrene into three tribes. Again, at tyrannical or possibly post-tyrannical Corinth, it seems (the evidence is some boundary markers published in 1968) that there was a tribal reorganization along *trittys* lines not dissimilar to, but earlier than, Cleisthenes' system.

Finally, there is the Roman analogy: the new system of tribes and centuries, a system based partly on residence, replaced a purely gentilitial system—i.e., one based only on heredity. The word *century* is a clue: although the term signifies a voting unit, it is military in character. It is evident that tribal reform was a fairly general Archaic solution to the difficulties experienced by states with large numbers of immigrants. Such states needed the human resources these immigrants represented, but they could not admit them under the old rules. The rules had to be changed.

One may end with religion, which has been called a way of "constructing civic identity" in the ancient world, where religion was something embedded, not distinct. Cleisthenes was a decisive innovator in the social sphere, above all in the new role he allotted to the deme, but he did not dismantle the older social structures with their strong religious resonances. (The phratry, which was associated with Zeus and Apollo, continued to be an important regulator of citizenship.) His 10 new tribes were all named after heroes of Athenian or Salaminian myth, and these tribal heroes were objects of very active cult: this is in itself a recognition of a craving for a religiously defined identity. Nor did the old four Ionian tribes altogether disappear as religious entities. They are mentioned in a sacrificial context in a late fifth-century inscription and continued to matter in imperial contexts. (In the period of the fifth-century Athenian empire, some eastern Aegean islands and mainland cities went on using the names of the old four Ionian tribes for their civic subdivisions. This may help to explain the importance of the tribes in the Ion of Euripides, a play written in perhaps 412 BC, a time of imperial crisis.) The Cleisthenic Athenian state was still in many ways traditional, and it is above all in the religious sphere that one sees continuity even after Cleisthenes.

THE WORLD OF THE TYRANTS

If the earlier Archaic period was an age of hospitality, the later Archaic age was an age of patronage. Instead of individual or small-scale ventures exploiting relationships of *xenia* (hospitality), there was something like free internationalism. Not that the old *xenia* ties disappeared—on the contrary, they were solidified, above all by the tyrants themselves.

Intermarriage Between the Great Houses

One very characteristic manifestation of this is intermarriage between the great houses of the tyrannical age, as between Cylon of Athens and Theagenes of Megara or between the family of Miltiades and that of Cypselus of Corinth. The Cypselids also were on good terms with the tyranny of Thrasybulus of Miletus in Anatolia (an indication that the Lelantine War alignments had been reversed, though no explanation for this is available).

The archetypal event of the Archaic age, however, was the sixth-century entertainment by Cleisthenes of Sicyon of the suitors for the hand of his daughter Agariste. This occasion looks back in some respects to the Homeric "suitors" of Penelope in the *Odyssey*. The novelty is that one is now in the world of the polis, and the suitors were men who had "something to be proud of either in their country or in themselves." They came from Italy (two of them, one from Sybaris, one from Siris), Epidamnus in northwestern Greece, Aetolia, Arcadia, Argos (the great-grandson of the great Pheidon), Eretria, Thessaly, and many other places. The winner was one of the two Athenians, Megacles the Alcmaeonid (the other Athenian, Hippocleides, had been well in front but lost the girl by dancing on a table with his legs in the air). Megacles' son by Agariste was the reformer Cleisthenes, named (as so often in Greece) after his grandfather. The suitors were made to perform in the gymnasia (if not too old, Herodotus says), but the decisive "match" at the Trial of the Suitors was held at the final banquet or symposium: proof of the centrality that athletics and communal banqueting had by now assumed.

Although some of the tyrants may (like the Athenian Peisistratids) have retained existing structures such as the archonship and so shown their respect for the status quo, the marriages even of the Peisistratids had politically defiant implications. They were more like pharaonic or Hellenistic sister marriage or like the close intermarrying in aristocratic families of the Roman Republic in that the tyrants had to take their wives only from strains as pure as their own. Yet in the tyrannical world the tyrant had no superiors or equals within his own state. More practically, such ties tended to guarantee political equilibrium. Another related feature that can be explained along similar lines was the practice of multiple marriages (Peisistratus had at least three wives). Breaking the normal social rules in this way had the function of placing the tyrant apart. It is an example of the games princes play.

A third aspect, both cause and consequence, of such intermarriage is internationalism. There also were other factors that contributed to creating something like a common culture or *koinē*. Some of these factors stemmed from an earlier period, such as that of the great Olympic Games (see near the beginning of this chapter "Colonization" and City-State Formation). Patronage of poets and artists was a newer phenomenon that helped to make the Greek world a *koinē* through the movement of ideas and individuals from one tyrannical court to another. (The general point must not, however, be exaggerated: cities retained their distinctive cultures, and there were sharp differences of style between one tyrant and another. Even in antiquity the Peisistratids and the Lydian tyrant Croesus were distinguished from monsters of cruelty such as Phalaris, tyrant of Sicilian Acragas.)

Poetry and Art

The poets Anacreon of Teos and Simonides of Ceos best exemplify the peripatetic lifestyle of the great cultural figures of the age. Both were brought to Athens by Hipparchus, the son of Peisistratus (Peisistratus himself did not summon poets and musicians to his court, perhaps preferring popular culture like the Dionysia and Panathenaic festivals). Anacreon had previously lived at the court of the splendid Polycrates, the sixth-century tyrant of Samos (who also patronized Ibycus, a native of Rhegium near Sicily). When Polycrates fell, Anacreon was dramatically rescued by

Hipparchus, who sent a single fast ship to take him away. Simonides, after the fall of the Peisistratids, moved to the court of the Scopad rulers in Thessaly. Pindar and Bacchylides, the writers of fifth-century victory odes for young aristocrats, were the successors of poets like these.

It would be wrong, however, to leave an impression that all the Archaic poets depended on the checkbooks of tyrants. On the contrary, the fragments of Alcaeus of Mytilene on Lesbos (*c.* 600 BC) include invective against the local tyrant Pittacus (just as the fifth-century Pindar, in one of his Sicilian poems, celebrates liberation from tyranny—i.e., the fall of one of the tyrants whose family he elsewhere extols). And the poetry of Alcaeus's contemporary from the same island, Sappho, has no political content at all but is delicate and personal in character, concerned with themes of love and nature.

More tangible in their achievements, but less easily identified by name, are the tyrannical architects and sculptors, who imitated each other across long distances. The enormous Peisistratid temple of Olympian Zeus is thought to be a direct response to Polycrates' rebuilding of the temple of Hera at Samos. Other huge efforts from the same period include a temple at Selinus in Sicily. This frenzied monumentalizing is surely competitive in character, and competition presupposes awareness. Again, Peisistratid interest in the water supply had a parallel not just in the activity of Theagenes at Megara but in a great Polycratean aqueduct at Samos, interestingly, built by a Megarian engineer.

Alcaeus

(b. *c.* 620, Mytilene, Lesbos [Greece]—d. *c.* 580 BC)

The work of the Greek lyric poet Alcaeus was highly esteemed in the ancient world. He lived at the same time and in the same city as the poet Sappho. A collection of Alcaeus's surviving poems in 10 books (now lost) was made by scholars in Alexandria, Egypt, in the second century BC, and he was a favourite model of the Roman lyric poet Horace (first century BC), who borrowed the alcaic stanza. Only fragments and quotations from Alcaeus's work survived into the Byzantine Middle Ages and into the modern world, but papyrus texts discovered and published in the 20th century considerably expanded knowledge of his poetry, enabling scholars to evaluate his major themes and his quality as a poet.

Alcaeus's poems may be classed in four groups: hymns in honour of gods and heroes, love poetry, drinking songs, and political poems. Many of the fragments reflect the vigour of the poet's involvement in the social and political life of Mytilene. They express a closed world of aristocratic values and conservatism, in which realism and idealism coexist—although the idealism is limited by the norms and goals of the poet's political faction.

This painting shows the two most famous poets of the Greek island of Lesbos. On the right, Alcaeus reads poetry to Sappho (seated left). Hulton Archive/Getty Images

At the end of the seventh century BC and the beginning of the sixth century, aristocratic families on Lesbos contended for power, among them the family of Alcaeus and his brothers, Antimenidas and Cicis. These families enrolled in hetaireiai *("factions"), societies of nobles united by an oath of loyalty and a community of ethical and political views. In the years 612–609 a conspiracy organized by Alcaeus's brothers and their ally Pittacus overthrew the tyrant Melanchrus. Alcaeus was probably too young to participate in the overthrow, but later he fought next to Pittacus in a war between Mytilene and Athens over the control of Sigeum, a promontory on the Troad peninsula near the Hellespont. He reportedly told his friend Melanippus how he had to abandon his shield to the enemy to save his own life.*

A new tyrant, Myrsilus, came to power in Lesbos, and Alcaeus became his fierce opponent. After the failure of a conspiracy, Alcaeus went into exile in Pyrrha, a small town near Mytilene. During his exile Alcaeus wrote bitter polemics against Pittacus, who had joined another faction. The poet greeted Myrsilus's death with fierce joy: "Now we must get drunk and drink whether we want to or not, because Myrsilus is dead!" With this death, Alcaeus was able to return to his home.

To replace Myrsilus, the city appointed Pittacus as aisymnētēs *("organizer"); he held power for a decade (590–580 BC). Pittacus enjoyed a reputation for benevolence and was later included among the Seven Sages (the sixth-century grouping of representative wise and clever men from all parts of Greece). For Alcaeus, however, Pittacus's rise to power meant a return to exile. (An ancient critic reported that he was exiled three times.) Alcaeus's poetry in this period dwells on his misfortunes, battles, and tireless rancour against Pittacus, whom he mocks for disloyalty, physical defects (including flat feet and a big stomach), rudeness, and low origins. There is little evidence regarding the poet's exile. He may have visited Egypt and perhaps Thrace and Boeotia. Pittacus may have recalled him from his second exile. His death is likewise a mystery, although he implied in his poetry that he was old, and some believe that he died in battle.*

Alcaeus's most influential image is his allegory of the ship of state, found in a number of fragments. Another common topic is wine, the gift of Dionysus, "the mirror of a man," which in every season offers the poet a remedy against his woes. This theme supports the theory that much of his verse was composed for symposia, a context that would explain his allusive language, full of references that presuppose the shared experiences, values, and aspirations of political partisans (hetairoi) *gathered together for drink and song. Horace reported that Alcaeus also wrote hymns and erotic verse for handsome young men.*

Other fragments of Alcaeus's work convey the atmosphere of everyday life in sixth-century Mytilene. He wrote of ships and rivers, of a girls contest, of a flock of wigeon in flight, and of the flowers that herald the spring. He managed to convey the spirit and the values of the city-states of the Aegean, as, for example, when he declares that true greatness lies "not in well-fashioned houses, nor in walls, canals, and dockyards, but in men who use whatever Fortune sends them."

INTERNATIONAL INFLUENCES

Such eastern Greek influences on thinking in the mainland imply a general Ionian intellectual primacy, which is most obvious in the sphere of speculative thinking. One sixth-century city above all, Miletus in Anatolia, produced a formidable cluster of thinkers (it is best to avoid the metaphor of a series, with its implication that intellectual progress was linear or organized). The cosmological theories of Thales, Anaximander, and Anaximenes are remarkable more for their method—a readiness to work with abstractions, such as water, or the unlimited, to which they accorded explanatory power—than for the actual solutions they reached. It is an interesting modern suggestion that all three were influenced by Persian or even ultimately Indian thought. The suggestion is especially plausible for Heraclitus (fl. 500 BC), because his native city of Ephesus, with its cult of Artemis (a goddess whose worship has features borrowed from that of her native counterpart Anahita) and its large Persian population, was always—down to and including Roman times—especially open to Iranian influences.

This raises the general question of intellectual awareness of the Persian empire, which conquered the Lydian kingdom of Croesus about 546 BC and so inherited Lydian rule over the Greeks of the Asiatic coastal mainland. The poetry of another poet-philosopher, Xenophanes, from the Ionian city of Colophon, addressed itself to problems of religion and concluded that if horses had gods those gods would be horses, just as Ethiopian gods are black-skinned and Thracian gods have blue eyes. Xenophanes' awareness of the differences between cultures could plausibly be linked to the turnover of empires around him, even if there were no confirmation in the form of a poem describing a symposium at which men "sit drinking sweet wine and chewing chick-pea, and asking each other 'How old were you when the Mede came?' " (The Medes were the predecessors of the Persians, and the Greeks sometimes, as here, conflated the two.) In his "sympotic" aspect—that is, his emphasis on the symposium—Xenophanes was a child of his age. He was more unusual in his rejection, in another poem, of athletic values because of what he thought to be their coarsening effects.

One way in which Persia influenced Greek thought was via individual refugees and refugee communities. Thus, Pherecydes of Syros has been seen as a theologian who emigrated from Anatolia to the west after Cyrus's arrival. (Whether there was a more general westward diaspora of Magi, members of the Persian religious caste, is disputable.) Whole communities left Anatolia under duress. Some of them became famous in later philosophical history, such as Phocaea, which founded Elea in Italy, a place famous for philosophy, and Teos, which founded Abdera in northern Greece, the home of the fifth-century atomists Democritus and Leucippus. Finally, one must allow for a considerable Egyptian and western Semitic influence on Archaic Greek religion, political organization, and thought, though its precise extent and the means by which it was mediated await proper scientific treatment.

The greatest literary stimulus provided by neighbouring cultures like the Persian was in the field of ethnography and history. The "inquiries" (*historiai*) of Herodotus, from Asiatic Halicarnassus, will be discussed later, but they would not have been possible without the writings of Hecataeus, another Milesian (*c.* 500 BC), who treated both geography and myth in works that survive today only in fragmentary form. Hecataeus was a "logographer," a prose writer as opposed to the poets so far considered. The gradual move from verse to prose as an intellectual medium goes together with a shift from oral to written culture. But that second shift was not complete even in Athens until well into the fifth century, and there is a case for thinking that even then and in the "document-minded" fourth century "oral" and "written" attitudes coexisted.

Inquiries of Hecataeus's kind had a certain practical application: knowledge of the world, in the most literal sense of that phrase, was of obvious usefulness in a city like Miletus with its colonial connections (in the Black Sea region) and its long-distance trade. (A close connection with Sybaris in southern Italy is implied by Herodotus's story that, when Sybaris was destroyed in 510 BC, the Milesians collectively went into mourning. And Herodotus says that at the beginning of the Ionian revolt, in 500–499, Miletus was at the height of its prosperity.) When the time came to confront Persia politically, after 500, Hecataeus had the standing to suggest initiatives for shared Ionian defense. Surely this standing was conferred as much by what Hecataeus knew as by who he was. On the longer perspective, it was awareness of Persia that helped the Greeks, as it helped the Jews about the same time, to define themselves by opposition. The existence of a great and menacing culture perceived as importantly different was thus a factor in the formation of a common late Archaic Greek culture.

These political and ideological consequences of Archaic Greek thought can be seen as a kind of practical application of theory. The greatest applied scientific achievements of the Archaic period, however, were in the sphere of military technology—the trireme and the hoplite. Some Middle Eastern influence can, it is true, be posited for each (Phoenician for the trireme, Assyrian for hoplite armour). Their refinement and effective use was Greek, however. The victories of the Persian Wars were won as much by the anonymous Archaic developers of the trireme and the hoplite as by the particular Greeks of 490 and 480–479.

CHAPTER 2

Classical Greek Civilization: The Persian Wars

Between 500 and 386 BC Persia was for the policy-making classes in the largest Greek states a constant preoccupation. (It is not known, however, how far down the social scale this preoccupation extended in reality.) Persia was never less than a subject for artistic and oratorical reference, and sometimes it actually determined foreign policy decisions.

The situation for the far more numerous smaller states of mainland Greece was different inasmuch as a distinctive policy of their own toward Persia or anybody else was hardly an option for most of the time. However, Eretria, by now a third-class power, had its own unsuccessful "war" with Persia in 490, and some very small cities and islands were proud to record on the "Serpent Column" (the victory dedication to Apollo at Delphi) their participation on the Greek side in the great war of 480–479. But, even at this exalted moment, choice of sides, Greek or Persian, could be seen, as it was by Herodotus, as having been determined either by preference for local masters or by a desire to spite an equal and rival state next door. (He says this explicitly about Thessaly, which "Medized"—i.e., sided with the Persians—and its neighbour and enemy Phocis, which did not.) Nor is it obvious that for small Greek places the change to control by distant Persia would have made much day-to-day difference, judging from the experience of their kinsmen and counterparts in Anatolia or of the Jews (the other articulate Persian subject nation). Modern Western notions of religious tolerance do not apply, however.

It remains true that Persia had no policy of dismantling the social structures of its subject communities or of driving their religions underground (though it has been held that the Persian king Xerxes tried to impose orthodoxy in a way that compelled some Magi to emigrate). Persia certainly had no motive for destroying the economies of the peoples in its empire. Naturally, it expected the ruling groups or individuals to guarantee payment of tribute and generally deferential behaviour, but then the Athenian and Spartan empires expected the same of their dependents. The Athenians, at least, were strikingly realistic and undogmatic about not demanding regimes that resembled their own democracy in more than the name.

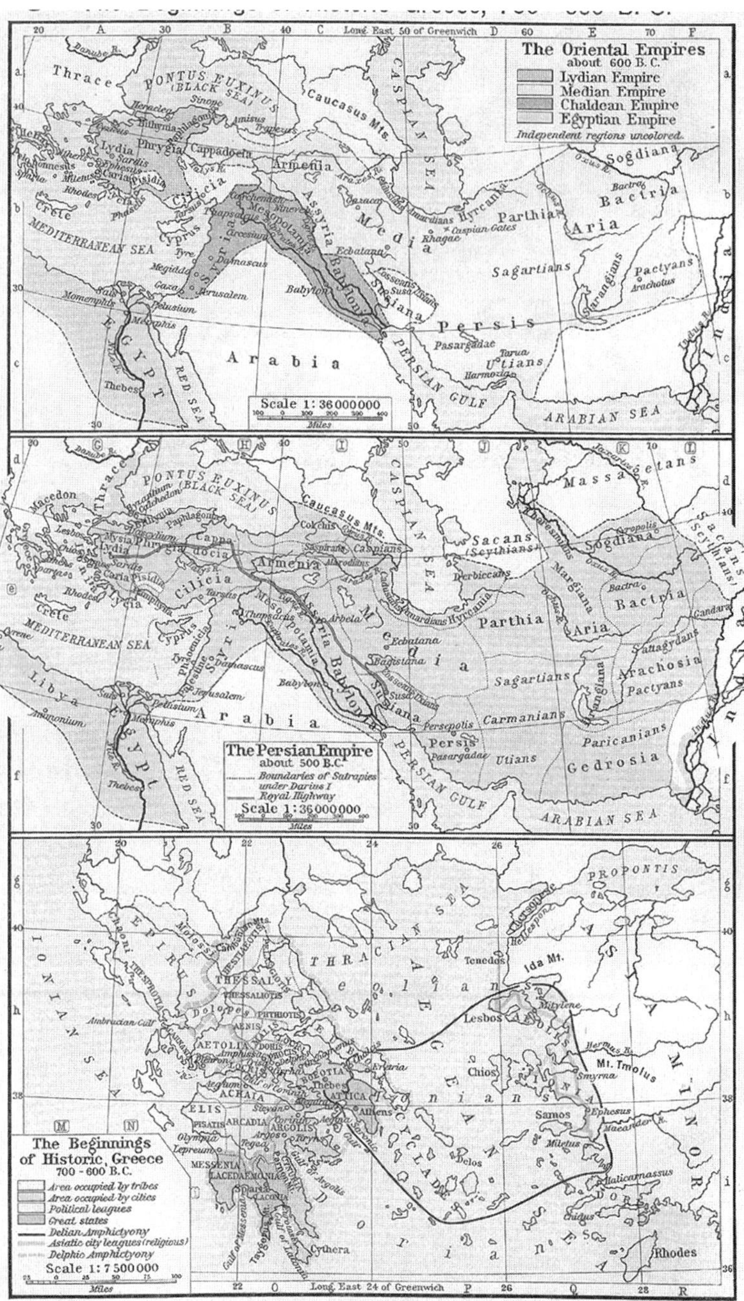

These maps show the ancient world from Greece to Persia in the years before the Persian war. Courtesy of the University of Texas Libraries, The University of Texas at Austin

THE IONIAN REVOLT

But the experience of the Asiatic Greek cities was different again, because it was precisely here that the great confrontation between Greeks and Persians began, about 500 BC. The first phase of that confrontation was the "Ionian revolt" of the Asiatic Greeks against Persia (despite the word Ionian, other Asiatic Greeks joined in, from the Dorian cities to the south and from the so-called Aeolian cities to the north, and the Carians, not Greeks in the full sense at all, fought among the bravest). The puzzle is to explain why the revolt happened when it did, after nearly half a century of rule by the Achaemenid Persian kings (that is, since 546 when Cyrus the Great conquered them. His main successors were Cambyses [530–522], Darius I [522–486], Xerxes I [486–465], Artaxerxes I [465–424], and Darius II [423–404]). Too little is known about the details of Persian rule in Anatolia during the period 546–500 to say definitely that it was not oppressive, but, as stated above, Miletus, the centre of the revolt, was flourishing in 500.

The causes of the Ionian revolt are especially hard to determine because the revolt was a short-term failure. (Concessions were made after it, however, and its longer-term consequence, the Persian Wars proper, resulted in the establishment of a strong Athenian influence in western Anatolia alongside the Persian.) Defeats lead, especially in oral traditions, to recriminations: "Charges are brought on all sides," Herodotus says despairingly about the difficulty of finding out the truth about the crucial naval battle of Lade (495).

Herodotus himself was contemptuously hostile, regarding the revolt as the "beginning of troubles"—a phrase with a Homeric nuance—between Greeks and Persians. This is odd, because it is inconsistent with the whole thrust of his narrative, which regards the clash as an inevitability from a much earlier date. It is part of his general view that military monarchies like the Persian expand necessarily (hence his earlier inclusion of material about, for instance, Babylonia, Egypt, and Scythia, places previously attacked by Persia). The reasons for Herodotus's hostility have partly to do with anti-Milesian sentiment specifically in fellow-Ionian Samos, where he gathered some of his material (the Samians seem to have tried to represent the failure as due to the incompetence and ambitions of Milesian individuals), and partly with the generally Ionian character of the revolt (Herodotus's home town of Halicarnassus was partly Dorian, partly Carian). In addition, he was influenced by defeatist mainland Greek sources, particularly by Athenian informants who resented Athens's unsuccessful involvement on the rebel side. And he genuinely thought that the Persian-Greek conflict was a horrible thing, although mitigated, in his view, by the fact that Persians and Greeks, particularly Spartans, gradually came to know each other and respect each other's values. There were always Greeks who were attracted to a Persian lifestyle.

CAUSES OF THE PERSIAN WARS

It should now be clear that Herodotus saw the revolt in terms of the ambitions of individuals (he singles out the Milesians Aristagoras and Histiaeus), and this must be part of the truth. But this must be supplemented by deeper explanations, because the rising was a very general affair.

Economic Factors

A simple economic explanation, such as used to be fashionable, is no longer acceptable. Perhaps one should look instead for military causes: Ionians disliked the military service to which they were then compelled (they did not even care much for the naval training they had to undergo, in a better cause, before Lade). Persia not only expected personal military service but punished attempts to evade it, even at high social levels. Its method of organizing defense and of raising occasional large armies (there was no large Persian standing army) was analogous to the method of later feudalism: "fiefs" of land were granted in exchange for political loyalty and for military service when occasion required.

Here perhaps is a clue, which permits the resurrection of the economic explanation in another more sophisticated form. Grants of fiefs in Anatolia are well attested in the fifth and fourth centuries. In the pages of the Greek historian Xenophon (431–350) one finds the descendants of Medizing Greek families still installed on estates granted to their ancestors after 479 (and inscriptions show the same families were still there well into the Hellenistic period). Grants by Persia of good western Anatolian land to politically amenable Greeks, or to Iranians, made good political and military sense. Such gifts, however, were necessarily made at the expense of the poleis in whose territory the land so gifted had lain. In this, surely, were the makings of a serious economic grievance.

Political Factors

Politically, the Greeks did not like satrapal control. This seems clear from the proclamations of isonomia (something more or less democratic is implied by this word) made at the beginning of the revolt. These were perhaps influenced by very recent democratic developments back in Athens. Political dislike of satrapal control is also implied by the concessions made after the revolt ended in 494: the Persians Artaphernes and Mardonius granted a degree of autonomy by instituting a system of intercity arbitration. They abstained from financial reprisals and from demanding indemnities and merely exacted former levels of tribute, but after a more precise survey. And above all, Herodotus says, they "put down all the despots throughout Ionia, and in lieu of them established democracies." The meaning and even the truth of this last concession are alike disputed. Although there certainly were still tyrants in some Persian-held eastern Greek states in 480, some improvement on arbitrary one-man government is surely implied.

Perhaps the answer is to be found in the formula recorded by a later literary source, the Greek historian Diodorus Siculus (fl. first century BC), who wrote that "they gave them back their laws." (When in 334 Alexander similarly claimed to restore to the Ionian and Aeolian cities their laws and democracies, he was largely indulging in propaganda.) Inscriptions, above all from Persian-occupied Anatolia in the fourth century, show that the cities in question held tribal meetings, enjoyed a measure of control over their own citizen intake, levied city taxes (subject to Persia's overriding tribute demands), and did indeed operate a system of intercity arbitration.

How different all this was from the situation before 500 is beyond retrieval, but the continuity of civic structures and cults in eastern Greek states from the Archaic period to Classical times implies that in many respects the Persian takeover of 546 was not cataclysmic. For instance, one reads at the very end of Herodotus's history (concerning the year 479) of a temple on Asian soil to Demeter of Eleusis that had been brought over by the Ionians from Attica in the early Dark Age and was still going strong, presumably without a break. So the improvements introduced after 494 consisted in the increase, not in the outright introduction, of local self-determination within the satrapal framework.

In any case, one is left with the problem of why political unrest boiled over, if boil over it did, in precisely 500. A large part of the answer is to be found in the changes recently made at the Ionian mother city Athens by Cleisthenes. Local arrangements that may have seemed tolerable before the end of the century seemed less so in face of the new political order at Athens, an order that had moreover shown its military effectiveness. The hypothesis that the example of Cleisthenic Athens induced restlessness elsewhere is plausible not just for its kinsmen in Ionia, which can be supposed to have had good "colonial" communications with Athens, but even for the Peloponnese, where in the first half of the fifth century Sparta had to deal with persistent disaffection.

ATHENIAN SUPPORT OF IONIA

Communication between Athens and Ionia in this period is, however, first firmly attested in the other direction, not to Ionia but from it. In 499 the Milesian tyrant Aristagoras arrived in Athens and Sparta (and perhaps at other places too, such as Argos) asking for help. The Athenians agreed, while the Spartans under their king Cleomenes (who ruled from 519 to shortly before 490) did not, thus showing, as Herodotus says, that "it seems indeed to be easier to deceive a multitude than one man." This is out of line with Herodotus's otherwise favourable assessment of Cleisthenic democracy and should be put down to particular hostility to the revolt and its consequences for Athens. The Athenians sent 20 ships. This was a major undertaking, considering Athens's resources and commitments. In 489 (when Athens's fleet was surely bigger than it had been a decade earlier) Athens had only 70 ships, of which 20 were borrowed from Corinth. The reason Athens had borrowed these ships from Corinth (actually it was a sale at nominal charge) was Athens's war, or series of wars, with Aegina, which had caused it to build a fleet. Corinth and Athens, both of which had naval outlets in the Saronic Gulf, had a shared interest in containing the power of Aegina, the greatest other power in that gulf, the "star in the Dorian Sea," as Pindar was to call Aegina. The Athenian-Aeginetan struggle, which may actually have continued after the Battle of Salamis in 480, having begun well back in the late sixth century with a shadowy precursor in the mythical period, meant that the Athenian help sent to Ionia was risky and heroic.

On a longer perspective the struggle against Aegina helped to make Athens a naval power through simple peer-polity pressure. Ancient versions of the Athenian ship-building program, however, put too much onto the Aeginetan factor, usually out of malice against the great Athenian politician Themistocles and reluctance to give him credit for anticipating the eventual arrival of the Persian armada of 480. The better tradition allows Themistocles an archonship in 493, during which he started the walls of the Piraeus, turning it into a defensible harbour, and so first "dared to say that the Athenians must make the sea their domain" (as Thucydides puts it with forgivable exaggeration). The Ionian revolt had failed disastrously, Miletus having been sacked in 494, and it was clear that the Persian finger was now pointed at Athens and that Darius wanted revenge for the assistance it had sent. The result was the Marathon campaign.

SPARTA'S FOREIGN RELATIONS

Sparta did not participate in the Battle of Marathon. Spartan policy toward Persia in particular, and its foreign policy in general in the years 546–490, is at first sight indecisive. Having expelled the pro-Persian Peisistratids, Sparta not only tried to put them back a few years later but declined to help the Ionians in 499. The reason given by Cleomenes on that occasion, after a glance at the position of the Persian capital Susa on the map, was that it was outrageous to ask a Spartan army to go three months' journey from the sea. This is a colourful way of saying that it was a tall order to ask Sparta to go to the help of distant Greeks, with few of whom it had kinship ties. The Spartans who had made the original, admittedly ineffective, alliance with Croesus against the Persians had not been so timid. But that was when the Persian threat had scarcely appeared over the horizon.

In 490 the reason for Spartan non-appearance at Marathon was a religious scruple: the Spartans had to wait until the Moon was full, probably because this was the sacred month of a festival. There is no good reason to doubt this, though it has been argued that there were special reasons why Sparta's leadership was half-hearted in the 490s and that it should be related to the scattered evidence for helot trouble at precisely this time.

Cleomenes' own career ended in disgrace not long before Marathon. It has been suggested that he fell foul of the domestic authorities at Sparta (who always had the power to discipline the kings) because he made promises to the helots: he proposed freedom in exchange for military service. If so, this must have been late in his career. The reply to Aristagoras in 499 looks straightforward. In any case, the theory rests largely on the equally speculative theory that replaces the religious explanation for Spartan absence from Marathon with a political one. To say this is not to deny the permanent threat posed by the helots, still less to deny that Spartan equivocation can often be explained in terms of it.

THE ROLE OF CLEOMENES

Large claims have been made for the statesmanship of Cleomenes, but his vision does not seem to have gone beyond the narrow issue of "What is best for Sparta?" For instance, Cleomenes crushed the old enemy Argos, then resurgent, at the great battle of Sepeia (near Tiryns) in 494. He was too shrewd, however, to destroy it completely, realizing that dislike of Argos was one of the factors that kept Sparta's Peloponnesian allies loyal. Argos was left to the control of a group described as "slaves" (hardly literally that, perhaps really members of surrounding subject communities), which was thoroughly traditional Spartan behaviour on Cleomenes' part. He surely does not deserve to rank as a forward-looking "Panhellenist"—that is, as a supra-Spartan enemy of Persia. While it is true that he did act on one occasion against Medizers on Aegina, he did so only at the 11th hour, perhaps as late as 491.

Even by the criterion of Sparta's local interests, Cleomenes, or more fairly Sparta's treatment of Cleomenes, had bad results. Cleomenes' offer of some kind of new deal to the Arcadians (better substantiated than his dealings with the helots) came to nothing with his spectacular death. He went insane (it was alleged), was imprisoned, and committed suicide. One form his alleged insanity took was poking other elite Spartans in the face with his staff. Such violence was (as noted) characteristically Spartan, but it was evidently not acceptable to turn it against other Spartans rather than against helots or other Greeks.

Some Arcadian states were certainly disaffected in the 470s and 460s and perhaps even anticipated fourth-century developments by forming a (numismatically attested) league of their own, though the chronology of this is far from secure. It is also tempting to link the new pattern of forces in the Peloponnese, which enabled Argos to recover sufficiently to

Battle of Marathon

During the Battle of Marathon, Greek soldiers pursued the routed Persians back to their ships. Hulton Archive/Getty Images

The decisive battle of the Greco-Persian Wars was fought in September 490 BC on the Marathon plain of northeastern Attica. During this battle the Athenians, in a single afternoon, repulsed the first Persian invasion of Greece.

Command of the hastily assembled Athenian army was vested in 10 generals, each of whom was to hold operational command for one day. The generals were evenly divided on whether to await the Persians or to attack them, and the tie was broken by a civil official, Callimachus, who decided in favour of an attack. Four of the generals then ceded their commands to the Athenian general Miltiades, thus effectively making him commander in chief.

The Greeks could not hope to face the Persian cavalry contingent on the open plain, but before dawn one day the Greeks learned that the cavalry were temporarily absent from the Persian camp, whereupon Miltiades ordered a general attack upon the Persian infantry. In the ensuing battle, Miltiades led his contingent of 10,000 Athenians and 1,000 Plataeans to victory over the Persian force of 15,000 by reinforcing his battle line's flanks and thus decoying the best Persian troops into pushing back his centre, where they were surrounded by the inward-wheeling Greek wings. On being almost enveloped, the Persian troops broke into flight. By the time the routed Persians reached their ships, they had lost 6,400 men. The Greeks lost 192 men, including Callimachus. The battle proved the superiority of the Greek long spear, sword, and armour over the Persian weapons.

According to legend, an Athenian messenger was sent from Marathon to Athens, a distance of about 25 miles (40 km), and there he announced the Persian defeat before dying of exhaustion. This tale became the basis for the modern marathon race. Herodotus, however, relates that a trained runner, Pheidippides (also spelled Phidippides, or Philippides), was sent from Athens to Sparta before the battle in order to request assistance from the Spartans. He is said to have covered about 150 miles (240 km) in about two days.

conquer Mycenae (460s) while Sparta was preoccupied elsewhere, with the activities of Cleomenes toward the end of his life and the expectations he had aroused only to disappoint. (Another plausible factor in Arcadia then, as in Ionia in 500 BC, was the unsettling effect of Cleisthenic democracy at Athens.) At least one can say that Spartan worries about Arcadia were relevant to the "Great Refusal" of leadership in 479, which made possible the Athenian empire.

AFTERMATH OF THE BATTLE OF MARATHON

The internal Athenian reaction to this latest military success of the Cleisthenic democracy was to take the development of that democracy a stage further. First, a change was made in the method of appointment to the chief magistracy, the archonship. From then on the archons were appointed by lot from a preliminary elected list instead of being directly elected, as the *stratēgoi* continued to be. There were nine archons and a secretary. Three of the archons had special functions: the *basileus*, or "king"; the *polemarchos*, originally a military commander (though after the institution of the Cleisthenic *stratēgoi*, military authority passed to this new panel of 10); and the "eponymous archon," who gave his name to the year. Interpretation of the significance of the change varies according to the view taken of the importance of the archonship itself in the period 508–487. Perhaps it was a young man's office and of no great consequence. The period is patchily documented, however, and in any case it would be eccentric to query the distinction of some of the names preserved. The point has a bearing on the composition and authority of the ancient Council of the Areopagus, which was recruited from former archons. The role of the Areopagus was to be much reduced in the late 460s, and if the archonship was after all not especially prestigious, then the importance of that subsequent attack on the Areopagus would be correspondingly reduced. A more substantial reason for thinking that the archonship mattered less after 508 than it had, for instance, under the Peisistratids lies in the "seesaw" argument that the rise of the *stratēgia* must have led to a fall in the power and prestige of the archonship.

The reform of 487 was probably the first time that lot or sortition (the casting of lots) had been used, though it is possible that Cleisthenes, or even Solon, used it as a device for distributing posts equitably among basically elected magistrates. This would not be unthinkable in the sixth century, when the Athenian state still contained so many aristocratic features. After all, the Romans used sortition in this way, not as a consciously "democratic" procedure but as a way of resolving the competing claims of ambitious individuals. If so, sortition did not necessarily entail a downgrading of the importance of the office of archon.

There is a further slight uncertainty about the system of "sortition from an elected shortlist." The usual and probably correct view is that this system was discarded, not long after 457, for the archonship and other offices appointed to by lot in favour of unqualified sortition. But there is enough evidence for the survival of the preliminary stage of election to have encouraged a theory that the hybrid system continued in use down to the fourth century. This, if true, would have serious implications for our picture of Athenian democracy, but the best evidence for the hybrid system is in untypically conservative contexts, such as appointment to deme priesthoods.

THE SYSTEM OF OSTRACISM

A further novelty of the early 480s was the first ostracism. This was a way of getting rid of a man for 10 years without depriving him of his property. First, a vote was taken as to whether an ostracism should be held in principle. If the voters wanted one, a second vote was taken, and, if the total number of votes now cast exceeded 6,000, the "candidate" whose name appeared on the largest number of potsherds, or *ostraca*, went into this special sort of exile. An obstinate tradition associates the introduction of ostracism with Cleisthenes, but this hardly matters because the evidence is explicit that no ostracism was actually held until 487. The object of this very unusual political weapon has been much discussed. Whereas some ancient writers considered it as a way of preventing a revival of the Peisistratid tyranny (hardly a real threat after 490), modern scholars see it as a device for settling policy disputes—that is, as a kind of ad hominem referendum. It is possible, however, to be too rational about ostracism. Of the large numbers of *ostraca* that survive, not all have been completely published, but one can see that their content is sometimes abusive and sometimes obscene. One accuses Cimon of incest with his sister, another says that Pericles' father Xanthippus "does most wrong of all the polluted leaders." The idea of the politician-leader as polluting scapegoat is a recurrent one in Greek political invective, and it is perhaps in terms of invective, or the need for a religious safety valve, that ostracism can best be understood.

GREEK PREPARATIONS FOR WAR

Evidently, the Athenian demos was growing more bold, as the *Constitution of Athens* puts it. This was equally true in foreign affairs. The year after Marathon, Miltiades made an attack on the Aegean island of Paros, which anticipates the more systematic imperialism of the period after 479. And it is possible that the Athenian duel with Aegina continued into the 480s. But the event with the greatest implications for foreign policy was a sudden large increase in the output of the Laurium silver mines (actually in a region called Maronea).

This model of a Greek trireme shows its main weapon—a battering ram on the prow that could pierce enemy ships under the water line, sinking them. SSPL via Getty Images

The evidence gives the crucial year as 483, but it is not known whether there was really a dramatic lucky strike just before that or whether this was merely the year when Athens decided how to spend the accumulated yield of several good years. One source does speak of "discovery" of mines, but the mining area had been worked since Mycenaean times, and the mines were certainly operational under the Peisistratids. It was decided to spend the windfall on building more triremes, bringing the total to 200 by 480, from the 70 attested for Miltiades' Parian expedition of 489. The precise method somehow involved the advancing of money to individuals, an interesting partial anticipation of the Classical system of "trierarchies."

Trierarchs, who are not specifically attested before the middle of the century, were wealthy individuals who, as a kind of prestige-conferring tax payment, paid for the equipping of a trireme (the state provided the hull). The source of the timber for this huge program is not known. Perhaps local Attic or Euboean supplies supplemented Italian timber. Themistocles, who is credited with the essential decision to spend the money on ships rather than on a distribution among the citizens, had western interests that make the Italian hypothesis plausible. If this is right, the feat of transportation should be admired almost as much as the crash building program itself. One consequence of the rapidity of the program was that much of the timber must have been unseasoned. This is relevant to the eventual Greek decision at the Battle of Salamis (480) to fight in narrow waters, where the resulting loss of speed (green timber makes ships heavier and slower) would matter less.

GREEK ALLIANCES

It was in Athens, then, that the most energetic action was taken. Xerxes had not lost sight of the old revenge motive, a motive that ought to have meant that Athens was the main or only target, but his aim this time was—as Herodotus correctly says—to turn Greece as a whole into another Persian province or satrapy. This called for a concerted Greek plan, and in 481 the key decisions were taken by a general Greek league formed against Persia. Quarrels like that between Athens and Aegina had to be set aside and help sought from distant or colonial Greeks such as the Cretans, Syracusans, and Corcyrans, whose extraordinarily large fleet of 60 ships (possibly developed against Adriatic piracy but also—surely—against Corinth) would be a prime asset. Corcyra, however, waited on events, and Crete stayed out altogether, while Syracuse and Sicily generally had barbarian enemies of their own to cope with, the Carthaginians. (Syracuse and other parts of Sicily were now under the tyranny of Gelon.)

Greek writers found the parallel between the simultaneous threats to eastern and western Hellenism irresistible and represented Carthage as another Persia. It has, however, been suggested that the imperialistic ambitions of Carthage have been generally exaggerated by Greek writers eager to flatter their patrons, such as Gelon. The reality of the Battle of Himera, however, in which Gelon decisively defeated the Carthaginians, is not in doubt. Like the Battle of Salamis, it was fought in 480, allegedly on the same day. Gelon did indeed have his own preoccupations. The Greeks may not have been altogether sorry: the tyrant Gelon would have been an ideologically awkward ally in a struggle for Greek freedom from arbitrary one-man rule.

Even without western Greek help, the Greek fleet numbered about 350 vessels, amounting perhaps to a third of the Persian fleet. The size of the Persian land army is reckoned in millions by Herodotus, and all modern scholars can do is replace his guess by far lower ones. Greek unity, though impressive, was not complete. Conspicuous among the "Medizers" was Thebes, while Argos's neutrality amounted, in Herodotus's view, to Medism.

An inscription found in 1959, the so-called "Decree of Themistocles," purports to contain further detailed decisions made about this time regarding the evacuation of Attica and the mobilization of the fleet. But the writing is of the fourth century, and the whole text is probably not a reinscribing of a genuine document but a patriotic concoction of the age in which it was written and erected.

THE LAST PERSIAN WARS

An initial plan to defend Thessaly was soon abandoned as unrealistic. Instead the Greeks fell back on a zone at the northeastern end of Euboea, where they hoped to defend Thermopylae by land and Artemisium by sea. Herodotus, who is often accused of failing to realize the interconnectedness of these two holding operations, did in fact stress that the two were close enough for each set of defenders to know what was happening to the other.

THERMOPYLAE

The Spartans had sent their king Leonidas to Thermopylae with a force of 4,000 Peloponnesians, including 300 full Spartan citizens and perhaps a helot contingent as well. They were joined by some central Greeks,

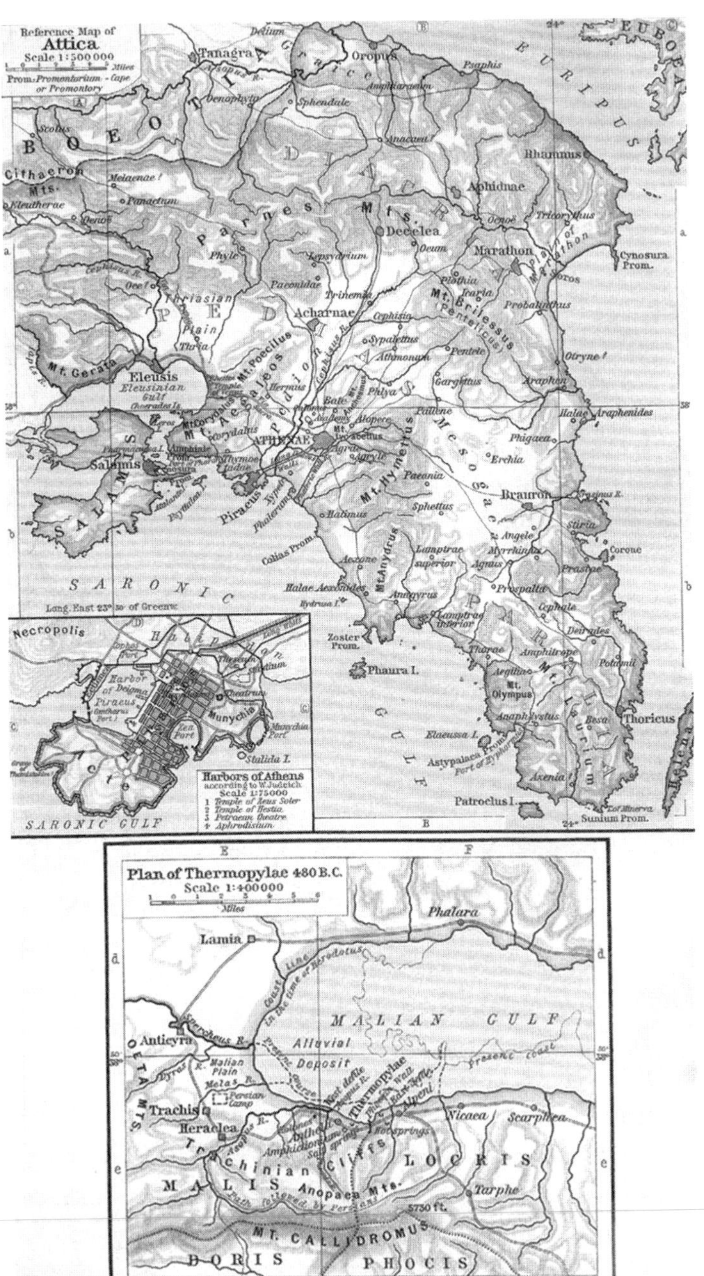

(Above) Map of Attica. (Below) Thermopylae, where the Battle of Thermopylae took place. Courtesy of the University of Texas Libraries, The University of Texas at Austin

including Boeotians from Thespiae and Thebes. The pass at Thermopylae could not be held indefinitely, as Leonidas surely knew, but he also knew that an oracle had said that Sparta would be devastated unless one of its kings was killed. Leonidas's exact "strategy" has been debated as if it were a puzzle, but perhaps one should not go beyond the oracle. The king must die.

Leonidas died, with his 300 Spartans (and the helots, Thespians, and Thebans, as should be remembered to the honour of all three). The other groups, Peloponnesians and central Greeks, were all dismissed. The naval action at Artemisium was inconclusive, the real damage to the Persian ships being done by a storm as they rounded Euboea.

Whether or not the Decree of Themistocles is genuine, it is a fact that Attica was evacuated and the Athenian Acropolis sacked by the Persians. This sacrifice of their city, like the victory of Marathon, is one of the cardinal elements in Athenian celebration of the Persian Wars. The Persians destroyed the temples on the Acropolis and carried off the statues of Harmodius and Aristogiton, the two men who had assassinated the tyrant Hippias's brother Hipparchus in 514. The symbolic importance to Athens of what happened on the Acropolis in 480 is illustrated by the subsequent history of those statues: they were returned to Athens by Alexander the Great a century and a half later as part of his claim to be punishing the Persians for their fifth-century impiety.

Salamis

The Persians entered the narrows of Salamis, where Themistocles had insisted the Greeks should be stationed, and they were comprehensively defeated under the appalled eyes of Xerxes himself. This defeat is a "David and Goliath" encounter only in the general sense that the Persian empire was vastly greater, in size and resources, than the realm of its Greek opponents. It is said that the Greek ships were actually heavier and less easy to maneuver than those of their opponents. Yet this Persian advantage, and that conferred by the greater experience of the Phoenician sailors on the Persian side, were canceled out by the Greek advantages of position: a fight in the narrows would enable them to board and fight hand to hand.

No doubt there was also a propaganda aspect. Themistocles had inscribed on the rocks of Euboea messages imploring the Ionians on the Persian side not to help in enslaving their Ionian kin. This looks forward to Athens's political exploitation, in the very near future, of its original role as Ionian mother city. For the moment it surely helped sap morale in the Persian fleet. Sound strategy might have dictated a Persian withdrawal, or an attempt to bypass Salamis and press on to the Isthmus of Corinth, before the battle had even begun, but the prestige of the Persian king was visibly at stake.

The Greeks celebrate their victory over the Persian navy in the Battle of Salamis in 480 BC. Hulton Archive/Getty Images

Plataea

Xerxes returned home, but the Persian general Mardonius remained for a final encounter with the Greeks at Plataea. The Spartans under Pausanias, regent for the underage Spartan king, advanced from the Peloponnese via the Isthmus and Eleusis. There had once been a question of making a stand at the Isthmus for the defense of the Peloponnese, but Salamis had made that unnecessary. Again the Persians were defeated, but this time the battle was primarily won, as Aeschylus was to put it in his play *Persians*, "under the Dorian spear"—that is, under the leadership of hoplite Sparta. (The army, however, was a truly Pan-Greek one and included a large infantry force of Athenians.)

Substantial fragments of an elegiac poem on papyrus by the great poet Simonides were published as recently as 1992. The poem describes the run-up to the battle of Plataea and more or less explicitly compares Pausanias to Achilles, the Greek leader of the mythical Trojan War. It thus equates the magnitude and importance of the Trojan and Persian wars. This remarkable find provides the missing link between epic, which had not hitherto normally treated recent historical events, and historiography proper. It is thus one of the most exciting literary discoveries in many decades.

These sculpted reliefs of warriors are from the archaeological site of Persepolis, Iran, once the capital of ancient Persia. Keystone/Hulton Archive/Getty Images

As much glory was to attach to Plataea itself as to Sparta. A Hellenistic geographer said with some impatience of the Plataeans that they had nothing to say for themselves except that they were colonists of the Athenians (strictly false, but an illuminating exaggeration) and that the Persians were defeated on Plataean soil. A great commemorative festival was still celebrated at Plataea in Hellenistic and Roman times. A third-century inscription discovered in 1971 mentions "the sacrifice in honour of Zeus the Liberator and the contest which the Greeks celebrate on the tombs of the heroes who fought against the barbarians for the liberty of the Greeks."

After the residue of the Persian fleet had been defeated at Mycale, on the eastern side of the Aegean, the Greeks were saved—for the moment. The Persians had, after all, returned to Greece after the small-scale humiliation of Marathon in 490. Thus there could be no immediate certainty that they would abandon their plans to conquer Greece after the far greater humiliations of 480 and 479. A leader was required in case the Persians returned.

CHAPTER 3

Classical Greek Civilization: The Athenian Empire

The eastern Greeks of the islands and mainland felt themselves particularly vulnerable to invasion and appealed to the natural leader, Sparta. The Spartans proposed an unacceptable plan to evacuate Ionia and resettle its Greek inhabitants elsewhere. This would have been a remarkable usurpation of Athens's colonial or pseudocolonial role as well as a traumatic upheaval for the victims. Samos, Chios, Lesbos, and other islanders were received into the Greek alliance. The status of the mainlanders was temporarily left in suspense, though not for long: in early 478 Athens on its own account captured Sestus, still under precarious Persian control hitherto. In this it was assisted by "allies from Ionia and the Hellespont"—that is to say, including mainlanders. The authority for this statement, which should not be doubted, is Thucydides, the main guide for most of the next 70 years.

THE FORTIFICATION OF ATHENS

The capture of Sestus was one manifestation of Athenian independence from Spartan leadership, which had gone unquestioned by Athens in the Persian Wars of 480–479, except for one or two uneasy moments when it had seemed that Sparta was reluctant to go north of the Isthmus. Another

Ruins of an ancient acropolis in Sparta, Greece. A. Garozzo/De Agostini/Getty Images

manifestation was the energetic building in the early 470s of a proper set of walls for the city of Athens, an episode elaborately described by Thucydides to demonstrate the guile of Themistocles, who deceived the Spartans over the affair. Whether the walls were entirely new or a replacement for an Archaic circuit is disputed. Thucydides implies that there was a pre-existing circuit, but no trace of this has been established archaeologically. The Themistoclean circuit, on the other hand, does survive, although the solidity of the socle does not quite bear out Thucydides' dramatic picture of an impromptu "all hands to the pump" operation carried out with unprofessional materials.

Sparta's reluctance to see Athens fortified and its anger—concealed but real—after the irreversible event show that even then, despite its cautious attitude to the mainland Ionians, Sparta was not happy to see Athens take over completely its own dominant military role. Or rather, some Spartans were unhappy, for it is a feature of this period that Sparta wobbled between isolationism and imperialism, if that is the right word for a goal pursued with such intermittent energy. This wobbling is best explained in factional terms, the details of which elude the 21st century as they did Thucydides. Thucydides disconcertingly juxtaposes the wall-building episode, with its clear implication of Spartan aggressiveness, with the bland statement that the Spartans were glad to be rid of the Persian war and considered the Athenians up to the job of leadership and well-disposed toward themselves. In fact, there is evidence in other literary sources for the first and more outward-looking policy, such as a report of an internal debate at Sparta about the general question of hegemony, as well as particular acts such as a Spartan attempt to expel Medizers from the Delphic amphictyony—i.e., pack it with its own supporters.

THE AMBITION OF PAUSANIAS

One easily identifiable factor in the formation of Spartan policy is a personal one: the ambitions of Pausanias, a young man flushed from his success at Plataea. Pausanias was one of those Spartans who wanted to see the impetus of the Persian Wars maintained. He conquered much of Cyprus (a temporary conquest) and laid siege to Byzantium. But his arrogance and typically Spartan violence angered the other Greeks, "not least," Thucydides says, "the Ionians and the newly liberated populations." These now approached Athens in virtue of kinship, asking it to lead them.

This was a crucial moment in fifth-century history. The immediate effect was to force the Spartans to recall Pausanias and put him on trial. He was charged with "Medism," and, though acquitted for the moment, he was replaced by Dorcis. Yet Dorcis and others like him lacked Pausanias's charisma, and Sparta sent out two more commanders. Pausanias went out again to Byzantium "in a private capacity," setting himself up as a tyrant to intrigue with Persia, but he was again recalled and starved to death after having taken sanctuary in the temple of Athena of the Brazen House in Sparta. (The end may not have come until late in the 470s.) The charge was again Medism, and there was some truth to this because the rewards given by Persia to Gongylus of Eretria, one of his collaborators, can be shown to have been historical. There was also a suspicion that Pausanias was organizing a rising of the helots, "and it was true," Thucydides says.

Despite its successes in 479, Sparta, then, was as much a prisoner of the helot problem as ever, and it could not rely on the loyalty of Arcadia or the Peloponnese generally: Mantinea and Elis had sent their contingents to the Battle of Plataea suspiciously late.

Delian League

*The Delian League was a confederacy of ancient Greek states under the leadership of Athens, with headquarters at Delos, founded in 478 BC during the Greco-Persian wars. The original organization of the league, as sketched by Thucydides, indicates that all Greeks were invited to join to protect themselves from Achaemenian Persia. In fact, Athens was interested in further supporting the Ionians in Anatolia and exacting retribution from the Persians, whereas Sparta was reluctant to commit itself heavily overseas. The Athenians were to supply the commanders in chief and to decide which states were to provide ships or money. Money was to be received and controlled by 10 Athenian treasurers (*hellēnotamiai*). Representatives of all member states, each with equal vote, met annually at Delos, where the league's treasury was kept in the temple of Apollo. The original membership probably included most of the Aegean islands, except Aegina, Melos, and Thera, most of the cities of Chalcidice, the shores of the Hellespont and Bosporus, some of Aeolia, most of Ionia, and a few eastern Dorian and non-Greek Carian cities.*

Action taken against Persia in the first 10 years was scattered: the Persian garrison was expelled from Eion, Thrace; an Athenian settlement (cleruchy) sent to that district was destroyed by the natives, but one sent to the island of Scyros was successful; the cities of the Thracian coast were won over; and Doriscus, unsuccessfully attacked, remained the only Persian garrison left in Europe. A major victory was achieved c. 467–466 when the Athenian commander, Cimon, heading a large confederate fleet along the southern coast of Anatolia, drove out Persian garrisons and brought the coastal cities into the league. He then defeated the Persian fleet on the Eurymedon at Pamphylia, sacked their army camp, and routed their Cyprian reinforcements.

League policy entered a new phase as relations between Athens and Sparta broke down in 461. The Athenians committed themselves to war with the Peloponnesian League (460–446), at the same time launching a large-scale eastern offensive that attempted to secure control of Cyprus, Egypt, and the eastern Mediterranean. While the Athenians and allies were campaigning successfully against the Spartans, subjugating Aegina, Boeotia, and central Greece, further expansion was checked when the league fleet was virtually destroyed in Egypt. Fearing the Persians would mount an offensive following such a naval defeat, the Athenians transferred the league treasury to Athens (454). Within the next five years, with the resolution of difficulties with Sparta (five-year truce, 451) and Persia (Peace of Callias, c. 449/448), the league became an acknowledged Athenian empire.

Athenian imperialism had been evident as early as c. 472, when Carystus, in Euboea, was forced into the league, and Naxos, wishing to secede, was reduced and subjugated. A Thasian revolt was crushed in 463, and during the 450s there were anti-Athenian movements in Miletus, Erythrae, and Colophon. The independence of the allies was progressively undermined, as Athenians interfered in their internal politics (imposing democracies and garrisons) and in their legal jurisdictions. League council meetings finally ceased, and the Athenians proceeded to use the league reserves to rebuild the Athenian temples destroyed by the Persians. Athenian participation in the Peloponnesian War (431–404) placed further strains on the allies: increased tribute to finance the war and increased military support to replace Athenian losses were demanded. But despite revolts at Mytilene (428–427) and Chalcidice (424) and widespread uprisings following Athenian defeat in Sicily (413), Athens was still supported by the democratic parties in most of the cities. After defeating the Athenians at Aegospotomi (405), Sparta imposed peace terms that disbanded the league in 404.

Ineffectual Spartan management of the former empire after 404 aided the revival of Athenian influence. By 377 Athens, with Cos, Mytilene, Methymna, Rhodes, and Byzantium, formed the nucleus of a new naval league, whose objective was to preserve peace and prevent Spartan aggression. Membership had grown to at least 50 states at the time of the defeat of the Spartans by the Boeotians in 371, but with the elimination of the common fear of Sparta that had kept the allies together, the league declined. It was effectively crushed by Philip II of Macedon at Chaeronea in 338.

PAYING TRIBUTE TO ATHENS

The Athenians first settled which allies should pay tribute in the form of money and which should provide ships. The details of this assessment were entrusted to the Athenian statesman and general Aristides. Tribute, the need for which was assumed rather than explained, was to be stored at Delos, which would also be the site of league meetings, or synods. Thucydides does not add that the choice of Delos, with its associations with Ionian Apollo, was essentially religious in motivation. Nor does he bring out more than the mercenary or revenge motive of the league (to get redress by devastating the king of Persia's territory).

The "booty" factor was indeed a major motive for much ancient warfare, and this war was no exception. But there is also evidence that the mood at the league's founding was positive and solemn, with oaths and ceremonies cementing the act of liberation (478–477). It is unlikely that there was much "small print" to which allies had to subscribe. League meetings were to be held, almost certainly, in a single-chamber organization, in which Athens had only a single vote, though a weighty one. There were perhaps undertakings, subsumed in the general oath taking, about not deserting or refusing military contributions.

Unfortunately there are no inscribed stelae, or pillars, as there are for the Second Athenian Confederacy a century later, recording precise pledges by Athens or (equally valuable) listing the members in the order of their enrollment. Apart from the big Ionian islands and some mainlanders, there were in fact Dorian members, such as Rhodes, and Aeolians, such as Lesbos. There even were some non-Greeks on Cyprus, always a place with a large Semitic component. (Some Cypriot communities probably joined at the outset.) Some Thracian

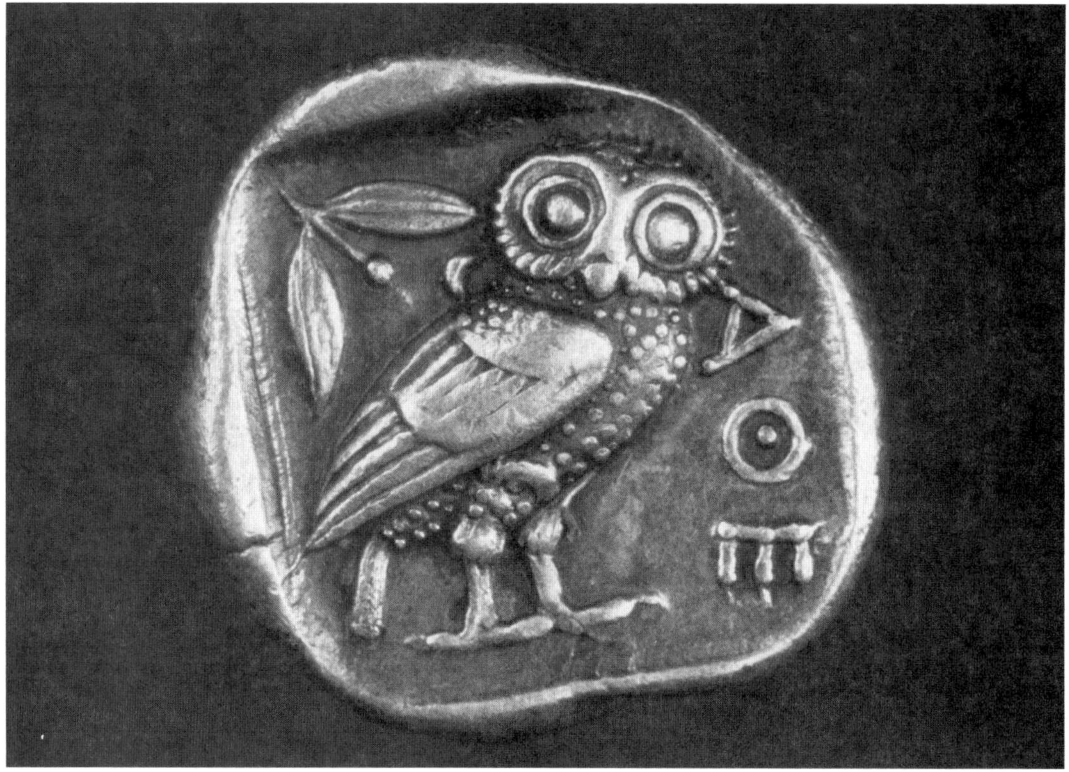

The silver owl tetradrachma coin of Athens was a popular currency across the ancient world. Private Collection/The Bridgeman Art Library/Getty Images

cities were surely enrolled very early. There was no doctrinaire insistence that the league should be exclusively maritime, though the facts of geography gave it this general character automatically. For instance, epigraphy (i.e., the study of inscriptions) suggests that by mid-century (in the period of Athens's decade of control of Boeotia, 457–446) the land-locked cities of Orchomenus and Akraiphia were in some sense members. Nor was the league necessarily confined to the Aegean: in 413, financial contributions from Rhegium in the south of Italy, among other places, were handled by the imperial "Treasurers of the Greeks." No inscribed records of tribute exist before 454 BC. After that point, one has the intermittent assistance of the "Athenian Tribute Lists," actually the record of the one-sixtieth fraction paid to the goddess Athena. It should be stressed that until roughly the late 450s there are virtually no imperial inscriptions at all.

STRAINS ON GREEK UNITY AND MOUNTING ATHENIAN AGGRESSION

Such lack of evidence makes it difficult to show in detail the increasing oppressiveness of the Athenian empire in the second half of its existence (450–404), particularly in the 420s when policy was affected by demagogues like the notorious Cleon. There is simply too little comparative material from the first three decades, and, in the absence of documentary material and of detailed information like that provided by Thucydides for the Peloponnesian War of 431–404, one must infer what happened from the very sparse literary account Thucydides gives for the years 479–439 and from supplementary details provided by later writers. Although it is right to protest, against facile talk of the harsh imperialism of Cleon, that imperialism is never soft, an important but sometimes overlooked chapter of Thucydides is nonetheless explicit that Athens suffered a loss of goodwill through its excessive rigour.

By the middle of the 470s, Greek unity had not come too obviously apart, though the reluctant withdrawal of Sparta was ominous. Even so, at the Olympic Games of 476, an unusually political celebration (the first after the last of the Persian Wars and held in the honoured presence of the Athenian Themistocles), there were still victorious competitors from Sparta, as well as from other Dorian states such as Argos and Aegina and from Italy and Sicily.

Cimon's Actions

Athens's capture of Eion on the Strymon River, also in 476, was perfectly in keeping with the ostensibly Panhellenic or anti-Persian program of the Delian League: Eion, an economically and strategically important site in northern Greece, was still held by a Persian commander. This, the first act of the league recorded by Thucydides, was undertaken by Cimon, the son of Miltiades the Younger, who had won the Battle of Marathon.

The next act of Cimon and the Athenians, the attack on the island of Scyros, was considerably more dubious. Cimon expelled the "Dolopians" (i.e., the indigenous inhabitants) allegedly because they were pirates. Protection against piracy was surely as real a justification for the Delian League as protection against Persia and more general in its application (vulnerability to Persia was very much a matter of geographic position). That Athens was effective in this respect is suggested by the evidence for recrudescent piracy in the early fourth century, when the Athenians no longer had the power to police the seas. Nonetheless, the treatment of these Dolopians, who were hardly a serious threat to peaceful commerce, certainly appears to have been an act of mere muscle flexing.

The enterprise had a propagandist point as well: Cimon brought back the bones of Theseus from the island to Athens, where they were housed in a shrine built for them, somewhere in or near the Agora—perhaps to the east of it. (The site has not been discovered. The so-called "Theseum" is generally agreed to be a temple to Hephaestus.) This magnificent piece of theatre must have been in imitation of the Spartan treatment of the bones of Orestes. This is not surprising, because Cimon was perhaps the first identifiable "Laconizer," or admirer of Spartan values, in Athenian history. Theseus had a special significance not only for Cimon but for the Athenian empire in general. It was Theseus who, according to the myth, had founded the great Ionian festival at Delos called the Delia, which Athens was to revive with much pomp in 426. Such exploitation of the cult of relics was a kind of manifestation of kinship diplomacy, a phenomenon already noted above. The Athenians practiced it again in the early 430s when they founded Amphipolis and made political use of the relics of Rhesus, a local Thracian hero.

Athens's Moves Against Other Greeks

More Athenian aggression followed, unequivocally directed against other Greeks: Carystus, at the southeastern end of Euboea, was forced to join the league. This was a stepping-up of an Athenian involvement in Euboea that goes back to the sixth century, when Athens installed a cleruchy on Chalcis soon after the Cleisthenic reforms. In the middle of the century inscriptions show that wealthy Athenians possessed land on the Lelantine Plain. Such ownership by individual wealthy Athenians of land in the subject cities of the empire is a telling phenomenon, because the land was usually acquired in defiance of local rules: landowning was normally restricted to nationals of the state in which the land was situated. For Athenians to acquire such land, otherwise than by inheritance as a result of marriage to a non-Athenian, was an abuse, and inheritance of this kind was much less likely after a law of 451 restricting Athenian citizenship to persons of citizen descent on both sides. After 451 "mixed marriages" must have been far less common.

A still more sinister move was the reduction of Naxos, probably in the early 460s. Thucydides equates the inhabitants' loss of freedom with "enslavement"—a strong metaphor. (The precise chronology of the whole period 479–439, and particularly the first 30 years, is uncertain, because Thucydides gives no absolute dates and there are none from other sources before the events in the northern Aegean of 465. The chronology followed here is the orthodox one, but some scholars seek to down-date the attacks on Eion and Scyros to 469—leaving the 470s implausibly empty of known imperial action—and Naxos later still.)

The anti-Persian aspect of the league had not, however, been forgotten, in spite of all this activity against Greeks. In 467 Cimon won the great Battle of the Eurymedon River in Pamphylia (southern Anatolia), a naval victory that made a great impression both in Greece (where it was celebrated by the dedication of a bronze date palm, or *phoinix*, at Delphi: a punning reference to the defeated Phoenician fleet) and among waverers, outside Greece proper, who had not yet joined the league. Many new allies were now recruited, such as the trading city of Phaselis on the Lycian-Pamphylian border. A rare early imperial inscription of the late 460s details the judicial privileges accorded to Phaselis.

Athens's Moves Northward

Greek success in the east was followed by some mixed achievement under Cimon in the north. A quarrel arose in 465 with the wealthy and fertile northern Aegean island of Thasos about the island's trading stations and mines along the mainland area just opposite it, and Thasos revolted. The word *quarrel* is obviously a euphemism for a piece of naked economic aggression by Athens. All ancient states wished to get their hands on as much precious metal for coinage as possible. Thasos was reduced and forced to give up all of its mines and mainland possessions. A further attempt at this time to extend Athenian northern interest, the colonizing expedition sent to the Nine Ways, the site of the later Amphipolis, was less successful. If silver was one coveted commodity, ship-building timber was another, and the desire for the latter was a large part of Athens's motive for getting a foothold in the Amphipolis region. The Nine Ways operation is a reminder that colonizing activity did not cease with the end of the Archaic period: 10,000 settlers were sent. But the entire force was destroyed at Drabescus. This was probably the occasion for instituting state burial for war dead, a democratic measure that anticipated the reforms at the end of the 460s.

Thasos signaled changes in foreign policy alignments all over Greece. The Thasians had appealed to Sparta for help, asking it to invade Attica, and the Spartans secretly agreed to do so. According to Thucydides, they would have done it had they not been detained by a massive revolt of the helots, who had taken advantage of an earthquake to occupy the strong position of Ithome in Messenia. Ithome, together with the Acrocorinth, the citadel of Corinth, was described by a Hellenistic ruler as one of the "horns of the Peloponnesian ox" that a would-be conqueror had to seize. It is indeed possible that the occupiers of Ithome planned not only an act of secession but, in fact, an attack on the famously unravaged city of Sparta itself. The earthquake not only shook Spartan nerve but must also have had serious demographic effects, though how long-term these were is disputed.

Sparta's Responses

The Spartan response to Thasos looked forward in its anti-Athenian aspect to the great Peloponnesian War of 431–404. It was one of three major episodes in the period up to that war when Sparta moved against Athens. The second was an aborted invasion of Athens under King Pleistoanax in 446. The third episode, in 440, revolved again around the issue of whether to intervene to prevent Athens disciplining a recalcitrant ally, this time Samos. The actual confrontation between Sparta and Athens did not happen in any of these cases. Among the reasons for this—apart from the helot revolt that took a decade for Sparta to put down—was the growing anti-Spartan restlessness in Arcadia.

The Athenian Themistocles, who had fallen from favour at Athens and spent time in the Peloponnese after his ostracism (perhaps 471), might have been behind this, though attempts to associate him with particular "synoecizing" developments in the Arcadian cities (i.e., developments whereby small communities coalesced into a single city) are speculative. Nor need such synoecizing (if it happened at this time) necessarily have been democratic and thus evidence that the communities in question were following the Athenian model rather than the Spartan oligarchic one. The evidence of Athenian tragedy (the *Suppliants* of Aeschylus) cannot be pressed to yield secure allusions to Themistocles.

Another reason was the continued revival of Argos. Its population had now recovered from the defeat at Sepeia (494), and the temporarily exiled descendants of the casualties of Sepeia, the "sons of the slain" as Herodotus calls them, a naturally anti-Spartan group, were now back in control (after ousting the slaves). Argos is on record as fighting a battle in perhaps the 470s, together with Arcadian Tegea, against Sparta, which also had to cope with "all the Arcadians except the Mantineans" at a strictly undatable battle of Dipaieis (which, however, should be put earlier than the Ithome revolt).

The "secret" promise to Thasos was followed by a more open rebuff to Athens. Sparta had invited the Athenians to help with the siege of the helots on Ithome, but with its usual catastrophic indecision Sparta then dismissed the Athenian contingent on suspicion of "revolutionary tendencies." Athens reacted by allying itself with Argos and Thessaly, which was a blow to Spartan ambitions both in its obvious stronghold, the Peloponnese, and in central Greece, an area into which one group of Spartans always seems to have wanted to expand.

THE EPHIALTIC REFORMS

This phase of foreign policy has to be somehow associated with internal change at Athens, the so-called Ephialtic reforms. In 462, together with the young Pericles, the Athenian statesman Ephialtes pushed through the decisive phase of the reforms, namely an assault on the powers of the Areopagus.

Legal Reforms

These powers heretofore exercised by the Areopagus—except for a residual jurisdiction over homicide and some religious offenses, and perhaps a formal "guardianship of the laws"—were redistributed among the Council of Five Hundred and the popular law courts. This is, in essence, the very bald and unhelpful account of our main source, the *Constitution of Althens*. There must have been more to it, but the problem is to know how much more. Probably the Areopagus ceased to hear crimes against the state, and such cases were transferred to the popular courts.

Alternative interpretations of the inadequate evidence, however, are possible: there are a handful of recorded treason trials earlier than 462 in which a popular element does admittedly play a prominent part, and, although these can be explained away in various ways, it can be held that the transfer of jurisdictional power to the people occurred earlier than 462. Alternatively, it is possible that Ephialtes' reforms in this area involved a mere transfer of "first-instance" jurisdiction (i.e., jurisdiction over cases other than those on appeal) from the Areopagus to the Council of Five Hundred. This requires the assumption of an unattested early fifth-century reform transferring capital appeals to the people.

More radically, and generally, the jurisdiction of magistrates (archons) was much curtailed. They now conducted a mere preliminary hearing, and the main case went to a large popular jury. The authority to conduct inquiries into the qualifications for office of the archons themselves (the *dokimasia* procedure) and into their behaviour after their terms of office had expired (*euthyna* procedure) was also taken away from the Areopagus and given to the Council of Five Hundred. This principle of popular accountability seems new, though the statement in Aristotle's *Politics*, that the right of popular *euthyna* goes back in some sense to Solon, has its defenders.

Political Reforms

There surely were other reforms. Certain features of the later democracy appeared after the rule of Cleisthenes but were in place by the Peloponnesian War (see following chapter). It is plausible to argue that they were introduced at this time, though there is a risk of circularity in characterizing Ephialtes as a comprehensive reformer by reference to strictly unattributed and undated changes. Thus, sortition (the casting of lots) for the Council of Five Hundred is not likely to have been earlier than 487, when the archonship ceased to be elective; but Athens imposed sortition for a comparable though smaller council on Ionian Erythrae in 453, surely not before there was sortition for the Council at Athens itself. Similarly, there is evidence for jury pay for the 460s (or less probably for the 450s), which makes it plausible to date Council pay, attested by 411, to the mid-century period also.

Taken together these reforms look like the result of careful thinking by particular individuals with a definite democratic philosophy. A case, however, can be made for seeing them all as part of a 30-year process, with a central action-filled phase, rather than as a single event. After all, the Areopagus was affected indirectly by the changes in the archonship in 487, though the archonship was formally opened to the *zeugitai* (the hoplite class) only in 457. But despite the great increase in work for the big popular juries and the granting to the courts of the right (which may go back to Ephialtes) to quash or uphold allegedly unconstitutional proposals, it is not likely that then or at any other time Athenians saw themselves as conferring sovereignty on the people's courts at the expense of the Assembly. The implied psychological distinction between juries of Athenians and political gatherings of the same Athenians is not a plausible one.

The Rejection of Cimon

Some of these changes were perhaps already in the air when the Spartans dismissed Cimon and his Athenians at Ithome. Cimon's absence seems to have given Ephialtes and Pericles their chance: the main Areopagus reform was passed at this time, and in 461 Cimon was ostracized. This rejection of Cimon, however, was a personal matter: he should not be seen as a "conservative" opponent of a reform that gave more power to the people and especially to the thetic class, which manned the fleet. For one thing, Cimon's victory at the Battle of the Eurymedon River was primarily a naval victory; for another, it was the Sparta-loving Cimon and his hoplites who were dismissed by the Spartans from Ithome for their subversive tendencies.

Most important of all, there is the general point that the interests of hoplites and *thētes*, now as at other normal times, coincided. Both were denied the chance of standing for the archonship before 457 (the hoplites were admitted to it in that year). On the whole, it is the top two "Solonian" groups, the *pentakosiomedimnoi* and the cavalry class who were bracketed together on the one hand (as by Thucydides in one military context), while the *zeugitai* and *thētes* tended to be bracketed together on the other. No built-in class cleavage existed between the hoplite or zeugite class and the *thētes*, and attempts to exploit one, by advocating or offering a "hoplite franchise," were short-lived failures. Cimon then should not be seen as champion of "conservative" hoplites against "radical" *thētes*. This view is wrong because the interests of hoplites and *thētes* were indissolubly linked.

Athenian Expansion

Athens's two new alliances, with Argos and Thessaly, were provocative (surely not just defensive), but they did not create direct danger of war. Far more serious was the friction at this time between Athens and Corinth.

Friction Between Athens and Corinth

Corinth had made no move to help Sparta, as far as is known, at the time of the Ithome disaster but seems to have pursued expansionist goals of its own in the Peloponnese, perhaps at Argos's expense. Now that Athens and Argos were allied, this indirectly tended to damage Corinth's hitherto good relations with Athens. (Corinth had fought well at Salamis, as even Herodotus was aware, though very different stories were circulating on this topic after 460.) More relevant than this was Athens's ready reception of a third ally, Megara. Like the Argives, the Megarians had also felt pressure from Corinth (one hears of a boundary dispute and a local war) and turned to Athens. This was the cause and beginning of the "violent hatred" between Corinth and Athens, which produced what modern scholars call the First Peloponnesian War.

The First Peloponnesian War (460–446) should probably be seen as essentially a conflict between Athens and Corinth, with occasional interventions by Sparta. Modern disagreement centres on the reasons why Sparta did not play a role: one line of explanation is purely military, invoking the difficulty of invading Attica while the mountains above Megara were policed by Athens. The other and more plausible view is that Sparta simply lacked the will to act consistently. Spartan inactivity should in any case not be exaggerated. There is a pattern to its interventions, which suggests that in this period, as at others, the "central Greek" lobby at Sparta, the closest thing to an identifiably imperialistic group to be found there, could sometimes prevail.

The Subjugation of Aegina

The first battle of the war, at Halieis in the Gulf of Argolis, was a Corinthian victory, but the next battle, at Cecryphalea (modern Angistrion), went Athens's way (459). Aegina, which was attacked and besieged in the same year, was reduced in the following year and forced to pay tribute to Athens, though some vague undertaking about autonomy may have been made. The alternative is to suppose a special clause about Aeginetan autonomy, or even a general autonomy clause, in the peace of 446, which ended the war. In any case, it seems likely that Athens did not honour their autonomy.

The alleged Athenian infringement of the autonomy of Aegina was one of the secondary causes of the main Peloponnesian War. In the meantime, the subjugation of Aegina, a great city of the Archaic age, whose proud Dorianism and traditions of seafaring and hospitality are stressed in lines of great beauty by Pindar in his *Nemean Odes* and elsewhere, was an event of cardinal importance. The pretense that Athens was merely leading a voluntary association of willing Ionian cities in need of protection could hardly survive the reduction of Aegina.

The Scale of Athenian Ambition

The real scale of Athenian ambitions is shown by four other developments of this period. First, Athens undertook a great and disastrous expedition to Egypt (460–454), in ostensible continuance of the fight against Persia. Egypt, however, had always been a rich and desirable Persian satrapy, exploited by absentee Persian landowners; and thus an economic motive for Athens cannot be excluded. Second, Athens made an alliance (almost certainly in 457) with an inland half-Greek Sicilian city, Segesta. This prepared the ground for a more tangible western policy in the 440s. Third, Athens now built the Long Walls connecting it to Piraeus and thus the sea and making it possible to depend for the future on the produce of its empire if absolutely necessary. The walls, however, should not be thought of as purely defensive in view of the constant connection made by Thucydides between walls and dynamic sea power. Fourth, Athens made an alliance (the inscription is strictly undatable) with the Delphic Amphictyony in the middle of the century. This must be connected with the Athenian alliance made with Thessaly in 461, because Thessaly controlled a

A view of the theatre in Delphi, Greece, overlooking the Sanctuary of Apollo. Mount Parnassus is in the background. Manuel Cohen/Getty Images

majority of Amphictyonic votes (always a reason why other states or rulers, like Philip of Macedon in the next century, were anxious to have a controlling interest in Thessaly).

It is interesting that Athens should thus extend its religious propaganda to include the sanctuary of Apollo of Delphi (Apollo Pythios) as well as that of Apollo of Delos. The oracle was always a distinct entity from the sanctuary, but it cannot be accidental that about now the oracle, normally favourable to Sparta in this period and conspicuously so in 431, declared Athens an "eagle in the clouds for all time."

The First Peloponnesian War can in fact be seen not as a straightforward political or military struggle but as a struggle for religious influence at certain of the great Panhellenic sanctuaries, above all Delphi and Nemea. The Athenians were vying for influence at Delphi with the Spartans, who significantly exerted themselves only twice during the whole war. The first time was the Tanagra campaign in defense of Doris, which was their mythical "metropolis" and the possessor of vital direct leverage in the amphictyony that controlled the affairs of the Delphic sanctuary. The Spartans themselves had no direct vote in the amphictyony. This explains why Doris mattered so much to them—it was a source of indirect Delphic influence. The second occasion was the so-called Second Sacred War, fought a few years later over control of the Delphic sanctuary. Corresponding to this struggle was a simultaneous struggle between the Corinthians and the Argives for influence over the Nemean Games, which were administered by the people of a small local city, Cleonae. Characteristically, Thucydides does not bring out these religious aspects at all clearly. They have to be reconstructed from other wisps of literary and inscriptional evidence.

Sparta's Resistance

The central Greek line of Athenian expansion was bound to bring a collision with Sparta. It entered the war in 458 in response to an appeal by its "mother city" Doris, the city from which the primeval Dorians were believed to have set out to undertake the invasion of the Peloponnese. This tiny state in central Greece was currently experiencing difficulties with its neighbour Phocis. The religious and sentimental factor in Sparta's response was not negligible, but Sparta may have had other aims as well. Not only is there the amphictyonic aspect already noted, but there is evidence in Diodorus Siculus, a Greek historian of the first century BC, though not in Thucydides, that Boeotia was a target.

It was on their return from Doris that the Spartans finally came to blows with Athens at Tanagra in Boeotia (458). The battle was of large scale—one hears of Argive involvement on the Athenian side—but indecisive. The Athenians, however, followed it up with a victory at

Oenophyta, which gave them control of Boeotia for a decade, an extremely important development passed over by Thucydides in half a dozen words. There was further aggressive Athenian action, first under the general Tolmides, who circumnavigated the Peloponnese (456) and perhaps settled the large number of Messenians at Naupactus alongside the original Naupactans, and second, under Pericles, who launched military expeditions in the Gulf of Corinth (454?). But the disastrous end to the adventure in Egypt (454) made Athens ready for a truce, and in 451 Athens came to terms with Sparta, while Argos concluded a 30-years' peace with Sparta on its own account.

Peace with Persia

Athens resumed the war against Persia with hostilities on Cyprus, but Cimon's death there made diplomacy imperative in this sphere also. This is where one should place the Peace of Callias (449), mentioned by Diodorus but one of Thucydides' most famous omissions. Thucydides' subsequent narrative of the Peloponnesian War, however, presupposes it at a number of points, especially in the context of Greek dealings with Persia in 411. More generally, a peace is made likely by the history of the 440s and 430s, which records no more overt Athenian warfare against Persia and a certain restlessness inside the Athenian empire. (This absence of warfare may be due to other factors as well. It is possible that the Treasury of the League, to which various states in the Delian League paid tribute, was moved from Delos to Athens in 454, a centralizing gesture that may have caused alarm. But the move may have happened earlier.)

Nonliterary evidence also points in the direction of a peace: the evidence of inscriptions makes it probable that no tribute was levied in 448. Perhaps it was recognized that the struggle with Persia was over and with it the justification for tribute. If so, the recognition was only momentary, because there was tribute again in 447. Furthermore, an inscription of the 420s appears to refer to a renewal of the peace on the death of Artaxerxes I. Finally, the commissioning of a new Temple of Athena Nike ("Victory"), and perhaps even of the Parthenon, may have been an aspect of the same mood. (The peace could be represented as a victory of a sort because it restricted the Persian king's naval movements.) Yet the close correlation of architectural with political history is to be avoided. Antibarbarian artistic themes on Greek public buildings need no special explanation at any time in the fifth century. Against all this there are a few ancient allegations that the peace was a later forgery, an implausible idea because such diplomacy was a matter of public knowledge.

Despite the truce with Athens in 451, Sparta had not withdrawn into its Peloponnesian shell completely. In addition to its campaign in support of Doris, Sparta successfully intervened in central Greece in a "Second Sacred War" against

Phocis, which, with the assistance of Athens, had gained control of Delphi. Sparta handed over Delphi to the Delphians, but this action was promptly neutralized by the Athenians, who restored the sanctuary to Phocis. Catastrophic revolts in Boeotia and Euboea (446), however, soon eroded that Athenian authority in central Greece of which the Delphic intervention was a manifestation.

REVOLTS OF ATHENS'S TRIBUTARY STATES

Athens's tributary states had much cause to rebel. Not only was tribute high, but Athenian interference in other economic, political, and legal matters soon became intolerable.

Economic Sources of Resentment

There was something ominous about the sheer physical scale of the first (in chronological order) of the stone blocks on which were carved, as a permanent record, the tribute payments due to Athena. The block, preserved in the Epigraphic Museum in Athens, is a towering 142 inches (3.61 metres) high and had plenty of room for many years of tribute. Evidently the Athenians of 454 expected the empire to go on indefinitely, despite the failure in Egypt, which must have made many observers reflect that peace with Persia could not be far away. Yet tribute, exactingly collected, as Thucydides says, was not the only grievance. It was not even the only economic grievance. In the period of the early Peloponnesian War there were, as inscriptions show, strict Athenian controls on the traffic of grain from the Black Sea, including "Guardians of the Hellespont." According to one view, these controls were a purely wartime expedient, but, given the state of the evidence, that charitable view is an abuse of the argument from silence. In any case, a prewar inscription does in fact attest a 10 percent tax on shipping from the Black Sea. Grain bound for Athens itself was probably exempt from this.

Still in the economic sphere, resentment against Athenian ownership of land—whether collectively (the so-called cleruchy system, stepped up at the end of the 450s) or privately, by wealthy individuals—can legitimately be inferred from the self-denying promises made by Athens in the days of its fourth-century confederacy. In this category should be included sacred precincts (*temenē*) in allied states, marked out by *horoi*, or boundary stones, which indicated land that might be leased out to other wealthy Athenians. The view that these precincts attest benevolently exported or adopted Athenian cults has been challenged.

Political and Legal Sources of Resentment

Another interference in the internal affairs of tribute-paying allies in the fourth century was the placement of garrisons and garrison commanders, attested as early as the Erythrae decree of 453. The same decree imposed a "democratic" constitution, according to a principle that the literary sources say was general Athenian policy. Yet it would be simplistic to think that such Athenian-influenced constitutions were necessarily a significant upholding of human rights. One must always ask what "democracy" can have meant in a small community.

At Erythrae, not only was the council less democratic than that at Athens, but there also was a property qualification for jurors. And at exceedingly few places other than Athens does inscriptional evidence for amendments from the floor exist. In any case, there are significant exceptions (Samos, Mytilene, Chios, Miletus, Potidaea, and possibly Boeotia) to the generalization that Athens insisted on democracies. What the allies thought of this is inscrutable. A statement by an Athenian speaker in Thucydides that the popular party everywhere supported Athens is matched by the reported view of another Thucydidean speaker that what the allies wanted was freedom from interference of any kind.

In the legal sphere the allies suffered from disabilities (such as the requirement to have certain types of cases heard in Athens). These were firmly maintained even in texts, such as the Phaselis decree, that accord specific limited legal privileges. Full legal privilege and status was reserved for full Athenians, a status whose definition was tightened by the citizenship law of Pericles in 451. Roman commentators pointed to Athenian (and Spartan) failure to integrate their subjects as citizens as the explanation of their more general failures as imperial powers. There is much in this. It is not an answer to say that there is no attested clamour for Athenian citizenship, when the allied view on so many points does not exist. Certainly, among the thousands disfranchised in the 440s by the new rules regarding citizenship, there must have been many immigrants from the empire. Colonial mother cities sometimes offered citizenship wholesale to their daughter communities. Imperial Athens borrowed many features of the colonial relationship, but not that one.

The Euboean Revolt

Boeotia revolted in 446 with help from Euboean exiles, and the Athenians were forced to accept this political reversal after a military defeat at Boeotian Coronea. The revolt of Euboea itself followed. Pericles crossed over to deal with it but only precipitated a third revolt, that of Megara. This was a serious military crisis, and it was compounded by a Spartan invasion of Attica: King Pleistoanax got as far as Eleusis and the Thriasian plain, but, as mentioned above, the invasion was not carried through. Pleistoanax and Pericles seem to have struck a deal: Sparta would not interfere in Euboea or invade Attica in exchange for Athens's acquiescence in the loss of Boeotia, the Megarid, and certain Peloponnesian sites.

An arrangement on these lines was formalized in a Thirty Years' Peace between Athens and Sparta, but it would be too ambitious to try to list all the terms. An essential undertaking was a renunciation of armed attacks if the other side was prepared to submit to arbitration. The prevalent modern view that the peace involved a formal recognition by the Peloponnesians of the Athenian empire rests on a misinterpretation of a passage in the first speech that Thucydides puts into the mouth of Pericles. Athens could now deal with Euboea, and inscriptions have preserved the terms of the firm settlement imposed on individual communities there.

Greek Communities in Italy and Sicily

Athenian buoyancy was not deflated even by these failures. For in 443 the Athenians advertised a big colonial venture to Thurii in Italy and about the same time made alliances with Rhegium in Italy and Leontini in Sicily (alliances renewed a decade later on surviving inscriptions).

Since the Persian Wars the most splendid of the western Greek communities had been tyrannically ruled until the fall of Gelon's family, the Deinomenids of Syracuse, in 466/467, soon after the death of Gelon's brother Hieron and the fall of the tyrannical house of Theron at Acragas in 472. Syracuse enjoyed a moderate democracy thereafter, disturbed only by a native rebel, Ducetius, whom it took surprisingly long to put down. In Italy, where Rome was preoccupied with the neighbouring Volsci and Aequi for much of the century, Hellenism maintained itself vigorously: the temples of Paestum dating to the fifth century, like those of Acragas or Segesta, were comparable to anything in mainland Greece, and there were philosophers and the philosophical schools of Croton, Taras, and Elea (Velia), all in southern Italy. At Elea, south of Paestum, interesting portrait statues were discovered in the 1960s, which showed that the philosophical school there had a medical aspect to it: a cult of Apollo Oulios, a healing god, was looked after by a clan of Ouliadai (which was associated with the medical organization, though the exact relationship is obscure), and even the famous Parmenides, better known as a philosopher, is called Ouliades.

Pythagoreanism, a philosophical school and religious brotherhood, flourished in southern Italy. In the early fifth century Pythagorean groups involved themselves in government, ruling Croton for a period. Nonetheless, there were tyrannies in southern Italy too, such as that of Anaxilas at Rhegium. Religious and social links with the Greek mainland were cultivated, above all by contacts with the sanctuary and games at Olympia and by patronage of poets like Pindar. Pindar's second and third Olympian odes display knowledge of Orphism, a religious movement whose initiates hoped to achieve at death the release of their souls from a sinful world. These odes were written for patrons in Sicily, where Orphism may have flourished.

The Athenian-inspired Thurii project represented a fairly substantial mainland Greek encroachment on western soil. This and a mysterious Athenian colonizing effort in the Bay of Naples region, undertaken perhaps in the early 430s by a western expert, Diotimos, must have caused unease to western-oriented Corinth. (There is even a Spartan aspect: Thurii was soon engaged in warfare with Sparta's only historical colony, Taras.) Nonetheless, when Samos revolted from Athens in 440, it was Corinth that in a congress of the Peloponnesian League voted against intervention against Athens on behalf of Samos (Corinth's attitude had no doubt softened with the detachment of Megara from Athens). Sparta, however, seems to have wanted to stop Athens in its tracks, though in the end it was typically unwilling to press this line of policy home. At this point Thucydides' main narrative stops for five crucial years, at the end of which tension between Corinth and Athens was again high, on the eve of the great Peloponnesian War. In historiographical terms we may call this vital period the Great Gap.

CHAPTER 4

Classical Greek Civilization: The Peloponnesian War

The causes of the main Peloponnesian War need to be traced at least to the early 430s BC—the Great Gap period—although if Thucydides was right in his general explanation for the war, namely Spartan fear of Athenian expansion, the development of the entire fifth century and indeed part of the sixth were relevant.

CAUSES

In the early 430s BC Pericles led an expedition to the Black Sea, and about the same time Athens made an alliance with a place close to areas of traditional Corinthian influence, Acarnania. (On another view this belongs in the 450s.) In 437 the Athenians fulfilled an old ambition by founding a colony at Amphipolis, no doubt on a large scale, though figures for settlers do not exist. This was disconcertingly close to another outpost of Corinthian influence at Potidaea in the Chalcidice, and there is a possibility that Athens subjected Potidaea itself to financial pressure by the mid-430s. That city was an anomaly in being both tributary to Athens and simultaneously subject to direct rule by magistrates sent out annually by Corinth. It clearly was a sensitive spot in international relations. Thus to the west (Acarnania and other places) and northeast (Amphipolis, Potidaea) Corinth was being indirectly pressured by Athens,

This map shows Greece and its territories at the start of the Peloponnesian War. Courtesy of the University of Texas Libraries, The University of Texas at Austin

and this pressure was also felt in Corinth's own backyard, at Megara.

Athens passed a series of measures (the "Megarian decrees") imposing an economic embargo on Megara for violations of sacred land. The religious aspect of the offense was reflected in the exclusions imposed: like murderers, the Megarians were banned from the Athenian marketplace and the harbours in the Athenian empire. But one should not doubt that Athens caused and intended to cause economic hardship as well or that the decrees were the first move in securing Megara as a military asset, a line of policy further pursued in the years 431 to 424. It should further be noted that the Black Sea, to which, as already mentioned, Pericles led a flamboyant expedition in the Great Gap period, was an area of colonial Megarian settlement. Here too one can legitimately infer an Athenian desire to pressure Megara, albeit indirectly.

Reactions to all this, within the empire and outside it, are hard to gauge. Athens's savage reduction of Samos, a member of the Delian League, in 440–439, did not stop Mytilene and most of Lesbos from appealing at some time in the prewar period to Sparta for encouragement in a revolt they were meditating. No encouragement was given: Sparta was standing by the Thirty Years' Peace and should be given (a little) credit for doing so.

For the period from 433 to 411 a vastly more detailed narrative is possible than theretofore, but the reader should be warned that this freak of scale is due to one man, Thucydides, who imposed his view of events on posterity. It would, however, be artificial to write as if the information for this unique period were no better than that available for any other.

The main precipitating causes of the war, thought of as a war between Athens and Sparta, actually concerned relations between Sparta's allies (rather than Sparta itself) and other smaller states with Athenian connections. The two "causes" that occupy the relevant parts of Thucydides' first, introductory book concern Corcyra and Potidaea. (Thucydides does not let his readers entirely lose sight of two other causes much discussed at the time—the Megarian decrees and the complaints of Aegina about its loss of autonomy. One fourth-century Athenian orator actually dropped a casual remark to the effect that "we went to war in 431 about Aegina.") Corcyra (present-day Corfu), which had quarreled with Corinth over the Corcyran colony of Epidamnus on the coast of Illyria (a colony in which Corinth also had an interest), appealed to Athens.

Taking very seriously the western dimension to its foreign policy (it was about then that the alliances with Rhegium and Leontini were renewed), Athens voted at first for a purely defensive alliance and after a debate, fully recorded by Thucydides, sent a small peace-keeping force of 10 ships. This was, however, trebled, as a nervous afterthought. No political background is given for this move, which, moreover, emerges only subsequently and in passing during the narrative of events concerning Corcyra itself. (This is a small illustration of the important point that Thucydides' presentation unduly influenced modern views on the general issue of Athenian belligerence, as on so many other issues. A different narrative, by emphasizing the escalation of the Athenian commitment and making it the subject of another full debate, might have left a different impression. It is, however, hard to be sure if Thucydides' postponement of the vital point was prompted by outright political bias in favour of Athens or if it was just a manifestation of a "Homeric" tendency to feed in information only at the point where it becomes most relevant). In fact, Corinthian and Athenian ships had already come to blows before the reinforcements arrived.

Then at Potidaea, a Corinthian colony, the Athenians demanded that the Corinthian magistrates be sent home. Potidaea revolted, and an unofficial Corinthian force went out to help. Potidaea was laid under siege by Athens. None of this yet amounted to war with the Peloponnesian League as a whole, but the temperature was as high as it could be, short of that. A congress of Spartan allies was convoked to discuss grievances against Athens, and the decision was taken for war.

The other Spartan ally seeking to involve Sparta in a private feud with an enemy was Thebes, whose attack on its neighbour Plataea (an Athenian ally) in time of peace was retrospectively recognized by Sparta as an act of war guilt. The Spartans should not have condoned it, nor should they have invaded Attica (despite the fact that the Athenians had placed a garrison in Plataea) so long as the Athenians were offering arbitration, as it seems they were.

THE INITIAL PHASE, 431–425

Athenian war strategy and the initial conduct of the war are presented by Thucydides very much in personal terms: the focus is on what Pericles, the dominant figure of this time, did or wanted. This method, like the Homeric emphasis on heroes, is to some extent literary spotlighting, for at no time was Pericles immune from criticism. In the 440s he had to deal with a major rival, Thucydides, son of Melesias (not the historian), who was ostracized in 443. Even after that, in the poorly documented 430s (before Aristophanes and Thucydides provide information about individual figures of second- or third-rate significance), there are suggestions of tension, such as a partial ban on comedy (with its potential for exposure) and indications in the sources that Cleon was really not a successor of Pericles at all but a highly critical contemporary. The reasons for Pericles' ascendancy remain a secret, and this in itself makes it necessary to allow for a large element of "charismatic" leadership.

Pericles

In the military sphere Thucydides is surely wrong to present Pericles as a one-man band. He says of Pericles that early in the war "the Athenians reproached him for not leading them out as their general should." If this sentence had survived in isolation, one would hardly have guessed that Pericles was one of the college of 10, subject to control and threat of deposition by the Assembly (Pericles was indeed deposed temporarily toward the end of his life). On the whole, however, Thucydides minimizes the degree to which Athenian generals enjoyed executive latitude, particularly in wartime. It may be suggested that the reason for this was his own exile, imposed in 424 as a punishment for failing, as commander in the region, to relieve Amphipolis. This impressed him deeply—and unduly—with the impotence and vulnerability of generals other than Pericles.

The reproach of "not leading out the Athenians" provides useful insight into Periclean strategy, revealing it to have been largely reactive. Whereas the Spartans sought to liberate Greece from tyranny, which required them to dismantle the Athenian empire, all the Athenians had to do was to avoid such demolition. In a way this suited neither side: initiative of the kind this demanded from Sparta was in short supply there (though never entirely absent). For the Athenians' part, the famously energetic and meddlesome population did not take kindly to the practical consequences of Periclean

This illustration shows the Athenian leader Pericles giving a speech during the time of the Peloponnesian War. Time & Life Pictures/Getty Images

strategy that required it to evacuate Attica and move its population behind the fortified walls of Athens, to rely on accumulated capital reserves and on the fleet as an instrument to hold the empire firmly down, and to avoid adding to the empire during wartime. By these means the Athenians would eventually "win through" (the Greek word is neatly ambiguous as between victory and survival).

Actually the Athenian position was not and could not be so simple. For one, the agricultural evacuation of Attica was not as complete as it was to be after 413 when the Spartans occupied Decelea in northern Attica. Nor did Pericles altogether abandon Attica militarily: there were cavalry raids to harass the dispersed foot soldiers of the enemy and to keep up city morale. Holding the empire down and holding onto capital were potentially inconsistent aims in view of the great cost of siege warfare (there was no artillery before the fourth century to facilitate the taking of fortified cities by storm). The destruction of Samos had been expensive—a four-figure sum in talents—and the siege of Potidaea was to cost 2,000. Athens, even with coined reserves of 6,000 talents at the beginning of the war, could not afford many Potidaeas. Pericles can be criticized for not foreseeing this, with the evidence of Samos behind him.

Sparta's Role

Sparta came as a liberator. This too called for money and ships, but the Spartans had neither accumulated reserves like Athens nor a proper fleet. Persia was a possible source for both, but assistance from Persia might compromise Spartan "liberation theology." This was especially true if Sparta set foot in Anatolia, where there were Greeks with as much desire for liberation (whether from Athens or Persia or both: some communities paid tribute in both directions) as their mainland counterparts. A further difficulty lay in the kind of regime Sparta itself could be expected to impose if successful. One revealing reason for the failure of the big colony at Heraclea founded in 426, a project with a strongly anti-Ionian and propagandist element, was the harsh and positively unjust behaviour of the Spartan governors, who frightened people away. Was the Spartan stick, or *bakteria*, too much in use by violent Spartan officers with too little self-control?

Again a few qualifications are in order. Money could be obtained from more acceptable sources than Persia—from the western Dorians, for instance. And subsidized piracy, of which one hears a little in the 420s, was another solution to the naval problem. Against harsh governors like those at Heraclea one has to balance Brasidas, who was as good a fighter in the battle for the hearts and minds as in the conventional sense.

Sparta's invasion of Attica set the tone of the first half of the Archidamian War (431–421 BC), named after the Spartan king Archidamus II, unfairly in view of the wariness he is said to have expressed at the outset. Athens moved its flocks from Attica across to Euboea, whose economic importance was thus raised further still. As if in recognition that this was a war brought about at the instance of Corinth, much early Athenian naval activity was devoted to stripping Corinth of assets in the northwest—of Sollium, Astacus, and Cephellenia. Yet there was also an Athenian raid on Methone in Messenia (the later Venetian strong point of Modon), foiled by Brasidas; a morale-boosting raid on the Megarid (such raids were repeated twice a year until 424); and some successful diplomacy in the north, where the Odrysian Thracians were won over.

At the end of this first campaigning year, Pericles delivered an austere but moving speech honouring the fallen men, which has become known as the funeral oration of Pericles. This famous oration, however, is largely the work of Thucydides himself. It is a timeless personal tribute to Athenian power and institutional strength but not, as has been argued, a key to unlock Athenian civic ideology. The speech, as preserved, is not peculiarly enthusiastic about democracy as such and has perhaps been over-interpreted in the light of Athens's later cultural fame. In particular, the Thucydidean Pericles is usually taken to have said that Athens was an education to Greece, but in context he says merely that other Greeks would do well to profit from its political example.

Continuing Strife

The second year of the war, 430 BC, began with another invasion of Attica. Thucydides, having scarcely brought the Peloponnesians into Attica, switches styles dramatically to record the outbreak of a dreadful plague at Athens. Although it cannot be securely identified with any known disease, this plague carried off one-third of the 14,000 hoplites and cavalry (there was a recurrence in 427). Pericles himself came down with the disease and died in 429, not, however, before leading a ravaging expedition against Epidaurus and other Peloponnesian places and defending himself against his critics. The speech Thucydides gives him for this occasion is as fine as the funeral speech, which has received so much more attention. It hints loftily at expansion to east and west of the kind that Pericles' initial strategy had appeared to rule out. It is possible that this speech is historical and that the purpose of attacking Epidaurus was to bar Corinth's eastern sea-lanes completely. Aegina had already been evacuated and repopulated by cleruchs in 430, perhaps as an initial step toward this end. In the north, Potidaea surrendered, and a cleruchy was installed here too, a further Corinthian setback.

Peloponnesian pressure on Plataea was stepped up in 429. A large expedition in the northwest under the Spartan Cnemus, who used barbarian as well as Greek forces in an effort to win back some of Corinth's losses, showed that there were adventurous thinkers before the northern operations of Brasidas later in the decade. It was, however, a failure, as was a Peloponnesian embassy to Persia asking for money and alliance. Intercepted by the king of the Odrysians, the ambassadors were handed over to Athens, where they were put to death with no pretense at trial. The Odrysians feature prominently at this time (but perhaps Thucydides' own family interests in Thrace have distorted the picture): the mass mobilization of a large Odrysian force, ostensibly in the Athenian interest, soon afterward caused general terror in Greece, but it came to nothing. There was more concrete encouragement for Athens in some naval successes of the great commander Phormion in the Gulf of Corinth.

Mytilene and Plataea

It is perhaps surprising that it was only in 428 that a revolt within the Athenian empire gave Sparta the opportunity to implement its basic war aim of liberating Greece. This was the revolt of Mytilene on the island of Lesbos, to which Athens reacted with a prompt blockade. It was a shrewd Spartan move to summon the Mytileneans and other injured Greeks to the Olympic Games at this point, thus emphasizing that one aspect of the war was the tension between Dorians and Ionians. (Athens was hardly formally excluded from the solemnities, but Olympia always had a Dorian flavour.) Alcidas, the Spartan commander sent to assist the Mytileneans, failed, however, to do anything for them. On its surrender (427) the city narrowly escaped the wholesale executions and enslavements Cleon had recommended, but only as a result of second thoughts on the part of the Assembly (these events and decisions form the context of the famous "Mytilene debate"). It is to the Athenians' credit that some of them were moved by the thought that their original decision was bloodthirsty.

There were no such doubters among the Spartans who supervised the final phase of Plataean fifth-century history. When the remaining Plataeans surrendered (some had already broken out to Athens), they were put to death to a man, after the "brief question" had been put to them, "Have you done anything for Sparta during the war?" This was a question that the Plataeans, despite some moving pleas, could answer only negatively. At least Cleomenes I in the sixth century and Agesilaus II in the fourth, both of whom applied much the same criterion as this in international affairs, made no pretense of being liberators of Greece. It is impossible for the modern reader to reflect on these two fully reported incidents at Mytilene and Plataea without coming to some general conclusions about Spartan behaviour. And Thucydides, too, was prompted to generalize in this fashion. His thoughts are attached to an account of civil strife at Corcyra, in the west, in 427. After a bloodbath, the democratic pro-Athenian faction prevailed over the oligarchical pro-Spartan party, with the Athenian commander Eurymedon making no attempt to stop it.

Speculation and Unease

About this time the Athenians speculatively pursued their western interests, sending at first an expedition of 20 ships under Laches and Charoeades (c. 427 BC) and then 40 more under Sophocles (not the tragedian), Pythodorus, and Eurymedon (426–425). This was a large force in total, given Athens's other commitments, but its goals are difficult to assess. Both radical and conservative motives are given, such as the desire to give the sailors practice (not a ridiculous motive, but an inadequate one), to cut off grain shipments to the Peloponnese (by which Corinth is presumably meant), or even to see if the whole island of Sicily could be brought under control, whatever exactly that might entail. (In 424, after mostly halfhearted warfare, the Sicilians put aside their internal differences at a conference in Gela, of which the Pan-Sicilian Hermocrates was the hero. The Athenian commanders returned home to an undeserved disgrace: their mandate for outright conquest had hardly been clear, nor were their resources sufficient.) The attempt by the Athenian general Nicias to take Megara by military means (427) had more immediate promise of success.

It is possible that even the Spartans were uneasy at what the main events of 427, at Mytilene and Plataea, had done for their image: they had been ineffective and brutal. Perhaps in partial redress, but also in pursuit of a traditional line of policy, they issued a general invitation to participate in a large (10,000 strong) colony at Heraclea in Trachis at the southern approach to Thessaly. This colonizing effort had intelligible short-term military motives, namely, a felt need to gain a hold on the Thracian region—the only part of the Athenian empire reachable by land—and a desire to deny Athens access to its larder on Euboea. But Thessaly had always featured and was always to feature in ambitious Spartan thinking. Indeed Sparta may already have planned to make use of the amphictyonic vote that one certainly finds Heraclea exercising in the fourth century. That is, the Spartans were seeking to improve the unsatisfactory state of affairs that had led, as noted, to their initial intervention in the First Peloponnesian War—namely, their inability to exert influence in the Delphic amphictyony except indirectly through their metropolis, Doris.

From the propaganda point of view, the exclusion of Ionians, Achaeans, and some others was telling. Sparta was presenting itself as a leader of Dorians, not just as a selfish promoter of Spartan interests. This was the redress offered to a Greek world well-disposed toward Sparta at the beginning of the war but now perhaps dismayed by the way things were going. It was a pity that the brutality and violence of Spartan governors at Heraclea helped to ruin the project.

Athens's magnificent refounding, also in 426, of the Ionian festival of Apollo on the island of Delos, where the Delian League had been established in 478 BC, must surely in part be seen as a response to Dorian Heraclea. (There were other motives too, such as desire for expiation for the plague, which had ravaged Athens a second time in the winter of 427–426.) Of the two great Panhellenic sanctuaries, Olympia had taken an ugly anti-Athenian look in 428, while the oracle of Delphi had actually approved the Heraclea colony. Athens, through Delos, was creating or inflating religious propaganda possibilities of its own. The same is true of an Athenian invitation to the Greeks at large, also (possibly) in the 420s, to bring offerings of firstfruits to Eleusis.

Land operations in the northwest occupied much of the purely military history of 426. They were conducted by one of the finest generals of the Peloponnesian War, the Athenian Demosthenes (no relation of Philip's fourth-century opponent). He was at first spectacularly unsuccessful in some ambitious campaigning, perhaps not sanctioned by the Assembly at all, in Aetolia, where his hoplites were nearly helpless against the light-armed tactics of the locals. He was, however, able to retrieve the position subsequently, in Amphilochia, in circumstances that brought further discredit on Sparta, whose commander deserted his Ambracian allies.

The Years 425–421

According to Thucydides' perhaps over-schematic account, 425 BC was the decisive year in the Archidamian War. Demosthenes, whose credit with the Assembly must now have been excellent, obtained permission to use a fleet round the Peloponnese.

Spartan Calls for Peace

Demosthenes and his troops used the fleet to occupy the remote Messenian headland of Pylos, a prominence at the north end of the Bay of Navarino, and to fortify it. The Spartans foolishly reacted by landing a hoplite force on Sphacteria, the long island to the south of Pylos. This force of 420 men, about half of them full Spartan citizens, was cut off by the Athenians, who thus acquired a potentially valuable bargaining chip. The Spartans sued for peace without reference to their allies (so much for liberation), but Cleon persuaded Athens to turn the offer down. Cleon made steep demands, including (in effect) the cession of Megara, showing that he—like Nicias in 427 and Demosthenes and Hippocrates in 424—grasped the strategic importance of Megara, even if the historian Thucydides did not.

One development which Thucydides does not report in its place, saving it for later mention, is the recall from exile in 427 or 426 of the Spartan king Pleistoanax, who is known to have favoured peace. Similarly, he notes only just before the Peace of Nicias of 421 that one Spartan worry was the imminent expiry in that year of their 30-year truce with the Argives. They did not want a war against Argos as well as Athens. This factor must in reality have been operative on Spartan minds for some years before 421. Like the return of Pleistoanax, this means that the capture of the Spartans at Pylos was by no means the only consideration making peace desirable at Sparta. Thus, 425 was less decisive than Thucydides sometimes suggests, perhaps because he was preoccupied with the activities of the Athenian Cleon.

Cleon's Influence

Thucydides disliked Cleon, as did another highly articulate contemporary, the playwright Aristophanes (see in particular his comedy *Knights*, of 425–424). The picture that emerges from their works of Cleon and figures like him as "new politicians," arising not from among the old or property-holding families but from the people, is largely a literary fiction. It was foisted on posterity by these ancient writers, who exaggerated the contrast between Pericles and his successors because they admired Pericles' style. In social background, political methods, and particular policies the difference was not great. The real change in Athenian politics came only with the loss of the empire in 404 and the resulting partial breakdown in the "consensus politics" that had prevailed hitherto (because all social classes stood equally to gain from the empire, which financed political pay, provided land for all, and cushioned the rich against the cost of furnishing the fleet).

There are two lines of policy one can safely associate with Cleon from evidence other than that of Thucydides. One is an apparently large theoretical increase in the level of allied tribute (425–424) documented by an inscription. But it is not certain that the increase was sudden (details of the immediately preceding reassessments do not survive) or that it was ever turned into actually collected tribute. The other line of policy is an attempt, attested by Aristophanes, to draw Argos into the war in some way (its peace with Sparta, as mentioned, was due to expire in 421, the year in which, unknown to Cleon in 425, the Archidamian War was to end).

By declining the diplomatic solution, Cleon found himself committed to a military one. He succeeded dramatically, capturing 120 full Spartans and taking them back to Athens. This operation, achieved partly with the use of light-armed troops, ensured that there would be no invasion of Attica in 424. Athens was free to establish a base on the island of Cythera south of Laconia and make a serious and initially successful attempt on Megara.

Spartan Recovery

At this point the balance of the war began to tilt again in Sparta's favour: Brasidas arrived, on his way to the north, and saved Megara by a whisker. Moreover, an ultra-ambitious Athenian attempt to reinstate the mid-century position by annexing Boeotia failed at Delium. This was a major defeat of Athens by a Boeotian army whose key component was Theban. Meanwhile, Brasidas had reached the north, where he had won over Acanthus by a blend of cajolement and threats and where, too quick for Thucydides (the historian) to stop him, he had taken Amphipolis. From there he proceeded to capture Torone. All this adventurous activity looks at first sight uncharacteristically Spartan, but Thucydides' picture of Brasidas as a romantic loner at odds with the regime back home is somewhat overdone, and there is reason to think that his liberation policies represented official Spartan wishes.

An armistice between Athens and Sparta in 423 did not stop further northern places from falling into Brasidas's arms—almost literally: at Scione the inhabitants came out to greet him with garlands and generally received him "as though he had been an athlete" (a rare Thucydidean glimpse of a world other than war and politics). He briefly won over Mende as well, but Athens recovered it soon after. Cleon arrived in 422 and won back Torone too. The deaths of both Cleon and Brasidas in a battle for possession of Amphipolis removed two main obstacles to the peace that most Spartans had been wanting for several years—in fact, since Sphacteria or even earlier (the return of Pleistoanax). As noted, the imminent expiry of the Argive peace was another factor, as was the occupation of Cythera, which provided a base for deserting helots (it is surprising that Athens did not make more use of the Spartan fear of their helots, a far from secret weapon of war). The essence of the Peace of Nicias (421) was a return to the prewar situation: most wartime gains were to be returned. Sparta had resoundingly failed to destroy the Athenian empire, and in this sense Athens, whatever its financial and human losses, had won the war.

The Peace of Nicias was seen by Thucydides as an uneasy intermission between two phases of a single war. Corinth and Boeotia rejected the peace from the outset, and an energetic young

Athenian politician, Alcibiades, tried to return to what may have been Themistocles' policy of stirring up trouble for Sparta inside the Peloponnese. Alcibiades' plans, like those of Themistocles, centred on Argos, once again a factor in Greek international politics after 421 and ambitious to revive mythical Dorian glories. This was a period of low prestige and unhappiness for the Spartans, who were actually excluded from the Olympic Games of 420 by their enemies, the people of Elis. They waited 20 years before extracting revenge for this and other insults (but contrary to most modern views, the Olympic ban almost certainly did not last for the whole intervening two-decade period).

An alliance of Athens, Argos, Elis, and Mantinea fought Sparta in 418 in the territory of Mantinea. Sparta, resolute in war as it was irresolute in politics, scored a crushing victory over its enemies. The shame of the Sphacteria surrender was wiped out in one day, and the Greek world was reminded of Spartan hoplite supremacy. If Athens, whose finances were now strong again, wanted outlets for its aggression, it would have to find them elsewhere than in the Peloponnese. It sought it first in Anatolia, second on Melos, and third in Sicily.

ATHENIAN AGGRESSION OUTSIDE THE PELOPONNESE

Athenian involvement in Anatolia began at some point after 425, when there was a routine renewal of the Peace of Callias. Their initial point of contact was the Persian satrap Pissuthnes, to whom Athens sent mercenary help, and subsequently perhaps to his natural son Amorges.

Entanglement with Persia

If this involvement began while the Archidamian War was still in progress, it was inexplicable provocation to Persia except on the assumption that Athens was too short of cash to pay these troops itself (a 1,000-talent reserve had been set aside at the beginning of the war, but there was resistance to touching this). If the entanglement began in the period of the Peace of Nicias, it was still dangerous adventurism because nobody could say how long the peace with Sparta would last.

Harsh Treatment of Melos

Thucydides says nothing about this Persian entanglement in its right place, despite its long-term importance: it was, after all, Persian intervention on the Spartan side that ultimately settled the outcome of the whole war. By contrast, he says a great deal about Athens's expedition in 416 against ostensibly unoffending Melos. Although militarily trivial, the subjugation and harsh treatment of Melos certainly had moral implications, which Thucydides explores in the famous "Melian Dialogue." It shows that the Athenians, who had made one attempt on Melos in 427 under Nicias, still wanted to round off their Aegean empire irrespective of the Dorian "ancestry" of Melos.

Thucydides' debate is framed in absolute terms, as if there were no question of provocation by Melos and the only issue were whether the weaker should submit to the stronger, as Melos in the end had to do. Yet there are points to be noted. First, Melos may have contributed to the Spartan war fund as early as 426. Second, Athens had assessed Melos at the high sum of 15 talents in the context of the (admittedly optimistic) general increase of 425. There was a fugitive sense in which Melos, which did not pay this exorbitant sum, could be seen as a recalcitrant subject. This, however, is not a line pursued by Thucydides' Athenians in the "Melian Dialogue." Third, some Athenian subject allies joined in coercing Melos in 416, evidence that Ionians and Aeolians could be mobilized against Dorians and perhaps even that they positively approved of all the implications of a notably ruthless action. And fourth, the Melians, unlike some other coerced subjects of the Athenians, were given a chance to submit but declined to take it.

The Sicilian Disaster

In 415 Athens turned to the third and most aggressive operation of the period, the great expedition against Sicily of 415–413, better known as the Sicilian disaster. The initial commanders were Alcibiades, Nicias, and Lamachus, but the expedition was weakened by the recall of Alcibiades to stand trial for impiety (he escaped and went to Sparta, which sent help to Syracuse at his suggestion).

Originally conceived in perfectly acceptable terms (a force of 60 ships to help Ionians and non-Greeks against the rising power of Syracuse), the expedition as ultimately sent was too ambitious. It consisted of a huge fleet of 140 ships—100 of them Athenian—reinforced by an additional 60. Thucydides speaks impressively but unspecifically about the cost of the expedition (he does report at one point that the Syracusans had spent 2,000 talents). An Athenian inscription is usually interpreted as showing that in a single transaction 3,000 talents was set aside for Sicily, though this restoration has been challenged.

A major problem was cavalry: Athens sent 250 cavalrymen without horses, but mounts were secured locally in Sicily, bringing the total to 650. (Athens also sent 30 mounted archers.) This total was not bad for a state that had never been a strong cavalry power, but it was scarcely more than half of the 1,200 that Syracuse was able to field. Even Athens's early successes in the field, and there were some, were neutralized by this disparity: pursuit of the enemy by victorious Athenian infantry became a dangerous matter because of harassment by Syracusan cavalry. When the Spartan Gylippus arrived to help the Syracusans and Athens failed to wall in Syracuse, the Syracusan cavalry made the Athenian position intolerable: those who went out from their camps foraging for food often did not come back. Nicias himself was ill but was kept in post by the Athenians, a great mistake not compensated for by the arrival of first the more energetic Demosthenes and then Eurymedon. (Lamachus had been

Spartans defeated the Athenians in the naval battle of Syracuse during the Second Peloponnesian War. Time & Life Pictures/Getty Images

killed in action.) The final catastrophic sea battle in the Great Harbour of Syracuse was fought in cramped circumstances that did not allow the Athenian fleet enough freedom of maneuver. The expeditionary force was virtually annihilated, including its main commanders.

THE SECOND PHASE OF THE WAR, 413–404

The blow to Athens's morale and prestige was perhaps greater than the strictly military reverse, for, with an astonishing capacity for replacement, Athens managed, after a crash building program, to achieve rough naval parity with the Peloponnesians. This was the more remarkable in view of difficulties at home. Already before the end came in Sicily, Sparta had reopened the Peloponnesian War. On the advice of Alcibiades, the Spartans had fortified Decelea (413) and, as a result, were able to occupy Attica. Athens, embarrassed economically for this and other reasons, decided to impose a 5 percent tax on shipping instead of the tribute (but the tribute seems to have been restored in 410).

Denied the use of Attica, Athens drew more heavily on Euboea for food, and this is relevant to Euboea's revolt in 411. By then, however, there had also been revolts in the eastern Aegean and in Anatolia (413–412). As regards Anatolia, another factor is relevant: the king of Persia, angered by the Amorges affair, had decided to back Sparta. Representatives of his satraps Tissaphernes and Pharnabazus, as well as ambassadors from Chios and Erythrae, invited the Spartans to carry the war across to the eastern Aegean. This Sparta did, and in some long, drawn-out diplomacy it agreed to abandon all claim to Anatolia as part of a deal for money and a fleet. The money given was hardly lavish, and the fleet did not materialize at all (perhaps, as Thucydides hints, because Tissaphernes wanted to wear down both sides, but perhaps because it was needed for use against Egypt. There is papyrus evidence for a revolt from Persian authority at this time, 411). For Sparta's part, it is possible that its abandonment of Anatolia was not quite final. A treaty of 408 may have stipulated autonomy for the Ionian Greeks. Despite the reservations on both sides, the possibility of a joint victory of Sparta and Persia over Athens had at least been conjured briefly into existence. For the moment, however, the war went on.

Athens's military resilience after its defeats in Sicily was remarkable, but the political credibility of the radical democracy had been battered: the rich had lost money, the *thētes* had lost men, all classes had lost their illusions. This was a situation ready to be exploited by intellectual activists, who disliked the democracy anyway. Thucydides gives a brilliant picture of the oligarchic revolution of 411 (the "Regime of the Four Hundred" oligarchs), but he can perhaps be criticized for not bringing out the importance of this intellectual factor, stressing instead the general atmosphere of suspicion and terror.

A complete analysis of the revolution ought, however, to allow for the influence, on oligarchic leaders like Antiphon and the less extreme Theramenes, and no doubt on others, of the subversive teaching of the sophists (rhetorically adept "experts" who professed to impart their knowledge of such politically useful skills as rhetoric, usually in exchange for money). Theramenes is said to have been a pupil of the sophist Prodicus of Ceos. Thucydides mentions sophists only once, and then not in the context of 411 at all. The first impetus to the revolution was given by Alcibiades, who certainly was a product of the sophistic age. His motives, however, were selfish and short-term (he was aiming to achieve his own recall from exile), and he abandoned the oligarchs when he failed to get what he wanted. Nor had Peisander and Phrynichos, two other leading oligarchs, always been hostile to democracy.

It is certain, however, that there were some who held, as a matter of sincere theoretical conviction, that there were merits in a "hoplite franchise"—that is, an undemocratic constitution in which the *thētes* would be barred from attending the Assembly or serving as jurors). Such a view, insofar as it was elitist, would naturally be attractive to the cavalry class, and it is an appealing suggestion that the original coup d'état was staged at the deme site of Colonus precisely because of its associations with the cult of Poseidon Hippios, "Horsey" Poseidon. But distinctions between extreme and moderate factions among the oligarchy must be made: Theramenes and Cleitophon were among the moderates who sought to justify the new arrangements by reference to Solon and Cleisthenes, who were wrongly represented, at this time, as having excluded the *thētes* from the Assembly. (Perhaps they used the slogan "ancestral constitution," but a contemporary sophist, Thrasymachus, implies that it was on everybody's lips.) However erroneous such an appeal to Solon was with regard to the facts—it is a good example of "invented tradition"—it is undoubtedly true that members of this group behaved more moderately than some of the other oligarchs (Theramenes helped to overthrow the Four Hundred).

The Law Against Unconstitutional Proposals, a democratic safeguard, was abolished, as was pay for most kinds of political office, and the old Council of Five Hundred was to be replaced by an elected Council of Four Hundred. These changes and plans did not go unopposed. Despite its losses in Sicily, there was still a fleet, at Samos, which was not at all pleased with what was happening. And the hoplites themselves, whatever theoreticians may have wished for on their behalf, were as enthusiastic for democracy as the *thētes*. The fleet sent a message to demand that the democracy be restored, and the extreme oligarchs were overthrown in favour of a more moderate oligarchy, the regime of The Five Thousand. This regime probably denied to the *thētes* the right of voting in the Assembly and law-courts, though this is controversial. In any case, it lasted a mere 10 months.

Full democracy was restored in 410, and a commission was set up to codify the law: it was evidently felt that constitutional history had been abused in 411 and that the abuse had been made possible through ignorance. Codification was to prevent a recurrence. It was expected to take four months but was still incomplete after six years. A fresh start was to be made in 403.

In 410 Athens had recovered sufficiently to win a battle against the Peloponnesian fleet at Cyzicus (this was a factor in the downfall of The Five Thousand), and the Spartans may have asked for peace. The offer, however, is not mentioned by Xenophon, who now replaces Thucydides as the main source. This was a remarkable reversal of the position in 413 when a Spartan victory must have seemed in sight. Athens, however, refused to come to terms.

Athenian success continued with further victories in the Hellespontine

Thirty Tyrants

The Thirty Tyrants, an oligarchy put in place by Sparta, ruled Athens (404–403 BC) after the Peloponnesian War. The thirty commissioners who composed the group were appointed to the oligarchy, which had an extremist conservative core, led by Critias, an Athenian citizen known to Socrates. Their oppressive regime fostered a bloody purge, in which perhaps 1,500 residents were killed. Many moderates fled the city. Gathering a force, they returned to defeat the tyrants' forces in a battle at Piraeus in 403. The 30 fled and were killed off over the next few years.

region, and Alcibiades, who had played a role in these victories, was able to return from exile in 407. He magnificently led the religious procession from Athens to Eleusis, thus atoning for, or giving the lie to, his alleged impiety in 415 when he was held to have joined in profaning the Sacred Mysteries. His subordinate Antiochus, however, lost the Battle of Notium in 406, which effectively ended Alcibiades' career. Athens managed yet another victory at Arginusae in 406. But the Athenian commanders, who failed to rescue survivors, were executed in an illegal mass trial. This was folly, and so was Athens's refusal of yet another Spartan peace offer after the battle. In this, as after the Battle of Cyzicus, it followed the advice of the demagogue Cleophon.

That a combination of Persia and Sparta could win the war easily can never have been in much doubt, even after the particular failures of trust and understanding in 411. The extra factor needed to bring it about was a combination of personalities. This happened quite suddenly after 408, with the emergence to prominence of a new Spartan, Lysander, and a new and extremely young Persian, the king's son Cyrus, sent to fight on Sparta's side. The two men got on instantly (it surely helped their relationship that Persia had made concessions, if make them it did, about the autonomy of the Greek cities). The result was the victory at the Battle of Notium and then, after the Athenian refusal of the peace offer after Arginusae, a final crushing defeat of Athens at Aegospotami (405). The Athenians were starved into surrender by Lysander (404). The Long Walls were demolished, the fleet was reduced to a token 12 ships, and the empire ceased to exist. Athens was to be governed by a Spartan-imposed oligarchy, the Thirty Tyrants.

CHAPTER 5

Greek Civilization in the Fifth Century BC

As noted earlier, some of the notable events of the fifth century BC in Greece included the Persian Wars and the Peloponnesian War. However, this century is also known for the brilliance of philosophical thought in Greece and elsewhere.

A number of observations may be made about fifth-century BC Greek civilization and its historical influences. A Persian influence on philosophy is notable, as are such movements as the rise of democracy and the growth of rhetoric as an art.

INTELLECTUAL ACHIEVEMENTS

Further, the effect of the Persian Wars on literature and art was obvious and immediate. The wars prompted such poetry as the *Persians* of Aeschylus and a dithyramb of Pindar praising the Athenians for laying the shining foundations of liberty and such art as the Athenian dedications at Delphi or the paintings in the Painted Colonnade at Athens itself.

The Effect of the Persian Wars on Philosophy

Less direct than their effect on literature and art was the effect of the Persian Wars on philosophy. Famous centres of philosophy, such as Elea and Abdera, owed their existence to the

Persian takeover of Ionia in 546. The thinkers for which those places were famous, Parmenides of Elea and Democritus from Abdera, were, however, products of the fifth century, and the title of "school" has been claimed both for the atomists of Abdera and for the Eleatics, who argued for the unreality of all change. A number of Ionian thinkers arrived at Athens after Xerxes' invasion perhaps because fifth-century Ionia experienced relative material poverty and was thus no longer an agreeable place or perhaps because they had escaped from the Persian army, into which they had been conscripted. This has been suggested for Anaxagoras of Clazomenae, who impressed Socrates by identifying mind as the governing power of the universe.

Another fifth-century Ionian who found his way to Athens was Hippodamus of Miletus, an eccentric political theorist, who made his own clothes and was famous for a theory of town planning. However, the laying out of cities on "orthogonal," or rectilinear, principles cannot quite be his invention (though he gave his name to such "Hippodamian" plans): such layouts are already found in Italy in the Archaic period at places like Metapontum. Hippodamus, nevertheless, may have had a hand in the orderly rebuilding of the port of Piraeus after the Persian Wars and even in the new colony at Thurii in 443. (A tradition associating him with the planning of the new city of Rhodes, almost at the end of the century, surely stretches his life span beyond belief.)

The more theoretical side of Hippodamus's political thought did not have much detectable effect on the world around him (he thought that communities should be divided into farmers, artisans, and warriors) except perhaps for his suggestion that a city of 10,000 souls, a *myriandros polis*, was the ideal size. This is the number of colonists allegedly sent out to Heraclea in Trachis by the Spartans; and the concept of the *myriandros polis* was to be very influential in the fourth century and Hellenistic period.

THE RISE OF DEMOCRACY

It has been plausibly claimed that there is a general link between the rise of a political system, namely democracy, and the self-critical speculative thinking that characterizes the Greeks in and to some extent before the fifth century. Democracy, it is held, was causally responsible for the growth of philosophy and science, in the sense that an atmosphere of rational political debate conduced to a more general insistence on argument and proof. To this it has been objected that there are already, in the Homeric poems, remarkable debates constructed on recognizable rhetorical principles and that Nestor in the *Iliad* defines a good leader as one who is a good speaker of words and doer of deeds, in that order. Great warriors always needed to be persuasive speakers as well. But political accountability was a cardinal principle of the Ephialtic reforms at Athens in the late 460s, and it is certainly attractive to suppose that intellectual accountability was a parallel or consequent development.

A further difficulty in assessing the relationship between intellectual activities consists in the lopsided ways in which the relevant evidence has survived. First, little is extant from any centre other than Athens, and this inevitably means that a treatment of fifth-century culture tends to turn into a treatment of Athenian culture. One can note the problem but not solve it. Second, some literary genres have survived more intact than others. Attic tragedy and comedy survive in relative abundance (the tragedies of Aeschylus, Sophocles, and Euripides, and the comedies of Aristophanes). The study of philosophy before Plato is, by contrast, a matter of detective work conducted from fragments preserved by later writers, whose own faithfulness in quotation and transmission may be suspect because of their own prejudices. (Christian apologists have perhaps been too readily trusted in this matter by students of the "pre-Socratics," or predecessors and contemporaries of Socrates.)

Hippocrates and the Fluidity of Genres

One set of texts that does survive in bulk and is neither Athenian in origin nor the work of poets is the Hippocratic corpus of medical writings. Hippocrates was a fifth-century native of the Dorian island of Cos, but the writings that have survived are probably not his personal work. Many of them contain references to northern Greek places such as Thasos and Abdera, a reminder that intellectual activity went on outside Athens.

The most striking feature of these writings, apart from the exactness of their descriptive passages, is their rhetorically conditioned polemical character. It was necessary for the practicing doctor not merely to offer the best prognosis and cure but to disparage his rivals and show by aggressive and competitive argumentation that his own approach was superior. In fact, it seems that on one specific major medical issue the "professional" doctors did not fare as well as an amateur commentator, the historian Thucydides, who in his description of the great plague was aware, as they were not, of the concepts of acquired immunity and contagion. In other words, he thought empirically and they did not. A basically competitive attitude as well as reliance on rhetoric are features of much early prose writing. For example, Hecataeus was criticized by Herodotus, who was in turn criticized by implication, though never named, by Thucydides.

Such shared features are a reminder that the fifth century, before the systematization of the fourth century associated with Aristotle or the organized Alexandrian scholarship of the third, did not yet make clear distinctions between literary genres. A distinction between prose and verse is perhaps implied by Thucydides' distinction between "poets" and "logographers," or writers of *logoi* (tales, accounts), and Pindar may hint at the same distinction. Thucydides' own

Hippocratic Oath

The ethical code attributed to the ancient Greek physician Hippocrates has been adopted as a guide to conduct by the medical profession throughout the ages and is still used in the graduation ceremonies of many medical schools. Although little is known of the life of Hippocrates—or, indeed, if he was the only practitioner of the time using this name—a body of manuscripts, called the Hippocratic Collection (Corpus Hippocraticum)*, survived until modern times. In addition to containing information on medical matters, the collection embodied a code of principles for the teachers of medicine and for their students. This code, or a fragment of it, has been handed down in various versions through generations of physicians as the Hippocratic oath.*

The oath dictates the obligations of the physician to students of medicine and the duties of pupil to teacher. In the oath, the physician pledges to prescribe only beneficial treatments, according to his abilities and judgment; to refrain from causing harm or hurt; and to live an exemplary personal and professional life.

Hippocrates, undated bust. © Photos.com/ Jupiterimages

The text of the Hippocratic oath (c. 400 BC) provided below is a translation from Greek by Francis Adams (1849). It is considered a classical version and differs from contemporary versions, which are reviewed and revised frequently to fit with changes in modern medical practice.

I swear by Apollo the physician, and Aesculapius, and Health, and All-heal, and all the gods and goddesses, that, according to my ability and judgment, I will keep this Oath and this stipulation—to reckon him who taught me this Art equally dear to me as my parents, to share my substance with him, and relieve his necessities if required; to look upon his offspring in the same footing as my own brothers, and to teach them this Art, if they shall wish to learn it, without fee or stipulation; and that by precept, lecture, and every other mode of instruction, I will impart a knowledge of the Art to my own sons, and those of my teachers, and to disciples bound by a stipulation and oath according to the law of medicine, but to none others. I will follow that system of regimen which, according to my ability and judgment, I consider for the benefit of my patients, and abstain from whatever is deleterious and mischievous. I will give no deadly medicine to any one if asked, nor suggest any such counsel; and in like manner I will not give to a woman a pessary to produce abortion. With purity and with holiness I will pass my life and practice my Art. I will not cut persons laboring under the stone, but will leave this to be done by men who are practitioners of this work. Into whatever houses I enter, I will go into them for the benefit of the sick, and will abstain from every voluntary act of mischief and corruption; and, further from the seduction of females or males, of freemen and slaves. Whatever, in connection with my professional practice or not, in connection with it, I see or hear, in the life of men, which ought not to be spoken of abroad, I will not divulge, as reckoning that all such should be kept secret. While I continue to keep this Oath unviolated, may it be granted to me to enjoy life and the practice of the art, respected by all men, in all times! But should I trespass and violate this Oath, may the reverse be my lot!

writings, however, like those of Herodotus, show an affinity to poetry, specifically to the epic poems of Homer. Indeed, an indebtedness to epic poetry is common both to the writings of Thucydides and to the Attic tragedy of the fifth century (it seems preferable to speak of shared influence of epic poetry on both the writers of tragedy and Thucydides rather than of direct influence of tragedy on Thucydides). And as noted, one now needs, since the discovery of the "new Simonides," to reckon with the influence on historiography of praise poetry about real military events.

GREEK DRAMA

Greek Tragedy

Greek tragedy was not itself intended as an immediate contribution to political debate, though in its exploration of issues, sometimes by means of rapid question-and-answer dialogue, its debt to rhetoric is obvious (this is particularly true of some plays by Euripides, such as the *Phoenician Women* or the *Suppliants*, but also of some by Sophocles, such as *Oedipus Rex* and *Philoctetes*). It is true that sometimes the *chorēgoi*, or rich men appointed by one of the archons to finance a particular play, were themselves politicians and that this is reflected in the plays produced. (Themistocles was *chorēgos* for Phrynichos, one of whose plays caused a political storm, and Pericles paid for the *Persians* of Aeschylus.)

One play with a clear contemporary resonance in its choice of the Areopagus as a subtheme, the *Eumenides* of Aeschylus (458), however, had for its *chorēgos* a man otherwise unknown. Nor is it agreed whether Aeschylus was endorsing the recent reforms or voicing reservations about them. The play treats the theme of the vengeful dead (Orestes is pursued by the Eumenides—*Erinyes* or Furies—for killing his mother on Apollo's instructions because she killed his father, Agamemnon). Such preoccupation with the vengeful dead was illuminated by the publication in 1993 of a remarkable mid-fifth-century law from Selinus in western Sicily, which mentions the Eumenides and gives Zeus the obviously related but hitherto unattested cult title Zeus Eumenes. The inscription deals with the steps to be taken to cope with pollution after bloodshed.

The *Suppliants* of Euripides contains much in apparent praise of democratic institutions, but it also includes some harsh words for the kind of politician that the democracy tended to produce. Euripides' associations with the sophists (the oligarchs Cleitophon and Theramenes are specifically linked to him) are another reason why it is difficult to treat his *Suppliants* as a straightforward endorsement of democracy. The political relevance of *Suppliants* has always been noted, but the *Ion* of Euripides, produced in perhaps 412, has at least as strong a claim to be regarded as a political play. It treats and reconciles the two crucial Athenian myths of Ionianism and autochthony—i.e., the essentially anti-Dorian and therefore anti-Spartan idea that the Ionian Athenians were not immigrants (unlike the arriviste Dorians) but had occupied the same land always.

The views, political or otherwise, of playwrights themselves cannot be straightforwardly inferred from what they put into the mouths of their characters. But it must be significant that the festival of the Dionysia, at which the plays were produced, was designed to reinforce civic values and ideology in various ways: war orphans featured prominently in a demonstration of hoplite solidarity, and there was some kind of parade exhibiting the tribute of the subject allies—all this taking place before the plays were actually performed. Not even this, however, entailed that the content of the plays was necessarily expected to reinforce those civic values. The opposite may even (it has been argued) be true of some plays; for example, both the *Ajax* and the *Philoctetes* of Sophocles question the ethic of military obedience, and his *Antigone* stresses the paramount claims of family in the sphere of burial at a time when the polis had made large inroads in this area. In general, however, it is hard to believe that Sophocles, who was a friend of Pericles and served as *stratēgos* and imperial treasurer, was a kind of subversive malcontent.

Aeschylus
(b. 525/524—d. 456/455 BC, Gela, Sicily)

Aeschylus was the first great tragic dramatist of Greece. He singlehandedly raised the emerging art of tragedy to great heights of poetry and theatrical power. His plays are of lasting literary value in their majestic and compelling lyrical language, in the intricate architecture of their plots, and in the universal themes that they explore so honestly.

Aeschylus's language in both dialogue and choral lyric is marked by force, majesty, and emotional intensity. He makes bold use of compound epithets, metaphors, and figurative turns of speech, but this rich language is firmly harnessed to the dramatic action rather than used as mere decoration.

Little is known of Aeschylus's youth. He was probably born and grew up in Eleusis, northwest of Athens. He was recorded as having entered the Dionysia, Athens's major dramatic competition, shortly after its reorganization in 501 or 500 BC. He won his first success in the theatre in 484 BC at age 41.

Among his many innovations, Aeschylus is said to have introduced into Greek drama the second actor. This allowed a play to contain more than one plot and decreased the role of the chorus. Aeschylean tragedy deals with the plights, decisions, and fates of individuals with whom the destiny of the community or state is closely bound up. In turn, both individual and community stand in close relation to the gods. Personal, social, and religious issues are thus integrated, as they still were in the Greek civilization of the poet's time. Theodicy (i.e., the justifying of the gods' ways to men) was in some sense the concern of Aeschylus, though it might be truer to say that he aimed through dramatic conflict to throw light on the nature of divine justice. Aeschylus and his Greek contemporaries believed that the gods begrudged human greatness and sent infatuation on a man at the height of his success, thus bringing him to disaster. Man's infatuated act was frequently one of impiety or pride (hubris), for which his downfall could be seen as a just punishment. In this scheme of things, divine jealousy and eternal justice formed the common fabric of a moral order of which Zeus, supreme among the gods, was the guardian.

Aeschylus died at age 69. After his death the Athenians took the unprecedented step of decreeing that his plays could be revived for festival competitions. He was awarded the title "Father of Tragedy."

Out of more than 80 known titles, 52 of his plays won first prizes. Only seven of the tragedies survive: the trilogy *Oresteia*, which includes *Agamemnon*, *Choephoroi*, and *Eumenides*; *The Suppliants*; *The Persians*; *Seven Against Thebes*; and *Prometheus*.

Sophocles

(b. *c.* 496, Colonus, near Athens—d. 406 BC, Athens)

The second of the three great Greek writers of tragic drama during the fifth century BC was Sophocles. Aeschylus preceded him, and Euripides was his successor. Sophocles is believed to have written 123 dramas, but only seven of these have survived. The best known is *Oedipus Rex* (also known as *Oedipus the King*). The others are: *Electra*, *Antigone*, *Trachinian Women*, *Ajax*, *Philoctetes*, and *Oedipus at Colonus*. Fragments of lost plays and poems also exist.

Information concerning Sophocles' life is sketchy. His father was a wealthy manufacturer of armour. Sophocles received a good education, studying music under Lamprus—the most noted musician of the time—and drama under Aeschylus. The date when he first entered the dramatic competitions at Athens is unknown, but his first victory was in 468 BC. On that occasion he defeated Aeschylus. Sophocles is credited with about 20 first prizes in drama contests. Oddly enough his greatest work, *Oedipus Rex*, only won second place.

The great Greek dramatist Sophocles. Hulton Archive/Getty Images

In addition to his extensive writing, Sophocles was much involved in the public life of Athens. He served as a general at least once and may have taken part in foreign embassies. He was 90 years old and still active when he died, just before the end of the Peloponnesian War.

Sophocles was a master of tragic drama, especially in his characterizations. His tragic women are probably his most outstanding characters—Electra, Antigone, Deianeira, and others. He also had great ability to devise well-constructed plots. Few dramatists have been able to handle situation and plot with more power and certainty. The frequent references in the *Poetics* to Sophocles' *Oedipus Rex* show that Aristotle regarded this play as a masterpiece of construction, and few later critics have dissented. Sophocles is also unsurpassed in his moments of high dramatic tension and in his revealing use of tragic irony.

The criticism has been made that Sophocles was a superb artist and nothing more. He grappled neither with religious problems as Aeschylus had nor with intellectual ones as Euripides had done. He accepted the gods of Greek religion in a spirit of unreflecting orthodoxy, and he contented himself with presenting human characters and human conflicts. But it should be stressed that to Sophocles "the gods" appear to have represented the natural forces of the universe to which human beings are unwittingly or unwillingly subject. To Sophocles, human beings live for the most part in dark ignorance because they are cut off from these permanent, unchanging forces and structures of reality. Yet it is pain, suffering, and the endurance of tragic crisis that can bring people into valid contact with the universal order of things. In the process, a person can become more genuinely human, more genuinely himself.

The typical Sophoclean drama presents a few characters, impressive in their determination and power and possessing a few strongly drawn qualities or faults that combine with a particular set of circumstances to lead them inevitably to a tragic fate. Sophocles develops his characters's rush to tragedy with great economy, concentration, and dramatic effectiveness, creating a coherent, suspenseful situation whose sustained and inexorable onrush came to epitomize the tragic form to the Classical world. Sophocles emphasizes that most people lack wisdom, and he presents truth in collision with ignorance, delusion, and folly. Many scenes dramatize flaws or failure in thinking (deceptive reports and rumours, false optimism, hasty judgment, madness). The chief character does something involving grave error. This affects others, each of whom reacts in his own way, thereby causing the chief agent to take another step toward ruin—his own and that of others as well.

Euripides
(b. *c.* 484, Athens—d. 406 BC, Macedonia)

Along with Aeschylus and Sophocles, Euripides was one of the three great tragic poets of ancient Greece. Of his life very little is known. He married a woman named Melito, and they had three sons. In 408 he left Athens for Macedonia, probably because of disgust with the seemingly endless Peloponnesian War with Sparta.

Euripides is believed to have written 92 dramas, but only 19 of them are now known. They show him to have been a tragedian of considerable merit. Euripides differed from Aeschylus and Sophocles in making his characters' tragic fates stem almost entirely from their own flawed natures and uncontrolled passions. Chance, disorder, and human irrationality and immorality frequently result not in an eventual reconciliation or moral resolution but in apparently meaningless suffering that is looked upon with indifference by the gods. The power of this type of drama lies in the frightening and ghastly situations it creates and in the melodramatic, even sensational, emotional effects of its characters' tragic crises.

As with those of the other tragedians, the plays of Euripides deal with legendary and mythological events of a time far removed from fifth-century Athens. But the points he made were applicable to the time in which he wrote, especially to the cruelties of the war.

During the last 20 years of his life, Euripides wrote a number of plays that might be called romantic tragicomedies. They were unusual in that they had happy endings. Among these were *Ion*, *Iphigenia in Tauris*, and *Helen*. In them he turned his back on the tragic real world and dealt purely in dramatic form. It is for his tragedies, however, that he is best remembered: *Medea*, first performed in 431 BC; *Hippolytus* (428); *Andromache*, *The Suppliants*, *Children of Heracles*, and *Hecuba* (all before 423); *Electra* and *The Trojan Women* (415); *Phoenician Women*

This photo shows a 1912 performance of Euripides' Iphigenia in Taurus. Topical Press Agency/Hulton Archive/Getty Images

(411–409); and *Heracles* (408) are among the best.

Euripides was known by his contemporaries as a dour and reclusive individual who spent much of his time writing in a cave overlooking the Saronic Gulf. Historians had long suspected that the cave was located on the island of Salamis. In January 1997, archaeologists from Greece announced that they had discovered a cave on the island of Salamis where they believed Euripides wrote several of his works.

Greek Comedy

Ancient Greek comedy was the second of three main forms of drama in classical Greece. There were three periods of Greek comedy: Old Comedy, Middle Comedy (which many place together with Old Comedy), and New Comedy. In the context of Greece in the fifth century BC, we are concerned only with Old Comedy.

Greek comedy arose out of the revels associated with the rites of Dionysus. Though tragedy evolved by stages that can be traced, the progress of comedy passed unnoticed because it was not taken seriously. The comic writing of fifth-century Greece is mainly known through the works of Magnes, Cratinus, and most illuminatingly, through the work of Aristophanes.

The 11 surviving plays of Aristophanes represent the earliest extant body of comic drama. What is known of Greek Old Comedy is derived from these plays, the earliest of which, *The Acharnians*, was produced in 425 BC. Aristophanic comedy has a distinct formal design but displays very little plot in any conventional sense. Rather, it presents a series of episodes aimed at illustrating, in humorous and often bawdy detail, the implications of a deadly serious political issue: it is a blend of invective, buffoonery, and song and dance. Old Comedy often used derision and scurrility, and this may have proved its undoing. Though praised by all, the freedom it enjoyed degenerated into license and violence and had to be checked by law.

Aristophanes
(b. *c.* 450—d. *c.* 385 BC)

Aristophanes was the greatest representative of ancient Greek comedy. Eleven of his plays survive almost in their entirety. They have stood the test of time, having been frequently produced on the 21st-century stage and in several media.

Little is known of Aristophanes' life. Most of what has been pieced together is based on references in his own plays. Although it is known that he was an Athenian citizen, his place of birth is uncertain. His first play was produced in Athens about 427 BC.

Most of his work is about the social, literary, and philosophical life of Athens. Many of his themes, however, relate to the folly of war, especially the Peloponnesian War (431–404 BC) between the city-states of Athens and Sparta. This war was essentially a conflict between imperialist Athens and conservative Sparta and so was long the dominant issue in Athenian politics. Aristophanes was naturally an opponent of the more or less bellicose statesmen who controlled the government of Athens throughout the better part of his maturity. Aristophanes lived to see the revival of Athens after its defeat by Sparta.

Aristophanes is thought to have written 40 plays in all, an average of one per year during his dramatic career. His success is attributed to his witty dialogue, comical though sometimes spiteful satire, brilliant imitations, clever and absurd scenes and situations, and charming songs.

The 11 works of Aristophanes that survive are: *The Acharnians, The Knights, The Clouds, The Wasps, The Peace, The Birds, Lysistrata, The Thesmophoriazusae, The Frogs, Women in Parliament,* and *The Plutus.*

GREEK SATYR PLAYS

The satyr play can be considered the reversal of Attic tragedy, a kind of "joking tragedy." The actors play mythical heroes engaged in action drawn from traditional mythical tales, but the chorus members are satyrs, guided by old Silenus. Satyrs are nature spirits who combine male human traits (beards, hairy bodies, flat noses, and an erect phallus) with the ears and tails of horses. The satyrs are contrasted with the main characters—who are more or less serious—by their dancing, their love of wine, and their diverting banter, often expressed in low language. This contrast, which is the special trait of satyric drama, served to alleviate the emotional tension of the tragic trilogy.

The usual interpretation is that the satyr plays were presented directly after the tragic trilogy, as the fourth play in competitions. They are regularly listed fourth in lists of plays put on at the Great (or City) Dionysia in Athens. Some satyr plays by Aeschylus seem to make more sense as the second play of the group, however, such as the Sphinx in his Theban trilogy and Proteus in his *Oresteia.* According to tradition, Pratinas of Phlius was the first to produce a satyr play, at Athens in the 70th Olympiad (499–496 BC).

Under the influence of comedy, the growing sophistication of Athenian audiences reduced the need for satyr plays to produce comic relief, as is seen in *Alcestis* (438 BC), the fourth drama produced by Euripides, which is almost completely lacking in the genre's traditional characteristics. Only one traditional satyr play, Euripides' *Cyclops,* survives. However, papyrus discoveries have revealed significant fragments of others, especially the *Dictyulci* ("Net Fishers") of Aeschylus and the *Ichneutae* ("Trackers") of Sophocles.

THE LITURGY SYSTEM

The choregic system is one aspect of a (for this period) very unusual institution by which individuals paid for state projects. The fifth-century BC Athenian economy, though it continued to draw on the silver of Laurium and was underpinned by the more recently acquired assets of an organized empire, nevertheless looked to individuals to finance both necessary projects like triremes and strictly unnecessary ones like tragedies. It is worth asking whether such distinction between necessary and unnecessary projects is too sharp: there was a sense in which the trireme, a noble achievement of human *technē* (art or craft), was an object of legitimate pride, which might have its aesthetic aspect. That, at least, is the implication of Thucydides' unforgettable account of the rivalry between the trierarchs en route to Sicily in 415. Thucydides describes the splendid flotilla, for which publicly and privately no expense had been grudged, racing from Athens as far as Aegina out of sheer pride, joy, and enthusiasm.

The psychology of contributions of this sort, the so-called liturgy system, was complicated. On the one hand, the system differed from the kind of tyrannical or individual patronage the poetry of Pindar shows still existed in, for example, fifth-century Sicily or at Dorian Cyrene, which still had a hereditary monarchy (the Battiads) until the second half of the fifth century. Athenians themselves liked to think that the system was somehow anonymous and that glory was brought on the city. That assumption was true of athletic as well as cultural success: Thucydides made Alcibiades claim the military command in Sicily during the Peloponnesian War because his Olympic chariot victories had brought glory on the city. Consistent with this, Athenian victors in the Panhellenic games were given free meals in the Prytaneium (the town hall), alongside the descendants of the tyrannicides Harmodius and Aristogiton. The evidence for this is an inscription of the 430s.

On the other hand, the liturgy system was exploited for individual gain. Thus Alcibiades' plea for political recognition was an individual and traditional one, recalling the seventh-century Olympic victor Cylon, who also sought political success by his attempted tyrannical coup. It was not altogether surprising that Alcibiades' contemporaries suspected that he too was aiming at tyranny. Alcibiades, it may be felt, can be written off as an exception and an anachronism. Far less famous speakers, however, in tight situations in the lawcourts, made comparable reference to their individual expenditure on behalf of the state, one of them frankly admitting that his motive in spending more than was necessary was to take out a kind of insurance against forensic misfortune. And generally the *History of Thucydides* does show awareness that athletic success still went hand in hand with political prominence.

Individuals might pay for the equipping of triremes, or even (like Alcibiades) own their own trireme. They might even help finance buildings like the Stoa Poikile of Peisianax (a relative of Cimon). But a building program such as that undertaken after 449 called for the full resources of the imperial state. The architects commissioned, Callicrates, Ictinus,

The ruins of the Parthenon in Athens, Greece, originally built in the fifth century BC. Hulton Archive/Getty Images

and Mnesicles, worked under the general supervision of the sculptor Phidias. Most of these men had personal connections with Pericles himself and with aspects of Periclean policy (Callicrates, for example, was involved in the building of the Long Walls). The main works on the Acropolis were temples, but even the great ceremonial gateway of Mnesicles (the Propylaea) was a lavish and expensive effort, though a secular one. The financial history of these buildings can be reconstructed with the help of inscriptions, though firm evidence for the Parthenon is lacking. Nonetheless, an inscription shows that the chryselephantine (gold and ivory) cult statue of Athena by Phidias cost somewhere between 700 and 1,000 talents, and the Parthenon itself, which housed the statue, may have cost something in the same region.

THE ROLES OF WOMEN AND SLAVES

The liturgy system, it should be noted, was not open to all alike. Only male citizens could participate in it. Some further examination should be made of the roles of women and slaves in this society.

Women

One Athenian group that can without absurdity be called an exploited productive class was the women. They were unusually restricted in their property rights even by comparison with the women in other Greek states. To some extent the peculiar Athenian disabilities were due to a desire on the part of the polis to ensure that estates did not become concentrated in few hands, thus undermining the democracy of smallholders. To this social and political end it was necessary that women should not inherit in their own right. An heiress was therefore obliged to marry her nearest male relative unless he found a dowry for her. The prevailing homosexual ethos of the gymnasia and of the symposium helped to reduce the cultural value attached to women and to the marriage bond.

Against all this, one has to place evidence showing that, whatever the rules, women did as a matter of fact make dedications and loans, at Athens as elsewhere, sometimes involving fairly large sums. And the Athenian orators appealed to the informal pressure of domestic female opinion. One fourth-century speaker in effect asked what the men would tell the women of their households if they acquitted a certain woman and declared that she was as worthy to hold a priesthood as they were.

In fact, priesthoods were one area of public activity open to women at Athens. The priestess of Athena Nike was in some sense appointed by lot "from all the Athenian women," just like some post-Ephialtic magistrate. (Both the inscription appointing the priestess and the epitaph of the first incumbent are extant.) The Athenian priests and priestesses, however, did not have the political influence that their counterparts later had at Rome. Only one anecdote attests a priestess as conscientious objector on a political issue (Theano, who refused to curse Alcibiades), and it is suspect. It is true that Athenian women had cults of their own, such as that of Artemis at Brauron, where young Athenian girls served the goddess in a ritual capacity as "little bears." Such activity, however, can be seen as merely a taming process, preparatory to marriage in the way that military initiation was preparatory to the male world of war and fighting.

Nevertheless, it was arguably in religious associations that the excluded situation of Classical Athenian women at the political level was ameliorated. At Athens and elsewhere, the rules about women and sacrifice seem to show that the political definition of female status was more restricted than the social and religious. As always, however, there is a problem about evidence. Much of it comes from Athens, yet there is reason to suppose that the rules circumscribing Athenian women were exceptional. The "Gortyn code" from mid-fifth-century Crete, for example, seems to imply that women held more property there than was usual at Athens in the same period.

Slaves

From the accounts of the Erechtheum, the temple of Athena on the Acropolis (built 421–405 BC), it is known that highly skilled slaves as well as metics (resident foreigners) participated in the work on the friezes and columns. The slaves, whose work on the building can hardly be distinguished from that of their free coworkers, received payment like the rest (but the money was presumably handed over to their owners). These slaves and those used as agricultural and domestic workers (e.g., the occasional nurse-companions mentioned by fourth-century orators) can be placed at one end of a spectrum. At the other end are the mining slaves working in the thousands under dangerous and deplorable conditions. Their life expectancy was short. It has been held that only condemned criminals were used in the mines, but the evidence for such "condemnation to the mines" is Roman, not Classical Athenian.

Slaves were thus necessary for the working of the economy in its mining and agriculture aspects, and they also provided skills for the architectural glorification of the Acropolis. It is disputed how much chattel slaves were needed as part of the infrastructure of Athenian life

The Acropolis

Many of Athens's bequests to the world are expressed in and around the natural centre of Athens, the Acropolis (designated a World Heritage site in 1987). Rising some 150 kilometres (500 feet) above sea level, with springs near the base and a single approach, the Acropolis was an obvious choice of citadel and sanctuary from earliest times. That it could be something more is evidenced in the Parthenon, one of the brightest jewels in humankind's, let alone Athens's, treasury.

As deceptively simple as Socrates' conversation, this columned, oblong temple is the expression—without a trace of strain or conflict—of a human ideal of clarity and unity. The architectural genius is concentrated in the exterior, for within was a shelter for the goddess Athena—the patroness who lent her name to the city—not a place for mass worship. Its spiritual quality, the sensation of being almost afloat, is enhanced by the lack of a single, straight, vertical line in the peristyle (the surrounding colonnade). Each vertical is almost imperceptibly bowed, theoretically meeting some 3,500 kilometres (11,500 feet) in the sky. The columns, of diminishing thickness toward the centre of the colonnade, with diminishing space between them, lean toward the centre, too; all these differences are virtually invisible to the beholder. Even the 20 flutings of each column diminish in width as they rise, and the humblest details of craftsmanship are perfect.

On the northeast corner of the interior are faint traces of Christian wall paintings dating from the temple's service as the Church of St. Mary, and in the southwest corner of the porch is the stair leading to the minaret that was added when the building was a Turkish mosque. The

The Acropolis, Athens. © Goodshoot/Jupiterimages

Parthenon was also used as a powder magazine, when, on Sept. 26, 1687, Venetian artillery, attacking the Turks from the Hill of the Muses, scored a direct hit. Francesco Morosini, the commander in chief, when reporting to the Venetian government, called it "a fortunate shot." Wishing to bring home more than just good news, he also tried to lower Athena's horses in the centre of the west pediment, but his men's dexterity was not as highly developed as their marksmanship and the masterpieces smashed to bits on the rock below.

The Turks regained possession of the Acropolis the following year and later began selling souvenirs to Europeans. The duc de Choiseul, formerly French ambassador in Constantinople, picked up a piece of the frieze and two metopes. In 1801 the British ambassador, Lord Elgin, arrived with an imperial decree permitting him to pull down Turkish houses on the Acropolis to seek fragments of sculpture. Among the 50 pieces he took home (the shipping charges were £75,000 [about $125,200], a huge sum for those days) was most of the remaining Parthenon sculpture, which he later sold to the British Museum for £35,000 (about $58,427). The Greeks have forgiven the clumsiness of the Venetian engineers, the accuracy of Venetian cannoneers, and the vandalism of the Turks, but they still nurture rancour against Elgin. The New Acropolis Museum (dedicated in 2009) was built in large part to house the "Elgin Marbles," and in anticipation of their return a top floor gallery of the museum, named Parthenon Hall, has been set aside for their display. Devoted, as its name suggests, to the Parthenon's construction and *adornment, the hall represents the pieces removed by Elgin with veiled plaster casts.*

When the Turks, who had occupied Athens since 1456, departed, they left the monuments in a state of ruin, the ground covered with garden plots, and several hundred small huts. After Greece won its independence, Otho, the first king of the Hellenes, had everything that postdated the Classical period swept away, set scholars to work identifying the remains, and encouraged some reconstruction.

Erechtheum, on the Acropolis, Athens, Greece. Alison Frantz

in that they provided the political classes, down to and including the *thētes*, with the leisure for politics and philosophy. The answer depends on population figures, which are far from certain. Perhaps the total slave population approached six figures (the adult male population in 431 was 42,000). Probably many *thētes* did own slaves. Although slaves were used for military purposes only rarely, they might exceptionally have been enrolled in the fleet. Slaves were always considered a dangerous weapon of war, but they occasionally figure prominently in descriptions of political struggle within cities. For example, at Corcyra in 427 the slaves were promised freedom by both sides but went over to the democrats. One cannot adduce this as support for an interpretation of Greek politics in terms of class struggle because the democrats may simply have made the more handsome offers.

MILITARY TECHNOLOGY

Greek military technology remained surprisingly static in the fifth century. The seventh century, by contrast, had witnessed rapid innovations, such as the introduction of the hoplite and the trireme, which still were the basic instruments of war in the fifth. The fourth century was to be another period of military change, although some of the new features were already discernible in the period of the Peloponnesian War (such as the more intelligent use of light-armed troops, as in the northwest and at Sphacteria in the 420s; the more extensive use of mercenaries; and the deepened right wing in the formation of the hoplite army used at Delium). But it was the development of artillery that opened an epoch, and this invention did not predate the fourth century. It was first heard of in the context of Sicilian warfare against Carthage in the time of Dionysius I of Syracuse.

CHAPTER 6

Greece in the Fourth Century BC

The loss of the Peloponnesian War at the end of the fifth century signalled many changes for Athens. One of those changes was the seizure of power by Dionysius I of Syracuse (*c*. 430–367 BC). Dionysius may be seen as a transitional figure between the fifth century and the fourth and indeed between Classical and Hellenistic Greece.

DIONYSIUS I OF SYRACUSE

Dionysius's career began in 405, after the seven troubled years in Sicily that followed the Athenian surrender in 413. For most of this period there was war with Carthage in North Africa, and there were internal convulsions that Carthage was constantly seeking to exploit. Sicily was always prone to tyranny and political instability, partly because the island was threatened by potentially hostile neighbours ready to encroach and partly because there was a large population of non-Greek indigenous inhabitants such as the forces mobilized by Ducetius.

Stasis, or civil strife, was always specially prevalent in Classical Sicily. The Selinus sacred law may have been a response to a particularly violent and bloody bout of stasis. Certainly it is significant that it is in a Sicilian context (in the Greek town of Leontini, 422) that one can find, in the pages of Thucydides, an early mention of the revolutionary slogan "redistribution of land," which in the fourth century and later was often associated with political upheaval of the sort feared by the possessing classes. Polis life in Sicily never struck deep enough roots, and populations tended to be mixed and were too often transplanted. Interesting lead tablets from Syracuse's daughter city Camarina, published in 1992, appear to indicate that the city reorganized its citizen body about 460, perhaps on "Cleisthenic" Athenian lines.

Immediately after the defeat of Athens, a radical democracy was installed in Syracuse, at the instigation of an extremist named Diocles. The leader of the moderate democrats, Hermocrates, who happened to be absent, was exiled in 410. He tried to return but was killed in 407 in an attempt (his enemies said) to establish a tyranny. Dionysius, who had been one of Hermocrates' followers (and married his daughter) seized sole power in 406. His tyranny lasted until his death in 367. It was mostly taken up by warfare, fought with fluctuating fortunes, against Carthage. Successes such as the capture of Motya in 397 were hard to consolidate, and none of several peace settlements was lasting. His significance lies elsewhere than in this inconclusive fighting. The first nontorsion artillery (i.e., artillery using mechanical means to winch back, by means of a ratchet, a bow of unusual solidity but of a basically conventional conception) is attested from the Sicily of this period.

Torsion artillery, which used the additional power of twisted substances like sinew or women's hair to act as strings for the projection of the missile and which did not need the bow element at all, was introduced in the middle of the fourth century. Torsion-powered stone-throwing machines could be huge and could batter down massive and sophisticated fortifications. Lack of torsion artillery prevented Agesilaus in the 390s from taking fortified cities rapidly and so making progress in his invasion of Anatolia. Possession of it, by contrast, helped Alexander later in the century to overrun the same area with relative ease. The preliminary discovery of nontorsion artillery in Dionysius's Sicily, however, was already a notable refinement on traditional siege technique.

In other military respects Dionysius looked to the future. His was essentially a military monarchy based on loyal mercenary power. War, which included large-scale munitions manufacture, was essential to his economy. In addition to taking on the Carthaginians in Sicily, he fought Greeks in Italy, even destroying the city of Rhegium in 386. Dionysius wanted to unite Sicily and southern Italy under his personal rule, and one need look for no subtler motive than the prestige and booty accruing from it. The kind of military monarchy he established was a crucial precedent for later figures such as Jason of Thessalian Pherae or Philip II and Alexander III the Great of Macedon.

Dionysius is called archon (an ambiguous title that can mean ruler or magistrate) of Sicily in an Athenian inscription, but he was surely thought of as king or tyrant by his local subjects. In this use of titles he has been compared to the fourth-century "Spartocid" rulers of southern Russia, Leucon I and his son Satyrus II, who (as inscriptions show) called themselves archon when dealing with their Greek subjects but king when describing their authority over the native population.

The Syracuse that produced Dionysius was a late fifth-century polis both in the literal sense and in features, such as appointment to office by lot, that it had adopted from the Athenians whose invasion had just been so vigorously resisted. Dionysius himself was helped to power by Sparta, the polis that above all others remained uncompromisingly "classical" in its repeated refusal, in later times, to come to terms with the victorious Macedonians. It is a striking fact, and a further betrayal of the liberation propaganda with which Sparta had entered the Peloponnesian War, that it ended it by installing at Syracuse a tyrant who was to last for four decades. This fact was not missed by the Athenian writer Isocrates. The particular Spartans sent to help Dionysius are figures of secondary importance, but it is reasonable to see behind them the hand of Lysander, who is attested as having visited Dionysius. (There is no overwhelming reason to doubt this.)

Spartan policy immediately after the Peloponnesian War looks imperialistic in the full sense: one hears of tribute and of "decarchies," or juntas of 10, imposed by Lysander, as, for example, on Samos. The government of the Thirty Tyrants, actually a Spartan-supported oligarchy, imposed at Athens is characteristic of this short phase. The seizure, by the Athenian democrat Thrasybulus, of the frontier stronghold of Phyle in northern Attica, however, created a focus for refugees, who flocked to join him. The democrats marched south, and the extreme oligarch Critias was killed in fighting in the Piraeus. Opinion at Sparta softened, and Lysander's tough policy was reversed at Athens and elsewhere (one of the Spartan kings, Pausanias, was instrumental in this, though he himself narrowly escaped condemnation at a trial held in Sparta). This episode perhaps deserves to rank as a rare instance in which moral scruple, or at least a qualm about what the rest of the Greek world might consider unacceptable, determined a foreign policy decision by Sparta. By the end of 403, democracy was restored at Athens.

Arguably, Athenian democracy was not merely restored but comprehensively rethought at this moment. As part of a general codification of the laws, now entering its second phase, it was made harder for the Assembly to legislate. Instead the passing of laws (or *nomoi*), with the important exception of those pertaining to foreign policy, was entrusted to special panels of sworn jurors. The Assembly henceforth passed only decrees. Pay for attendance in the Assembly was introduced at this time, and the hillside meeting place, the Pnyx, was physically remodeled, making it easier to control admission. The Council of Five Hundred also may have been tampered with, if it is right that "bouleutic quotas"—that is, the total of councillors supplied by demes—were now altered to take account of changes in settlement patterns brought about by the Peloponnesian War. The case for discontinuity has, however, not been proved.

Other post-403 changes, some not strictly datable, may be mentioned here. The Assembly no longer heard treason trials after about 350. Perhaps this was because jury trial was cheaper now that the Assembly was paid. (Juries also were paid, but Assembly attendances were larger.) For the same financial reason, and perhaps also in the mid-fourth century, a limit was imposed on the hitherto unrestricted number of meetings of the Assembly per prytany, or council month lasting one-tenth of the year: the limit imposed was at first three meetings, though this was later increased to four. Generals received more specialist functions in the course of the century, while financial officials, especially those in charge of funds for disbursing state pay, acquired great elected power. The climax of this development was the financial control exercised in the third quarter of the fourth century by first Eubulus and then Lycurgus. All this tended toward efficiency and professionalism but away from democracy. There is no doubt that the Athens of the fourth century was less democratic than the Athens of the fifth.

THE CORINTHIAN WAR

The restored Athenian democracy may have been less democratic in certain respects than that of the fifth century, but it was no less suspicious of, and hostile to, Sparta. These feelings, along with the straightforward hankering at all social levels for the benefits of empire (a strong and well-attested motive that should be emphasized), were to be exploited by Thebans at Athens in 395 in their appeal to Athens to join in war against Sparta. This war, called the Corinthian War (395–386) because much of it took place on Corinthian territory, was fought against Sparta by a coalition of Athens (with help from Persia), Boeotia, Corinth, and Argos. Sparta eventually won the war, but only after the Persians had switched support from Athens to Sparta. In fact, the winning side was the old combination that had proved victorious in the Peloponnesian War.

The causes of the Corinthian War lie in the policies pursued by Sparta after its victory in 404. Persian participation on Athens's side needs a special explanation, which is to be found in two ultimately related sets of operations conducted by Sparta east of the Aegean. In 401 Lysander's old friend Cyrus, the younger brother of the new Persian king, Artaxerxes II (reigned 404–359), made an attempt on the throne with Spartan help. The expedition was a military failure. Cyrus was killed at the Battle of Cunaxa north of Babylon, and the Greek army had to be extricated and brought back to the Black Sea region. It became famous, however, because a participant, first as a soldier of fortune and after Cyrus's death as a commander of the Greek force, was

Xenophon, who made these exploits the basis of his *Anabasis* or "March Up-country" of the Ten Thousand. Lysander's support of Cyrus provided grounds for a change of attitude toward Sparta on the part of the new Persian king. The battle, though a short-term failure, had long-term propaganda importance because it fixed in Greek minds the possibility of a better-organized "march up-country," a project that was to be preached by the Athenian orator Isocrates, planned by Philip of Macedon and realized by Alexander the Great.

Cyrus had been given help in the early stages of his revolt by some Greek cities of Anatolia. When the Persian Tissaphernes, the victor of Cunaxa, threatened reprisals against them, they appealed to Sparta, which sent out Thibron (400). This was the beginning of the second Spartan operation in Anatolia, related to the first because the Ten Thousand were eventually able to attach themselves to Thibron, having meanwhile been harried by Tissaphernes.

Thibron's expedition was followed by that of Dercyllidas (399–397), but the most ambitious of all was led by the new Spartan king, Agesilaus, in 396. At the least (and Xenophon, a great admirer of the Spartan king, attributes to him some very grand ideas indeed) Agesilaus seems to have wanted to establish a zone of rebel satraps in western Anatolia. It is therefore not surprising that in 397 the Persians began to build a new fleet to deal with the menace of a Spartan army in Asia. (Sparta's help may, however, have had some technical justification if, as is possible, there had been diplomacy in 408 that renegotiated a more favourable position for the Ionian cities than they had been left in at the end of 411.) It may have been a further irritant that Sparta was helping another anti-Persian rebel in Egypt. The fact that Egypt maintained its independence from Persia until the 340s was a serious economic loss to the Persian landowners who had been exploiting it at a distance.

The Greece that Agesilaus had left behind was uneasy under its new Spartan masters, despite the glory of Sparta's victory over the Athenian fleet at Aegospotami (405), duly commemorated at Delphi, and the personal prestige of Lysander, who may even have received at this time some kind of cult at Samos (though perhaps only after his death in 395). In fact, Sparta was not even secure in its local dominance in Laconia and Messenia: the old helot problem recurred in 399 with the attempted revolt of Cinadon, already noted in its helot aspect. A little farther away, Sparta's former Peloponnesian and extra-Peloponnesian allies were unhappy with what they saw as alarming extensions of Spartan territorial interests, though in fact some of these were very traditional.

One powerful Spartan enemy was Thebes, which had emerged much strengthened from the Peloponnesian War. After the expulsion of the Athenians in 446, Boeotia had reorganized itself federally. The detailed arrangements are preserved in a valuable papyrus account by the so-called Oxyrhynchus Historian. After the destruction of Plataea in 427, Thebes took over Plataea's vote and some of its territory. This was one reason for Theban strength. Another lay in the depredations that the Thebans had been able to carry out in Attica as a result of the occupation of Decelea. When Agesilaus prepared to leave for Anatolia, he tried to sacrifice at Aulis "like Agamemnon" before the Trojan War, but the Boeotian federal magistrates stopped him. Although they had little to fear from a Spartan presence in Anatolia, hardly a normal object of Theban ambition, Theban alarm can be explained by developments nearer home.

In central Greece in the early 390s, the Spartans reinforced their position at Heraclea in Trachis and had a garrison at Thessalian Pharsalus. Initially, Lysander seems to have been at the back of this northward encroachment (good evidence connects him with Thrace and the Chalcidice). Yet because this was always a direction in which Sparta expanded if given the chance, Sparta did not pull out of central Greece during Lysander's temporary eclipse after 403. From the point of view of Thebes and Corinth, there was a risk of encirclement by Sparta. Another factor making for specifically Corinthian resentment may have been Sparta's interference in Corinth's colony, Syracuse. Unlike Thebes, Corinth had emerged badly from the Peloponnesian War. Its prosperous middle class had been eroded, and this made possible a remarkable turn of events: Corinth and democratic Argos, in a unique if short-lived political experiment, became fully merged at this time. Argos, for its part, never needed much excuse to act against Sparta.

By 395 then, all Sparta's enemies were ready and willing for war. The precipitating cause was a quarrel between Locris, abetted by Boeotia, and Phocis. When the Phocians appealed to Sparta, Lysander (now back in qualified favour at Sparta) invaded Boeotia. He was immediately killed at the battle of Haliartus, however, a grave military loss to Sparta. Agesilaus returned from Asia and fought two large-scale hoplite battles but could not prize the Athenian general Iphicrates out of Corinth, where for several years he established himself with mercenaries and light-armed troops. At sea, more progress was made against Sparta: Pharnabazus and the Athenian commander Conon won a decisive battle off Cnidus (southern Anatolia) in August 394. The war might well have ended at this point, especially since Sparta faced a renewed helot threat as a result of the occupation by Pharnabazus and Conon of the island of Cythera. It was this as much as anything that made Sparta offer peace terms in 392, which would have meant the final abandoning of its claims to Asia. Artaxerxes, however, had not yet forgiven the Spartans for supporting Cyrus, and the war continued. Nor was Athens yet in a mood for peace.

In the years immediately following 392, the Athenians made such nuisances of themselves in Anatolia under

Thrasybulus, who revived a number of fifth-century Athenian imperial institutions, that Persia—which was anxious to end rebellions not just in Egypt but also in Cyprus—eventually realized where its true interest lay. Consequently, it changed its support to Sparta. The Spartans under Antalcidas now blockaded the Hellespont with help from Persia and Dionysius of Syracuse, and Athens was once again starved into surrender.

THE KING'S PEACE

The ensuing Peace of Antalcidas, or King's Peace, of 386 specified that Asia, including Cyprus and Clazomenae, were to belong to the king of Persia. (Ionian Clazomenae was included because Athens had interfered there and also because its status—whether it was an island or part of the mainland—was unclear. It was in fact a peninsular site. Cyprus was included because Athens had been helping the rebel Cypriot king, Evagoras.) The other Greek cities great and small, including the other islands, were to be autonomous, but Athens was allowed to keep Lemnos, Imbros, and Scyros, three long-standing cleruchies. Modern argument centres on the question of whether there were additional clauses, not supplied by the main account (that of Xenophon). For instance, the Athenian navy was perhaps ordered to be broken up and the gates on the Piraeus removed, but these may have been consequences, not clauses, of the peace. The same is true of Sparta's position under the peace, which was certainly much strengthened. There is no agreement, however, that Sparta's enhanced position was officially recognized by some such description as "champion" of the peace. Argos's merger with Corinth was cancelled, and, more important (in view of the relative power of the states concerned), Thebes had to relinquish the control of Boeotia that it had been exercising in an unrecognized but progressively real way since 446.

In Anatolia there was little immediate change—the Spartans had after all pulled out of Anatolia some years before, though an inscription (published in 1976) suggests that the Ionian cities may have clung to a precarious autonomy until 386. One difference after 386 lay in the status of possessions up to then held by various Greek islands on the mainland of Anatolia. These possessions had hitherto been anomalous enclaves of Greek control within basically satrapal Asia, but the King's Peace surely assigned them formally to Persia in general. Anatolia now became the political property of Persia and the satraps for the 50 years until Alexander's arrival. Occasional adventures, such as Greek flirtation with the Revolt of the Satraps in the 360s, do not seriously affect this generalization.

The activities of those fourth-century satraps (and of dynasts without the satrapal title but recognized by Persia) are of great interest, though documented more by inscriptions and archaeology than by written sources. The most energetic of them was the Hecatomnid dynasty of Caria, which took its name from Hecatomnus, the son of Hyssaldomus. Hecatomnus was appointed satrap of the new separate satrapy of Caria, perhaps in the mid-390s, as a counterpoise to Sparta. He ruled his pocket principality under light Persian authority until 377 and made dedications in Greek script at a number of local sites and sanctuaries. The major Hellenizing force, however, was his son Mausolus (Maussollos on the inscriptions), satrap from 377 to 353, who gave his name to the Mausoleum, the tomb he perhaps commissioned for himself.

The Mausoleum itself, a creation of Greek artists and sculptors but with some barbarian features, has long been known from surviving sculptural fragments and from Greek and Latin literary descriptions. It was constructed at Halicarnassus, which, after a move from inland Mylasa, became the Hecatomnid capital, with palace and harbour built on monarchical lines that surely owed some inspiration to Dionysius of Sicily. The importance of other sites associated with the Hecatomnid dynasty, above all that of Labranda in the hills not far from the family seat of Mylasa, would not have been guessed from the literary sources.

Inscriptions placed in aggressive prominence on fine temples and temple-like buildings at Labranda (and published in 1972) attest the wealth and the Hellenizing intentions of the rulers (the dedicants include Mausolus's brother and eventual successor Idrieus). They also illustrate the range of the family's diplomatic contacts (for instance with faraway Crete) and their relations with the local communities, both Greek and native Carian. For example, in a text from Labranda, a semi-Greek community called the Plataseis confers tax privileges and citizenship on a man from Cos. The grant is ratified by yet another Hecatomnid brother and satrap, Pixodarus. And a remarkable trilingual inscription in Lycian, Greek, and Aramaic (a Semitic script used for convenience in many parts of the Persian empire), found in 1973, proves the family's interests to have spread eastward into Lycia. The text illustrates the cultural, social, and religious heterogeneity of southwestern Anatolia in the period before Alexander's arrival. Hellenization was well under way before he came.

The same conclusion is compelled by such dynastic (rather than strictly satrapal) edifices as the Nereid monument from Lycia (early fourth century) or the caryatids (roof-carrying female sculpted statues) from Lycian Limyra, a place ruled by a Hellenizing prince significantly named Pericles.

Hellenization at the cultural level and tolerance of the social structures of small local places with no military muscle did not necessarily entail favouring the political interests of the Greek states to the west. In fact, Mausolus, despite a brief and cautious insurrectionary moment in the late 360s when he joined the great Revolt of the Satraps (a movement in which there was also tentative Athenian and Spartan participation), is found actively damaging Athenian interest in the Aegean in the 350s.

In 386, however, the political dividing line between Greek and Persian interests looked relatively clean, although it was usually with the help of Greek mercenaries that over the next decades Persia made its series of attempts on the recovery of Egypt, the immediate task in the sequel to the King's Peace. Unsuccessful there, Persia had better fortune in Cyprus. In Greece, Sparta's supremacy looked as militarily imposing as in 404, though with the abandonment of Asia its moral authority was much weakened.

FROM 386 BC TO THE DECLINE OF SPARTA

The autonomy guaranteed to the Greek cities by the King's Peace in 386 represented in principle an advance in interstate diplomacy. But then as now the word *autonomy* was elastic, and Sparta by its behaviour soon made clear its intention to interpret it in the way most favourable to itself. That is, it applied the old criterion of "what is best for Sparta."

Spartan Adventures

Sparta's first move, in 385, was to break up the polis of Mantinea into its four constituent villages. This move was intended to dismantle the physical polis of Mantinea as well as its democracy. In the particular Mantinean context the return to the villages strengthened the political influence of the wealthy and oligarchic landowners, whose estates adjoined the villages. The "troublesome demagogues," as Xenophon calls them, were expelled. Sparta could perhaps have represented the original fifth- or possibly sixth-century Mantinean synoecism, whereby the villages had been joined into a polis, as a breach of local autonomy (that is, of the right of the separate villages to exist as political units), but it is doubtful that Sparta even bothered to formulate any such justification. It would have been too hollow a reply to the more obvious interpretation that it was simply exploiting its supremacy to infringe on the autonomy of the Mantinean polis.

Soon after, Sparta responded to an invitation, surely welcome in view of its previous northern and central Greek involvements, to interfere against the rising power of Olynthus in northern Greece. Grown populous and powerful since its synoecism in 432 at the instance of Perdiccas II of Macedon, the city had survived the military reorganization of Macedonia by Perdiccas's successor Archelaus (413–399). Now another Macedonian king, Amyntas III, who had succeeded to the Macedonian throne about 393 after a series of short, weak reigns, joined two Greek cities, Acanthus and Apollonia, in an appeal to Sparta against Olynthus. The Spartans sent Phoebidas north, but in a momentous development he was asked into Thebes en route by a pro-Spartan faction there. Without reference (naturally) to the authorities at home, Phoebidas installed a garrison on the Cadmea, the Theban acropolis (382).

The occupation of the Cadmea was a famous instance of Spartan high-handedness. Indeed, it produced such a revulsion of feeling that Sparta lost its leadership of Greece. Had Phoebidas's act been promptly disowned by Sparta, the damage could have been contained. King Agesilaus, however, approached the matter solely from the point of view of Spartan advantage. He once again posed the question of whether this action had been good or bad for Sparta, with the result that Phoebidas was punished with a fine but then reemployed elsewhere, and the garrison in Thebes was retained. Meanwhile (380), Olynthus was reduced.

The Second Athenian Confederacy

Agesilaus, however, gave the wrong answer to his own question. The Cadmea episode meant that Sparta would no longer have things its way. When a group of Theban exiles liberated the Cadmea in 379, they were helped by Athens, though at first unofficially. Athens, whose foreign policy in the years 386–380 had been cautious in the extreme, evidently felt it could not risk Spartan reprisals for its help to Thebes without seeking moral and military support from other Greek states. It now made a series of alliances, with Chios, Byzantium, and Methymna on Lesbos, which prefigure the formation of the Second Athenian Confederacy, formally inaugurated in 378. The charter of the new confederacy was issued at the beginning of 377. Athens was right to suspect Spartan anger. An attempted raid on the Piraeus by the Spartan Sphodrias at this time is best seen as a response to the new mood in Athens. The raid failed in its object, whatever exactly that was. Once again Sparta did not pursue the offender.

The aims of the new confederacy are set out on an inscription of cardinal importance, the "charter" document. The enemy singled out is Sparta, while the main ally is Thebes. Hostility toward Sparta, however, though it was certainly the motive shared by Athens and Thebes, does not adequately explain the participation of islanders such as the Rhodians and Chians. In these islands the main fear must have been of encroachment by such Persian satraps as the energetic Mausolus. In this respect the new alliance recalls the early 470s, when alarm felt in eastern Aegean waters about Persia's intentions had led to the formation of the old Delian League. Yet the charter says nothing about Persia or the satraps in so many words. That would have been too provocative given Athens's naval weakness at the time. On the contrary, it is likely that a clause actually spelled out an intention to remain within the structure of the King's Peace. But this is not quite certain because the relevant lines were subsequently erased, probably in a moment of Panhellenist ardour.

Action against Persia may, then, have been once again envisaged, but in other respects the precedent of the Delian League was explicitly avoided. There was to be freedom and autonomy for all as well as an allied chamber, or *synedrion*, that could put motions directly before the

Athenian Assembly. An inscription from 372 shows that this chamber had an allied president. In other words, an improvement was intended on the old synod of the Delian League, which met (presumably) only when Athens called it and had no way of influencing policy in an immediate or effective way. For instance, there is no sign of allied influence in Thucydides' detailed account of the preliminaries to the great Peloponnesian War. The *synedrion* was to decide on the membership of the confederacy, and it had some financial competence. There was to be joint judicial action: although there would not exactly be a joint court, the *synedrion* was to participate in treason trials alongside the Athenian Assembly and Council. It is possible (according to a late 20th-century reinterpretation of the relevant inscriptions) that, within the framework of the confederacy, the Athenians operated an enlightened policy of arbitration and used "foreign judges," thus anticipating sophisticated Hellenistic methods of settling interstate disputes.

The restrictive policies adopted by Athens are interesting as showing awareness of what had been fifth-century grievances. There was to be no tribute, no governors, no garrisons, and no cleruchies. Land outside Attica was not to be cultivated by Athenians, and "unfavourable stelae" (inscribed pillars) were to be taken down. (Perhaps this is a reference to grants of the right to own land in the empire. It does not seem, however, that much or any land had survived in Athenian hands after the end of the empire in 404, and the importance of this clause may be merely symbolic.) Except for the pledge against private cultivation of land outside Attica, every one of these pledges was to be broken sooner or later, mostly sooner. There is even a hint by an orator of a private Athenian estate on the island of Peparethus, and thus one perhaps should make no exceptions at all.

Athens now began to reorganize its public finances and to build ships. A new system of levying taxes by taxation groups, Symmories, was introduced. To make sure there were no cash-flow difficulties, rich individuals were expected to produce money for the state from their own resources and then recoup it from their taxation group. The new Athenian navy defeated Sparta in the battle of Naxos (376), a victory won under the command of the Athenian Chabrias. In western waters another great Athenian commander, Timotheus, won the battle of Alyzia. These successes produced new members for the confederacy (some states had cautiously stood aloof at first). In Boeotia, which Sparta, under King Agesilaus and initially the other king, Cleombrotus I, repeatedly invaded in the years after the liberation, there was a surprising land defeat of some Spartan contingents at the hands of the Theban "Sacred Band," a crack professional force. This, the battle of Tegyra (375), anticipated the more famous Spartan defeat at Leuctra four years later. The very existence of a Sacred Band was militarily significant, indicating that Spartan professionalism was now being copied by others who would soon overtake Sparta.

By 375 these efforts had exhausted all parties, and they were ready to make peace, or rather to accept another King's Peace. (Greeks felt uncomfortable about their involvement in this kind of Persian-inspired diplomacy, in which the various peaces were "sent down"—i.e., imposed—by the Persian king. As a result, the Persian aspect to this and other initiatives tends to be minimized or ignored by some literary sources, notably the "Panhellenist" Xenophon.) This time Athens's improved position was acknowledged in a clause specifically giving it the leadership by sea.

THEBAN EXPANSION

After its expulsion from Thebes, Sparta had steadily lost ground in central Greece. The Thebans energetically centralized Boeotia under their own leadership. For instance, they gained control of Thespiae and—yet again—of the unfortunate Plataea, which must have been resettled at some point, or perhaps just gradually, after the Peloponnesian War. In addition, a new power arose in Thessaly, that of Jason of Pherae, an ally of Thebes and until his assassination in 370 a military despot on the Dionysius model. Sparta was unable to respond to local Thessalian appeals against Jason, proof that Spartan ambition in central Greece had finally come to an end.

Theban expansionism was bound to drive Athens and Sparta together before long. Despite renewed fighting between Athens and Sparta in the west (374 and 373) and despite Thebes' continued, though increasingly reluctant, contributions to the Athenian navy (373), it was becoming clear that Thebes was the real threat to both Athens and Sparta. In this respect the Second Athenian Confederacy, with its political justification in terms of anti-Spartan sentiment, had already been superseded by events. There were other causes for concern within the confederacy. Tribute by another name had been levied for the western operations of 373, not altogether unreasonably: ships cost money, and Athens did not have great reserves, as it had in the fifth century. Perhaps more disquieting in its implications was the Athenian garrison on Cephallenia, attested by an inscription of 373. There may, however, have been special factors, and it is not known how long the garrison remained.

At a famous peace conference held at Sparta in 371 (which, in fact, resulted in another King's Peace), Sparta tried to prevent the Thebans from asserting and formalizing their local pretensions by signing on behalf of the whole of Boeotia. After a breach in the negotiations, signaled by a rhetorical duel between Agesilaus and the Theban Epaminondas, "a man famous for culture and philosophy," as his fellow Boeotian Plutarch described him half a millennium later, the Spartans invaded Boeotia. Twenty days after the peace conference, Sparta was defeated by Thebes on the field of Leuctra, the Theban commander

Epaminondas showing more than cultural and philosophical qualities.

This was a major and decisive battle in Greek history. Politically, it was to loosen Sparta's hold even on its Peloponnesian dependencies and to end its long subjection of Messenia. It introduced a decade of Theban prominence (which was, however, too inconclusive in its results to deserve its usual name of the "Theban hegemony"). Militarily, the battle was innovative in several ways, not only in the sheer professionalism of the Sacred Band. The left wing of the army was deepened to 50 men, in a further development of the Delium arrangement of 424. This provided a flexible "tail," or reserve force on the left that could be deployed as the course of the battle suggested. The decision about whether, when, and how to deploy it would be the general's, whose influence on the outcome of the battle was thus greater than had been usual hitherto. By placing the best troops on the left, the Thebans aimed to knock out the best Spartan troops, who were positioned opposite them, occupying the right wing in the traditional hoplite manner. Finally, by marching forward obliquely (rather than straightforwardly, as was customary), the Thebans increased the punch administered by this deepened left.

Perhaps the Spartan defeat needs no explanation other than Theban superiority. The Spartans lost about 1,000 men, 400 of them full Spartan citizens. It is disputed, however, whether manpower problems were the most serious factor in the defeat. Aristotle, on the one hand, explicitly made the connection between the defeat at Leuctra and shortage of men. There were not enough ways for talented or physically vigorous outsiders to acquire Spartan citizenship and too many ways by which full citizens could lose their status. Thus full citizens might be degraded in status for alleged cowardice in battle, or they might fall into debt through inability to pay their mess bills (these debts often resulted in the takeover of land by women, whose social and economic position was stronger at Sparta than elsewhere). In addition, the number of full citizens was reduced by unavoidable demographic disasters such as the earthquake of 465. On the other hand, it has been replied that non-Spartans (either degraded Spartans, the so-called "inferiors" like Cinadon, or citizens of the surrounding communities) might be and probably were brigaded alongside full Spartans, at least in the fourth century.

After Leuctra there was a second peace of 371, this time at Athens. It is disputed whether Sparta participated, but it is certain that the Thebans were again excluded. It is also certain that the peace included undertakings to accept "the decrees of the Athenian allies"—a possible reference to the Second Athenian Confederacy and in any case a further strengthening of Athens's position.

Sparta's position, by contrast, now began visibly to crumble. In Arcadia, not merely did the Mantineans organize themselves into a polis once more, but Arcadia as a whole became a federal state on the initiative of a Mantinean named

Lycomedes. (The capital was to be at Megalopolis, the "Great City," a new foundation made necessary by the ancient rivalry between Tegea and Mantinea.) Both these movements were obviously anti-Spartan, and the Arcadians or federation badly needed military support from some powerful quarter. The Arcadians found it at Thebes, after being rejected by Athens (if Athens had responded positively to this appeal, major Peloponnesian developments of the 360s might never have taken place).

Federal Arcadia was in origin a local growth, but there is no doubt that Theban support was crucial for its subsequent success. Theban promotion of federalism here and in central Greece is a notable political contribution, for which the evidence is largely inscriptional. Federations are attested in this decade not just in Arcadia but north of the Gulf of Corinth, in Aetolia, an ally of Thebes since 370, and in western Locris. There was also an intriguing Boeotian federal organization of Aegean states in the 350s, complete with *synedrion* on the Athenian model. All these federations arguably betray the influence of the Thebans, who evidently sought to export the federal principle long familiar in Boeotia itself. On a skeptical view, however, the development was a natural one and merely approximately simultaneous with the period of maximum Theban power.

In 370–369 Epaminondas invaded the Peloponnese (the first of several such invasions) and weakened Sparta irreparably by refounding Messene as a physical and political polis. The "state-of-the-art" fortifications of fourth-century Messene, an artillery-conscious circuit, stretched for nearly 6.4 kilometres (4 miles) over Mount Ithome. They are the best preserved in mainland Greece except perhaps for Aegosthena at the east end of the Gulf of Corinth. In Anatolia only Heraclea on Latmus, in Mausolus's Caria, is comparable. The loss of Messene crippled Sparta economically. In particular, Sparta no longer had a helot population to provide the economic surplus necessary for its military life-style. The combined impact of Leuctra, Megalopolis, and Messene was, however, not immediately obvious. In the "Tearless Battle" of 368, Sparta still managed to win a victory over a force of Arcadians. But Sparta was no longer a leading power.

ATHENS AND THEBES

In the 360s the main focus of Greek history shifted from Sparta to the struggle between Athens and Thebes. Neither power was really strong enough to impose a definitive solution. Nor were outside forces available to give either side a decisive margin of superiority in the way that Persia had allowed Sparta to prevail in the Peloponnesian War. The 360s were a period of satrapal revolts in the western half of Artaxerxes' empire, and the subjugation of Egypt continued to elude him. In effect, though there also was some Persian-sponsored inter-Greek diplomacy in this decade, there was even less threat of force behind it than usual (the King's Peace of the 380s and that of the 370s had not been backed up by Persian men or ships). Dionysius I had added his weight on the Spartan side in 386, and his troops were found operating against Thebes as late as the early 360s. After his death, however, Sicily was not a serious factor in mainland Greek politics. Dionysius's son Dionysius II did send help to Sparta, enabling it to recover control over some formerly subject communities in 365, but that was about the limit of his interference. Dionysius II ruled precariously in Syracuse and southern Italy. He recovered Syracuse only to be finally driven to exile in Corinth by the Corinthian Timoleon in the 340s. This mid-century period of Syracusan history is of interest because of Plato's involvement in the politics of the tyranny. Dion, a relative of the older Dionysius by marriage, brought Plato to Syracuse in 367 to tutor Dionysius II in science and philosophy and generally to educate him to become a constitutional king. The visit, however, was not a success.

In central and northern Greece, the energetic rule of Jason (which might have given a push to the plans of his Theban allies) had ended abruptly in 370, and his eventual aims remained and remain an enigma. Macedon was the power of the future, but that was far from obvious in the 360s. After the death of Amyntas in 370, Macedon relapsed into a period of short unstable reigns, as in the 390s. Thus neither Thessaly nor Macedon was in a position to tilt the balance of power.

Thessaly and Macedon, however, were valuable prizes. Thessaly was not only enormously fertile but also had good harbours and religious influence in the Delphic amphictyony. Macedon had ship-building timber and great natural resources (though few outlets to the sea because Greek colonial poleis stood in the way). Sparta could no longer compete for these assets, but Athens and Thebes could. Not long after the peace of 371, Athens restated an old claim to Amphipolis and added a claim to the Chersonese. In 368 it sent its general Iphicrates to Amphipolis. Thebes reacted to the Athenian claims by sending its other great man of the fourth century, Pelopidas, to Thessaly and Macedon. Theban activity in these areas did not add up to much in the end (one incidental result was that the young Philip, son of Amyntas, spent a period in Thebes as a hostage. The relevance, for Philip's subsequent army reforms, of his exposure to the methods of the first military state in Greece has often been noted). It did, however, show the Greek world the scale of Theban ambitions.

By 367, affairs in Thessaly and Arcadia were temporarily stalemated, and a peace conference was held at Susa, inside the Persian empire. Pelopidas asked that Sparta be made to give up Messenia formally and (more importantly, in view of Sparta's relative impotence at this time) that Athens be requested to give up its fleet. When these proposals inevitably failed, Thebes seized the valuable border territory of

Oropus, and Athens was after all obliged to accept what was probably a King's Peace (366). There was, however, no question of Athens dismantling its navy. On the contrary, its claims to the Chersonese (reachable only by sea) were recognized in exchange, it seems, for acceptance of Theban leadership of Boeotia, including Oropus.

Athens's pursuit of essentially private Athenian aims, such as control of Amphipolis and the Chersonese, cannot have pleased its allies in the confederacy. It was costly, and it was unsuccessful. (Securing the recognition of Athenian claims in theory was not the same thing as making good those claims in practice.) On the other hand, Athens, shortly after the peace of 366, did send help—a force under Timotheus—to a rebel satrap, Ariobarzanes, in the eastern Aegean. This showed a perhaps encouraging willingness to defend Greek interests against Persia, especially since Timotheus ejected a Persian garrison he found installed on Samos. This Persian garrison was a violation of Persia's side of the original King's Peace. It may seem surprising that Athens should act against Persia so soon if the peace of 366 was really a King's Peace, but the risk of reprisals just then was slight. In any case, Timotheus's somewhat contradictory instructions were to keep to the King's Peace while also helping Ariobarzanes.

Timotheus's next move, however, the installation of an Athenian cleruchy on Samos, was a capital error. An inscription published in 1995 shows that the Samian cleruchs were indeed resident and that the cleruchy featured a council of 250 members, exactly half the Athenian model or prototype. This was a large and serious influx of Athenian settlers. Timotheus's action could be technically justified: Samos was not a member of the Athenian Confederacy, and Persia had violated the King's Peace by installing its garrison. Thus the cleruchy could be seen as a military response to Persian provocation in an area not covered by the rules of the charter of 377. Nonetheless, its effect on Greek opinion was damaging, and the Thebans quickly tried to exploit it.

Some naval interest on the part of Thebes can perhaps already be inferred from its designs on Thessaly, with its good harbours. After 365, however, Theban rivalry with Athens became explicit. Thebes planned a fleet of 100 triremes, lured away Athenian allies such as Rhodes and Byzantium, and induced a revolt on Ceos. This scheme was no more successful in the long run than the Thessalian entanglement, except that the Athenian loss of Byzantium seems to have been permanent. This was a serious setback for the Athenian corn supply, given Byzantium's geographically controlling position. Thebes' Aegean *synedrion* may have been founded at this time. Byzantium was certainly a member of it in the 350s.

In Thessaly, Pelopidas was killed in 364 at Cynoscephalae. Although the immediate outcome of the battle was favourable for Thebes and although

Thessaly was reorganized in a way that gave Thebes for the first time an absolute majority of votes on the Delphic Amphictyony, active Theban interference in Thessaly was over.

In the meantime the Arcadian federation in the Peloponnese had split in two. The Tegean party appealed for help to the Thebans (who in turn had for allies the Argives and Messenians), and the Mantineans to Athens and Sparta. The great Battle of Mantinea (also called "Second Mantinea" to distinguish it from the events of 418) was a technical victory for Thebes in the strictly military sense, but (as Xenophon noted) it was actually indecisive: Epaminondas's death permanently crushed Theban hopes of leadership in Greece. The peace after the battle in effect recognized the independence of the Messenians, thus settling at the diplomatic level an issue that in reality had been settled for years. The death of Agesilaus in 360 marked the end of one era and the beginning of another, the age of Philip and Alexander.

The Rise of Macedon

In 359 two new strong rulers came to the throne, Artaxerxes III of Persia and Philip II of Macedon. The last decade of the long reign of Artaxerxes II had been blighted by revolts in the western half of his empire—at first sporadic, then concerted. Already in the late 370s Datames, the governor of Cappadocia, had established his independence. Then, by the middle of the decade, Ariobarzanes of Hellespontine Phrygia went into revolt, assisted by Timotheus of Athens and Agesilaus of Sparta. The last and greatest phase of the revolt was led by Orontes, described by the sources as satrap of Mysia. (Possibly an enclave in the Troy region of Anatolia, "Mysia" could, however, also be an error for "Armenia." If so, the geographic spread of the insurrectionist satraps was still greater.) The other rebelling satraps were Mausolus of Caria (briefly) and Autophradates of Lydia. Some participation by local Greek cities in Anatolia is possible, though perhaps they merely followed the lead of their satrapal overlords. Athens and Sparta seem surreptitiously to have helped.

The aims of the revolt are a matter for speculation, but it looked serious for a long moment: a second and successful Cunaxa was a possibility. (One speculation sees the affair in dynastic terms: Orontes, who was well born, presented a greater danger to Artaxerxes than local men like Mausolus, whose ambitions were by definition limited. No one would follow a native Carian in an attempt on the kingship of Persia. It is significant that Mausolus returned to his allegiance so promptly.) At the date of Artaxerxes' death in 359, the revolt was over, the traitors's cause having been ruined by treachery among themselves. Despite setbacks, Artaxerxes II and the empire had weathered the Revolt of the Satraps.

The new king Artaxerxes III promptly ordered the satraps to dismiss their mercenary armies, thus preempting future trouble of the same sort. This was an early indication of the vigour with which he intended to rule and which was to regain Egypt for him.

In Macedon, Amyntas had eventually been succeeded by Perdiccas, the second of his sons by Eurydice. This happened in 365, after a turbulent five-year interval of two brief reigns, those of Alexander II and Ptolemy, and one intervention by a pretender, Pausanias. Perdiccas himself was killed in 359 in a catastrophic battle against the Illyrians, Macedon's permanent enemies, and his younger brother Philip, the last of Amyntas's sons by Eurydice, succeeded.

The achievements of Philip's predecessors have naturally been overshadowed by his own, just as Philip's were to be eclipsed by Alexander's. To some extent the historical injustice is beyond redress, because the literary sources gave no systematic attention to Macedon until it was obvious that the activities of its kings were to be the determining factor in Greek history. That realization came later than 359, when Philip's chances must have looked little better than those of his

These ruins are of Verghina, in Macedonia, Greece. Francoise De MulderRoger Viollet/ Getty Images

immediate predecessors. Thus there is not even proper information about Philip's early consolidation of power.

Fortunately, Thucydides was specially interested in the north, for personal reasons, and he speaks with admiration of the way Archelaus had pulled Macedon together militarily in the last years of the fifth century. Regarding the culture, there is valuable evidence from Herodotus and from excavations, particularly those conducted in the 1970s and 1980s at Macedonian Verghina. The Macedonian kings of the fifth century were sufficiently Hellenized to compete in the Olympic Games (as Herodotus attests) and at the games for Argive Hera (as proved by a dedicated prize tripod found at Verghina). The poets Euripides and Agathon both moved to Macedon at the end of that century, and so evidently did first-rate Greek artists in the course of the next, judging from the paintings discovered in the Verghina tombs. In 1983 investigators discovered, again at Verghina, an inscription in extremely beautiful Greek lettering recording a dedication by Philip's mother, "Eurydice daughter of Sirras," which is further proof of the Hellenism of Macedon in this period.

Modern belief in the Greekness of the Macedonian language was strengthened by the publication in 1994 of an important curse tablet from Pella that appears provisionally to indicate that the Macedonian language was a form of northwest Greek. Macedonian religion looks Greek; there are local variations, but that is equally true of incontestably Greek places in, for instance, the Peloponnese. Many Macedonian personal names resemble Greek ones, and it has been suggested that such onomastic evidence indicates that the Macedonian settlers originally migrated from northern Thessalian Perrhaibia and the region around Mt. Olympus—as already suggested by a poem ascribed to the Archaic poet Hesiod.

Cultural Hellenization, however, was compatible with a social and military structure that was alien to Greek tradition, resembling instead the feudalism of later societies. (In some respects the contemporary society having most in common with Macedon was Achaemenid Persia.) The fourth-century Macedonian kings made grants of land in exchange for military service. This system is hinted at by literary sources and illustrated by inscriptions. Given the size and fertility of the areas controlled by the Macedonian kings, there was huge potential for military achievement, provided Macedon's chronic enemies and invaders could be appeased or crushed.

Philip needed to buy time by means of the first method, appeasement, in order to build the army that would enable him to crush where appeasement failed. (Philip always preferred diplomacy to force, dissimilar in this respect to his son Alexander, whose preferences were the reverse.) Although Philip must have seemed unlucky in coming to the throne at so unpromising a moment in Macedonian history, there were in fact compensations, especially if one looks beyond such real but local enemies as the Illyrians and assumes that from the outset Philip's vision rested on the far horizon. The greatest hoplite power in Greece, namely Sparta, was preoccupied with regaining Messenia, just as Persia was preoccupied with Egypt. Thebes had lost Epaminondas and was soon to overextend itself badly in the Third Sacred War. Athens still had a naval empire of sorts, but this was already showing signs of breakup. In any case, if Philip was to be stopped, it would not be by sea. He could and arguably did time his operations so as to make it impossible for a fleet to get at him (ships could not sail north when the Etesian winds were blowing). On the positive side, the productivity of the silver and gold mines of the Pangaion region would be a huge asset to Philip, and thus it was encouraging that they were currently controlled by a dwarf among imperial powers, Thasos. Although Thasos seems to have been extending its mainland interests remarkably in the 360s, it was not Athens and could be dealt with.

First Philip needed to reorganize his army, which he accomplished by introducing more rigorous training and employing mercenaries. This enabled him to inflict defeats on the Illyrians and other northern enemies. At the same time he made a string of advantageous "marriages," some more official than others and scarcely amounting to more than politically slanted concubinage. One of these was to an Illyrian princess, Audata. In 357, however, all of these were effectively displaced by his marriage to the formidable Olympias, who on or about July 20, 356, gave birth to Alexander. In 358 Philip made a preliminary visit to the strategically and politically crucial area of Thessaly. He was now poised for a "blitzkrieg" against Amphipolis, which he besieged and captured in 357. Then he moved on to conquer Pydna and the mining city of Crenides, renamed Philippi (356). In 356 he formed an alliance with the Olynthians, who had good reason to be alarmed at Philip's dazzlingly rapid progress, which continued with the taking of Potidaea in 356 and the successful siege of Methone (355–354). An inscription shows that the Olynthian alliance was recommended by the Delphic oracle, interesting evidence that the oracle was still politically active. The Olynthian alliance is a reminder that Philip was always happy to operate diplomatically if at all possible. In fact, the Athenians had been kept quiet at the time of Philip's assault on Amphipolis by promises that he would hand it over to them. He never did. The territory of Amphipolis was distributed to Macedonian feoffees.

After the conquest of Methone came some successes in Thrace, which Athens was unable to prevent despite attempts, a little halfhearted and a little late, to strengthen the independent Thracian princes through alliances with itself. Even the great Athenian orator and statesman Demosthenes (384–322) was slow to realize that Athens's interest required a united, not a divided, Thrace.

Athens had difficulties of its own at this time. In 357 the "Social War," the war against its allies, broke out. Already in the 360s in the aftermath of the Samian cleruchy, trouble had occurred on Ceos and elsewhere. In addition, Mausolus of Caria, once more loyal to Persia and its new king Artaxerxes III, and surely remembering Epaminondas's example, incited Rhodes, Chios, and Byzantium to revolt against Athens (though, as stated, Byzantium was probably already detached). Dislike of Athens was as much a factor in the outbreak of war as the intriguing of Mausolus, which Demosthenes (naturally) stressed in his search for an outside scapegoat. (Mausolus's help, however, is a fact and should not be doubted.) To Athens's costly obsession with Amphipolis and the Chersonese should be added its various breaches of the promises made in 377. (For instance, Athens had, despite the charter, installed garrisons and cleruchies and had even levied tribute under the euphemistic name of "contributions.") In fact, it did not even respect its most basic political guarantees: at the end of the 360s, the Athenian commander Chares actually helped an oligarchy to power on Corcyra.

The war went badly for Athens, and it was forced to accept a disadvantageous peace in 355 when the Persian king threatened to intervene on the rebel side. It is disputed how far the inefficiency of the Athenian navy was responsible for the defeat. There are plenty of complaints by contemporary orators to the effect that the trierarchic system was not working properly. Still, there was no absolute shortage of ships, and it has been pointed out that some features denounced by orators, such as the hiring out of trierarchic obligations to third parties, actually tended to promote professionalism, because such hired trierarchs built up expertise.

Macedonian Supremacy in Greece

In 353 Philip was in undisputed control of a much-enlarged Macedon. He was brought into Greece itself as a result of the Third Sacred War of 355–346. This war originated in a more or less gratuitous Theban attack on Phocis, which in 362 had refused to send a contingent for the Mantinea campaign. The time lag is to be explained in terms of power politics: the Thebans had suffered a reverse on Euboea in 357, when Theban ascendancy was suddenly and humiliatingly replaced by Athenian, and they were looking for a victim. Phocian behaviour offered an excuse. The Thebans, who since 364 had influence over the preponderance of votes in the Delphic Amphictyony, persuaded it to condemn Phocis (autumn 357) to a huge fine for the usual technical offense, "cultivation of sacred land." The hope was that if, or rather when, Phocis was unable to pay, Thebes would be awarded the conduct of the ensuing Sacred War. It all went wrong. The Phocians seized the temple treasure in 356 and recruited a mercenary force of such size and efficiency that the Thebans could not defeat them. The Phocian leaders were Philomelus, followed by Onomarchus, Phayllus, and finally Phalaecus. The actual declaration of the Sacred War was delayed until 355, partly because it was only in that year that the relative impotence of one of Phocis's hitherto most impressive-looking allies, the Athenians, was revealed by the miserable end to the Social War in the Aegean.

After Philomelus's death, Onomarchus formed alliances with the rulers of the Thessalian city of Pherae. Thessaly as a whole had been willing enough to declare war on Phocis in keeping with an enmity of immemorial antiquity already remarked on as long-standing by Herodotus in the context of the Persian Wars. Nonetheless, Thessalian unity on the one hand and Theban ability to influence events in Thessaly on the other were both less than complete, and Onomarchus evidently succeeded in exploiting this fluid situation. Yet another city, Larissa, responded by issuing an invitation that was ultimately to be disastrous to Greek, as well as merely to Thessalian, freedom. It called in Philip.

The immediate consequence, a victory for Onomarchus's Phocians over Philip, his only defeat in the field, was totally unexpected. The Phocians seem to have had a "secret weapon," in the form of nontorsion artillery. In the following year (352) this defeat was, however, completely reversed at the Battle of the Crocus Field. Philip, who had already perhaps been officially recognized as ruler of Thessaly before the Crocus Field, now took over Thessaly in the full sense, acquiring its ports and its revenues. A further asset was the Thessalian cavalry, which was used to augment Macedon's own "companion cavalry" in the great battles of Alexander's early years in Asia.

Southern Thessaly was the gateway to Greece proper, as Thermopylae had illustrated in 480 and the Spartans had recognized by their foundation of Heraclea in Trachis. A probe by Philip on Thermopylae itself was, however, firmly repelled by Athens. Philip could afford to wait and perhaps was obliged to do so by Thracian trouble closer to home (end of 352). When he laid siege to a place called Heraeum Teichos, Athens sent a small contingent in September 351. At some date not long before this, perhaps June 351, Demosthenes delivered his "First Philippic," a denouncement of Philip and Macedonian imperialism. He decried the Athenian moves to counter Philip as always being too little and coming too late. He also urged the creation of a task force and larger emergency force. It is not clear how influential Demosthenes' advice was—or how influential, at this stage, it deserved to be: at about the same time, and perhaps actually after the "First Philippic," Demosthenes was found advocating, in the "Speech on the Freedom of the Rhodians," a foolish diversion of resources to the southeastern Aegean against the encroachments of Mausolus's family. The situation there was, in fact, beyond repair.

In summer 349, with Etesian winds about to blow, Philip, despite the alliance of 356, attacked Olynthus, the centre of the Chalcidic Confederation. Olynthus turned to the only and obvious place for help, Athens. This was the occasion of the three "Olynthiac Orations" of Demosthenes. One of Demosthenes' pleas was to make the reserves of the so-called Festival, or *Theoric*, Fund immediately available for military purposes—in fact, to finance an Olynthian expedition. There is no agreement that his stirring patriotism was correct from the point of view of policy. Perhaps the decision to build up Athens's financial resources slowly in preparation for the time when Philip had to be confronted nearer home was right. This unglamorous, though not actually dishonourable, policy is associated with the name of Eubulus, the Athenian leader of the pacifist party, whose caution helped to make possible the prosperous Athens of the time of the statesman and orator Lycurgus.

Olynthus fell in 348, despite the Athenian help that was eventually sent. Many of the inhabitants of the city were sold into slavery. Although Greek warfare always permitted this theoretically, the treatment of Olynthus was, nevertheless, shocking to Greek sentiment. In addition, there was no comfort for Athens from the events on its doorstep. Euboea, which Eubulus and his supporters agreed should always be defended, successfully revolted in 348.

At Athens, it must have seemed that there was no immediate further point in fighting, with Amphipolis and Olynthus gone. Philip, moreover, had been putting out peace feelers for some time. The Sacred War, however, brought Philip back into Greece, when desultory warfare in 347 caused the Boeotians to call him in. In alarm Phocis appealed to Athens and Sparta. The Phocian commander Phalaecus, however, unexpectedly declined to allow the Athenians and Spartans to occupy Thermopylae, and Athens was forced to make peace. This was the notorious Peace of Philocrates—notorious because of the attempts by various leading Athenian orator-politicians to saddle each other with responsibility for what was in fact an inevitability.

The Phocians surrendered to Philip, who received their Amphictyonic votes. Many individual Phocian troops, branded as temple robbers, had already fled. Some of them eventually joined Timoleon in Sicily. The cities of Phocis were physically destroyed and the remaining inhabitants distributed among villages. It is doubtful whether Philip ever seriously intended any other solution to the war in its Phocian dimension. Demosthenes was later to allege that Philip at one point had a different plan—namely, to crush Thebes and save the temple robbers in Phocis. This, however, would have been an implausible renunciation of a valuable weapon, the leadership of a Sacred War. Any such threats or promises can have been no more than feints.

Philip was for the moment supreme not merely in Phocis but in Greece. Athens, as its chief concession, had to abandon claims to Amphipolis formally. It also had to enter into an alliance, as well as make peace, with Philip. This raises the interesting question of whether Philip was already thinking of a grand crusade against Persia as early as 346. Some of the sources make such a claim, but they may be contaminated by hindsight. He probably was considering such a move. For one thing, the idea of punishing the Persians for their sack of Athens in 480 was not prominent before 346 but was much heard of thereafter. Moreover, Philip had triumphantly ended one religious war and demonstrated his Hellenism and suitability for the leadership of the Greeks. Nothing would be more natural than that he or his propagandists should have hit on the idea of exploiting the still greater moral appeal to the Greeks of an all-out war of revenge for Persian impiety.

In fact, the idea of a Macedonian spillage into Anatolia was a very old one indeed, and a natural one. About half a millennium earlier, the Phrygian kingdom of Midas, the predecessor of the Lydian dynasty of Croesus, had emerged as a result of a mass movement of peoples from Macedon. An Asiatic expedition is an idea that Philip could surely have thought of for himself: he did not need Isocrates to urge him, as he did in his pamphlet called the *Philippus* of 346, to settle the Persian empire with wandering Greeks (or resettle them: some of these wanderers must have been mercenaries rendered unemployed by Artaxerxes' demobilization edict of about 359). Information supplied by Artabazus, a satrap who had fled to the Macedonian court at some time in the late 350s, may have been helpful to Philip. Artabazus could have told Philip—and the very young Alexander perhaps—about the complex Persian system of supplies and travel vouchers for high-ranking officials, a system revealed to historians only in 1969, with the publication of the Persepolis Fortification Tablets. In addition, Philip seems to have had contacts elsewhere in western Anatolia, for instance with Hermias of Atarneus, a fascinating minor ruler at whose court Aristotle stayed. Whatever Philip's plans may have been, the Persian empire was not yet as debilitated or ripe for takeover as it was to be in the 330s. On the contrary, Persia suppressed revolts in Cyprus and Phoenicia in the mid-340s, and, the greatest success of all, in Egypt in 343.

In Athens after 346 there was a group who seemed to want war against Persia, and this entailed good relations with Philip. However, Demosthenes, who constantly worked against this policy, argued that Philip was untrustworthy; he pointed out that in the second half of the 340s Philip was a persistent peacebreaker, as, for instance, in the Peloponnese and on Euboea. In 344 Demosthenes even persuaded the Athenians to reject a proposed renegotiation of the peace terms offered by Philip in the person of an orator from Byzantium named Python.

Philip had preoccupations closer to Macedon in this period, which themselves make it unlikely that he wanted to upset the arrangements of 346—at least not yet. In 345 he had to deal with the

Illyrians again, which he did at the expense of a bad leg wound. The strains of his intense military life had by now left their effects on his appearance. He must have looked older than his age, scarcely more than the mid-30s, because he had already lost an eye at Methone. (It is possible that a skull found in Macedonian Verghina bearing traces of a missile wound over the eye may in fact be the actual skull of Philip II of Macedon. This possibility encouraged the forensic reconstruction in 1983 of the entire head, by techniques used for rebuilding the features of unknown crash victims with a view to identification.) Philip's leg wound of 345 did not incapacitate him completely. In 344 he had the energy to reorganize Thessaly into its four old divisions, or "tetrachies." It helps to explain, however, why he was relatively inactive in Macedon until 342, when he made another and final move against Thrace, removing the first local recalcitrant, a ruler named Cersebleptes. From the economic as well as the political point of view, subduing the Thracian rulers was well worth the effort: the gorgeous Thracian Treasure from Rogozen in Bulgaria, discovered in 1986, consists of 165 high-grade silver and gilded vessels. One of them is inscribed "Property of Cersebleptes."

Philip attacked the Greek city of Perinthus in 340. Perinthus was helped by Byzantium and other Greek communities, including Athens, and even by the Persian satraps (which represents the first collision between the two great powers, Macedon and Persia). Despite all Philip's efforts (and artillery), Perinthus held out. In 340 an exasperated Philip declared war on Athens. He also switched his siege engines from Perinthus against Byzantium, but he made no easy headway there either. It is possible that the reason for Philip's abandonment of at least the second of these sieges was not military (siege engines were now virtually irresistible when applied to their target over time) but political. Philip's gaze was now fixed on Athens, the greater enemy and the greater prize.

The pretext for Philip's final involvement in Greece was trivial: still another (Fourth) Sacred War, declared this time against the petty city of Amphissa. Philip, its designated leader from the first, entered Greece toward the end of 339. This perilous occasion prompted Demosthenes' famous rallying call to Athens, reported by its author nearly a decade later in the speech "On the Crown." He urged sending an embassy to Thebes at this moment of danger for Greece as well as for Athens. Thebes responded magnificently, and the joint Greek army took up position at Chaeronea in Boeotia. The battle, fought in August 338, settled the political future of Greece until the second-century Roman conquest. No accurate account survives of the course of the battle, but it ended in a total victory for Philip. Tradition insists (probably rightly) on the valuable contribution of Alexander on the Macedonian left and suggests (perhaps wrongly) that Philip executed a feigned retreat. The Theban Sacred Band had simply ceased to exist. Athens was treated mildly, its prisoners being allowed to return home without ransom.

Philip's political settlement is illustrated by a speech wrongly attributed to Demosthenes and by an inscription much restored with the help of the speech. The settlement was a masterly construction, the League of Corinth (337). Philip had perhaps waited a little while for the inevitable pro-Macedonian reaction to set in inside the leading Greek cities. Only in Sparta, arrogant but powerless, was there no willingness to adjust. Philip invaded Laconia but did not interfere further than that. Thebes had to receive a garrison. Philip's overall goal was general acquiescence and cooperation in the war against Persia, which was now a certainty. In fact, he wanted an alliance, and without doubt the arrangements of 337 secured one. To this end most of the great federations of Greece were left intact. Only Athens's naval confederacy was dissolved (though its cleruchy on Samos was retained) and, less certainly, the Aetolian League suppressed in a punitive measure.

Like the King's Peace and the Second Athenian Confederacy, the new league guaranteed freedom and autonomy. Unlike the Athenian organization, however, this new league put the emphasis on property rights. There were specific bans on "confiscation of property, redistribution of land, cancellation of debts, or freeing of slaves with revolutionary intent."

The real novelty of this league was the fact that it had a king at its head and garrisons at crucial places, such as Chalcis and Corinth, to maintain the peace. The military requirements made of each state were set out in detail. Philip may have borrowed some of the features of the new arrangement, such as his politic use of titles, from precedents other than the Second Athenian Confederacy. Thus he may have absorbed a lesson about the politic use of titles in his mother's kingdom of Epirus. Although it had been ruled by kings, the officials in the confederacy over which they presided were given Greek-sounding titles such as "secretary." Other examples may have been provided by Dionysius I of Syracuse and Leucon of Bosporus, who took different titles for use in different contexts (indeed, this may have suggested to Philip the expedient of avoiding royal titles when dealing with the Greeks: for them he would be "general with full powers").

In fact, the fourth century saw a thorough mixing of political categories, of which Philip's new league is a sophisticated example. A cruder example is present in a curious decree from Labranda, which begins with the words "It seemed good to Mausolus and Artemisia" (his sister and also his wife). Here, one finds combined a regular formula for a Greek city-state with a highly irregular decision-making body—namely, a Persian satrap and his incestuous wife.

Mixing of political categories, however, was unwelcome at home in Macedon.

Perhaps some Macedonian soldiers, who might have preferred Athenian loot to an Athenian alliance, were puzzled about Philip's motives. Thus it may have been for the benefit of such doubters that, after planning his Asiatic war and sending an advance force under Attalus and Parmenio, Philip had himself depicted in a domestic Macedonian context (he would surely not have risked such a thing in Greece) as a "13th Olympian god." (Inscriptional evidence indicates that Philip may have received cult at Philippi, but cult for such founders was well established.) Further speculation about Philip's motive for this action, which is as remarkable in its way as anything he ever did, is unprofitable. For it was at this moment (336) that he was struck down by an assassin, whose own motives have never been ascertained.

ALEXANDER THE GREAT

Unless Alexander was himself ultimately responsible for his father's assassination (an implausible view, but one already canvassed in antiquity), he cannot have foreseen the moment of his own succession to a father who, though grizzled, was in the prime of life. His reaction to the turn of events was remarkably swift and cool. Two highly placed suspects were killed immediately. Not many actual rivals had to be eliminated, however, because Alexander's succession was not in serious doubt. A son of Philip's brother Perdiccas, Amyntas, was still alive, but there was no reason for Alexander to see him as a threat. In any case, he was probably dead by 335.

Alexander and the Greeks

Alexander began his career of conquest in 335. He started with lightning campaigns against the Triballi and Illyrians, which took him across the Danube. Thebes was next: the Thebans had risen in the optimistic belief that Alexander had died in Illyria. He reached Thessaly in seven days and was in Boeotia five days later. Then followed the destruction of Thebes. The blame for this act is differently distributed in the two main literary traditions about Alexander, that of Arrian and that of the vulgate. Arrian, a Greek historian and philosopher of the second century AD, relied on the works of two writers nearly contemporary with Alexander, Ptolemy (subsequently king of Egypt) and the historian Aristobulus. Arrian's tradition, which is regarded as the more "official" of the two, shifts the blame away from the Macedonians. The tradition of the vulgate, which is often fuller than that of Arrian, can be used to supplement or correct his. Although the vulgate tends toward the sensational, the greater reliability of Arrian can never be lightly assumed. For instance, on the Theban question, the vulgate more credibly puts the responsibility firmly on the Macedonians.

Soon after his accession, Alexander had been voted the leadership of the Persian expedition by the League of Corinth. He set out for Asia in the spring

(334). Ancient writers sometimes speak in an implausible way of wars being planned by a father and executed by a son (such as the Macedonian king Perseus's war against Rome, allegedly planned by his father, Philip V). Alexander's invasion of Asia, however, is surely a clear case where a son does seem automatically to have taken over a great project, one that had been in the cards since the Battle of Cunaxa at the beginning of the century. Philip had created the army, the prosperity, and the human resources that enabled Alexander to embark on his Asian campaign. He left behind his general Antipater as governor of Greece, with 12,000 foot soldiers and 1,500 cavalry, while taking 40,000 foot soldiers (12,000 of them Macedonians) and more than 6,000 cavalry with him to Asia. To what extent Alexander needed to reorganize the army at the outset of the expedition is unclear. It is certain that he made changes during it. For instance, he incorporated Iranian troops to deal with special circumstances in his eastern campaigning and changed the structure of the cavalry so as to reduce the politically dangerous territorial affiliations of the individual brigades (*ilai*, squadrons of Macedonian cavalry, were replaced by hipparchies). From the first, however, he must have given thought to problems of reconnaissance and supply. Whereas Greek armies expected to live off the land to some extent, Alexander used wagons, despite a tradition that Philip had forced his soldiers to carry their own provisions and equipment. The core of the infantry was the Macedonian phalanx, armed with the long *sarissa*, or spear. The pick of the cavalry were the Companions, led by Alexander himself on the right wing. Philip's great general Parmenio commanded the Thessalian cavalry on the left. In addition, there were lighter armed troops, such as the scouts, and less-coordinated but highly effective contingents of slingers and other irregulars, usually from the parts of Greece where the concept of polis was imperfectly developed. This army was a formidable machine in the metaphorical sense. There also were literal machines—stone-throwing siege engines that could be assembled on the spot. The Thessalian siege engineers associated with Philip certainly continued into Alexander's reign and enabled him to conquer Anatolia and Phoenicia at comparatively high speed, given the fortified obstacles confronting him.

The Spartan Agesilaus may have hoped merely to construct a belt of rebel satraps, and Philip's ultimate aims are inscrutable. Alexander, however, as soon as he had crossed the Hellespont, cast his spear into Asian soil and openly declared that he laid claim to all Asia (admittedly a geographically fluid concept). At Troy he visited the tombs of the heroes Achilles and Ajax, paying them due religious honour. This was an early and emphatic statement that he saw himself and his expedition in epic, Homeric terms. The conquest of Asia (in the sense of the Persian empire) was more feasible than in 346: Artaxerxes III had died in 338–337, and the king now reigning was the much weaker Darius III (he succeeded in 336, after the brief reign of Arses, whom the trilingual inscription found at Xanthus in 1973 shows to have borne the title Artaxerxes IV).

It was in this region, at the Granicus River, that Alexander was confronted by a Persian army—not the central army of the Persian king but a very sizable force levied by the satraps from Anatolia itself. Alexander attacked in full daylight (the vulgate tradition of a "dawn attack" should probably be rejected). The Persians lined the opposite riverbank—impressively but suicidally. Alexander's victory was achieved in part by his own conspicuous example. He led the right wing with a battle cry to the god of battles. Such "heroic leadership" is, indeed, one of Alexander's main contributions to the history of generalship.

Alexander immediately appointed satraps in the parts of Anatolia thus acquired, thereby giving an early signal that he saw himself as in some sense the successor and continuator of the Achaemenid Persian kings, not merely as an outsider devoted to their overthrow. At the same time, he proclaimed democracy, restored law, and remitted tribute in the Ionian cities. This illustrates how seriously Alexander took the propaganda purpose of the war as revenge for the Persian impieties of 480: it is noticeable that the places he accorded specially favourable treatment in his passage through Anatolia often turn out to be places with a "good" record in the Ionian revolt or the Persian Wars; that is to say, they had been prominent rebels. Alexander felt no scruple about subjecting to direct satrapal rule the tracts of territory outside the poleis. Whether the Greek cities of Anatolia joined the League of Corinth is an intractable question. Some of the islanders certainly did, as, for instance, Chios, where an inscription recording the terms of Alexander's settlement proclaims bluntly that "the constitution is to be a democracy" and refers to the "decrees of the Greeks." As for Asiatic cities like Priene, there is no certainty, but the probability is that they joined the league.

Priene was a very old city indeed, one of the Ionian "Dodecapolis," but it was physically derelict. It is possible that Alexander in some sense refounded this and other western Anatolian Greek cities, such as Heraclea south of Latmus and Smyrna. (There is, however, an almost equally strong case for associating their physical reconstruction with the Carian Hecatomnids, the family of Mausolus.) If Alexander was their founder, this would be the first good evidence of the urbanizing that was a marked feature of his policy for the conquered territories to the south and east. In this respect, however, as in others, credit should be given to Philip for his example: Philippi (the renamed Crenides) was not his only city foundation.

At Halicarnassus, Alexander met his most serious resistance so far from a defended city, in mid-334. Miletus had not delayed him long (nor was it punished very severely—it had after all been the leader of the Ionian revolt). The siege of Halicarnassus was a far tougher operation. The city had good defenses, both natural and artificial, and had been chosen as the local Persian military headquarters. The fighting was severe, though in the apologetic tradition used by Arrian the severity is minimized. At one moment Alexander was forced to the extremity of having to send a herald to ask for the bodies of some Macedonians who had fallen in front of the walls. After the city was taken—the citadels held out for another year or two—Alexander reappointed the native princess Ada as satrap (his earlier satrapal appointees had been Macedonians). She was the sister of the great Mausolus, and her reinstatement prefigures Alexander's shrewd subsequent policy of allowing local men and women to remain in post (though usually, like Ada herself, under the superintendence of a Macedonian troop commander). A romantic story makes her "adopt" Alexander as her son, a gesture graciously accepted by Alexander. That gesture of conciliation toward the native population was good politics.

After the conquest of Halicarnassus, Alexander moved east, meanwhile sending to Macedon for drafts of reinforcements. The scale of these demands through the whole campaign and their effects on the domestic situation in Macedon are not easy to estimate. The record of the literary sources is too fitful and episodic. According to one view, Alexander's legacy was one of lasting damage. He had exhausted the manpower of Macedon to such a point that the Macedon of Philip V and Perseus inevitably succumbed to the Romans with their almost infinite capacity for replacement. On the other hand, one must allow in the reckoning for a good deal of voluntary emigration by Macedonians to the armies and cities of the successor kingdoms in the Hellenistic period. Thus Alexander was not the only culprit. There were more intangible demographic forces at work.

Alexander's path took him from Carian Halicarnassus to Lycia and Pamphylia. At about the Lycian-Pamphylian border a strange natural phenomenon occurred that allowed Alexander and those with him to enjoy a freak dry passage along the coastline. This was greeted by his supporters as a portent and a recognition of Alexander's divinity (the sea "doing obeisance" to the great man). It was the first believable suggestion that special religious status could be claimed for Alexander.

In early 333 Alexander moved through Pisidia, where the nearly impregnable mountain city of Termessus, a remarkably well-preserved site some 35 kilometres (20 miles) northwest of the modern Antalya, managed to hold out (even Alexander's early years in Asia were not an uninterrupted success story). Morale and self-esteem had to be satisfied with the taking of Sagalassus and some minor places. Thus it was high time for a piece of propaganda and political theatre, especially since the Aegean he had left behind him was not altogether quiet. A Persian counteroffensive was achieving some notable reconquests (but eventually troop drafts were required by Darius for the campaign that finally took shape at Issus, and the Aegean war shriveled to nothing).

Alexander found his opportunity for propaganda some distance farther north in the Anatolian interior at Gordium, the old capital of the Phrygian kings (themselves, as stated, ultimately of Macedonian origin). There occurred the famous episode of the "cutting of the Gordian knot." The old prophecy was that whoever unloosed the knot or fastening of an ancient chariot would rule Asia. Alexander cut it instead—or perhaps pulled out the pole pin, as one tradition insisted. Either way, he solved the problem by abolishing it.

The visits to Pisidia and Phrygia had been a huge detour, evidently designed to show that Alexander had conquered Anatolia. This statement raises problems of definition. *Conquest* was a relative term when there were large tracts of Anatolia, such as Cappadocia, that Alexander had scarcely touched, not to mention the mixed achievement at Pisidia.

A more obvious way of achieving conquest was to defeat the king in open battle. The time had come to face Darius, whose army was already in Cilicia. In fact, Darius got ahead of Alexander, occupying (after a protracted delay) a position to the north of the Macedonians. The numerical advantage at the ensuing Battle of Issus, fought toward the end of 333, was heavily with the Persians, but they were awkwardly squeezed between the sea and the foothills of a mountain range close by. Alexander's Companion cavalry punched a hole in the Persian infantry, making straight for Darius himself, who took flight. The Persian mercenaries were routed by the Macedonian phalanx. After the battle, Darius's wife and mother both fell into Alexander's hands. In an exchange of letters Alexander grandly offered that Darius could have them back—"mother, wife, children, whatever you like"—if he recognized his own claim to be lord of Asia and addressed him as such for the future. Darius, of course, refused the offer.

Alexander did not immediately follow Darius eastward. Instead he continued southward in the direction of Phoenicia and eventually Egypt. The Phoenician cities of Byblos and Sidon submitted willingly, but Tyre was a major obstacle. Its walls were not finally breached until summer 332, after various contrivances had been tried, including a huge and elaborate siege mole. The siege of Gaza occupied much of the autumn. When the city at last surrendered, Alexander dishonoured the corpse of Batis, its commander, in the way that Achilles in the *Iliad* had treated the corpse of Hector. Alexander's imitation of Homeric heroes had its less attractive side.

This was the part of the world in which the Jews might have encountered Alexander. No doubt there was some contact, but virtually all the available evidence is unreliable and romantic or even fabricated to give substance to later Jewish claims to political privileges. Alexander's effect on the Jews was indirect, but no less important for that: he surrounded them with a Greek-speaking world.

Alexander in Egypt

Egypt was taken without a struggle, an indication of the dislike the subject population felt toward Persia. (Even though Egypt had been reconquered by Persia hardly more than a decade before, it is possible that there had been yet another revolt since 343.) Alexander's period in Egypt was marked by two major events, the founding of Alexandria and the visit to the oracle of the god Ammon at Sīwah in the Western Desert. Although the sources disagree about which event came first, the foundation probably preceded the visit to the oracle.

The new city of Alexandria, the first as well as the most famous and successful of many new Alexandrias, was formed by joining a number of Egyptian villages (April 331). Alexander supervised the religious ceremonies of foundation, including Greek-style athletic and musical games (an indication of his intentions to Hellenize these foundations, at least as far as their cultural life was concerned). He thought that the site was an excellent one and hoped for its commercial prosperity. It is quite certain, from an inscription, that early Hellenistic Alexandria possessed a civic council. This and other self-governing institutions such as an assembly probably go back to Alexander's time. Not all Alexander's foundations were run on this liberal model, though some were inaugurated with similar symbolic gestures in the direction of Hellenism. One hears of "satraps and generals of the newly founded cities," a phrase that does not imply much self-government. No doubt some of Alexander's "new foundations" were little more than military camps. And one should assume that in all the far eastern Alexandrias the native population was forced to perform menial or agricultural tasks.

The oracle of Ammon at Sīwah, to which Alexander now made a pilgrimage, was already well known in the Greek world. Pindar had equated Ammon with Zeus, the oracle had been consulted by Croesus in the sixth century and Lysander in the fifth, and there was a sanctuary to Ammon at Athens in the first half of the fourth century. Alexander had a *pothos*, or yearning, to visit Ammon (the word *pothos* is often used by the sources to describe his motives and is appropriately suggestive of far horizons, even if it does not reflect a usage of Alexander's own). He wanted to find out more about his own divinity, the implication being that he already had an inkling of it. He was told what he wanted to hear. More than that (some sources offer a great deal more) was probably speculation to fill a gap.

To the Persian Gates

Alexander then crossed Phoenicia again to meet Darius for the second and last time in the open field at Gaugamela (between Nineveh and Arbela) at the beginning of October 331. The tactic was to be the usual one—a leftward charge by Alexander from the right wing toward the centre, while Parmenio held the left wing firm. Parmenio seems, however, to have encountered unusual difficulties and had to summon help from Alexander, who was already in victorious pursuit of Darius. The mechanics of this "summons" are not clear, and the story may be a fabrication intended to discredit Parmenio. Alexander and his troops won the battle, sealing the fate of the Persian empire, but Darius managed to escape. Alexander then moved to Babylon, where in another gesture of conciliation toward the Iranian ruling class he reappointed Mazaeus as satrap, with Macedonians to supervise the garrison and the finances.

This kind of gesture has been much discussed. It can be both overinterpreted and unduly minimized. Ideas that Alexander, then or ever, planned to forge a harmony between nations at a mystical level have no solid basis in the evidence. There is nothing odd, however, in supposing that his intentions toward Persians like Mazaeus (or Abulites, confirmed in the Susa satrapy about the same time) were positive. Also, the idea of such "fusion" was not entirely new. Greeks such as Xenophon earlier in the century had by their writings and actions anticipated Alexander's policy of fusion, and the cooperation of Cyrus and Lysander was just the most famous example of mutual understanding between Persian and Greek. Nor is it convincing to interpret Alexander's policy of integrating army and satrapy as a repressive device. Macedonians like Peucestas (appointed satrap of Persia) learned Persian and were rewarded for it. And Hephaestion's position of favour with Alexander is largely to be explained by his support of Alexander's Orientalizing policies. Admittedly, after leaving Iranian territories, Alexander returned to employing Macedonians as, for instance, in the Indus lands. But even there one finds native appointees like the Indian king Porus. Military integration—the use of Iranian horse-javelin men—is first firmly attested soon after the battle of Gaugamela. This is to be explained in purely military terms: the Companion cavalry on their own were not entirely suited to the more disorganized warfare lying ahead against the fierce opponents waiting to the east and north of Iran proper.

After some spectacular campaigning in Persis proper, Alexander occupied the palace of Persepolis, where the strong defensive position known as the "Persian Gates" was taken only after an unsuccessful and costly initial assault. The palace of Persepolis was looted and burned (spring 330). The less creditable tradition of the vulgate maintains that the fire started when a drunken Athenian courtesan named Thais led a revel that got out of hand, and this may well be right. The event, however, could be exploited afterward as a signal to dissident Greeks at home that the "war of revenge" was complete.

To establish securely the propaganda value of the burning of Persepolis would require a more precise chronology for the phases of that Greek dissidence than is ever likely to be achieved. The last fling of fourth-century Sparta was a revolt led by its king Agis III. It was probably still going on in 330 when it culminated in a narrow victory by the Macedonian general Antipater over the Spartans at Megalopolis. If this is right, the burning of Persepolis at about this time makes good propaganda sense. Athens had not participated in the revolt. The quiescence of Athens in the early years of Alexander's campaigning is to be explained partly by the policy of civic retrenchment associated with the name of Lycurgus (a phase of Athenian history that included a remarkable building program, the first since the fifth century) and partly by a well-attested grain shortage in Greece, which may have sapped the will to fight.

The Conquest of Bactria and the Indus Valley

By the middle of 330 Darius had been killed—not by Alexander but by his own entourage. Alexander now adopted symbolic features of Persian royal dress, but one of Darius's noble followers (and murderers), Bessus, the satrap of Bactria, also proclaimed himself king. The reckoning with Bessus, however, had to be postponed until the middle of 329. Alexander, who had initially followed Darius north, now moved steadily east, through Hyrcania and Areia, where Satibarzanes was confirmed as satrap. Alexander planned an invasion of Bactria and the elimination of Bessus. Satibarzanes, however, revolted almost instantly, and Alexander turned south again to deal with this rebellion. Having done so (though without taking the satrap himself), he maintained direction southward, toward Arachosia and Drangiana, home satrapies of Barsaentes, another of Darius's murderers. Barsaentes, however, fled to India.

At Phrada, capital of Drangiana, occurred the most famous conspiracy of Alexander's expedition, that of Philotas, the son of Parmenio and a commander of the Companion cavalry. There was little solid evidence for the prosecution to go on, but it is clear that Alexander's Orientalizing tendencies and the ever more personal style of Alexander's kingship had begun to irk his Macedonian nobility, accustomed as they were to express themselves freely, as in the outspoken court of Philip's day. Philotas had no doubt spoken very incautiously on some sensitive subjects, such as Alexander's visit to Ammon. The execution of Philotas entailed the execution of his father Parmenio as well, not because there was any serious suggestion that he too had been plotting but as a matter of practical politics. The family group of Parmenio, which can be elucidated by means of prosopography (the investigation of family ties with the help of proper names), had considerable power.

The year 329 saw the final elimination of Satibarzanes and the capture of Bessus in Sogdiana, north of the Oxus River from Bactria. In Sogdiana,

Alexander founded the city of Alexandreschate, "Alexandria the Farthest," not far from the site of Cyropolis, a city of Cyrus II the Great, whom Alexander highly admired. This is a reminder that Persian urbanization in Central Asia had not been negligible. (At the interesting Bactrian site of Ai Khanum, which cannot definitely be identified as an Alexandria, there is evidence of Achaemenid irrigation.) Alexandreschate was a prestige foundation, designed, as explicitly stated by Arrian, for both military and commercial success. Alexander had already planted a number of new Alexandrias in central Iran, including Alexandria in Areia (Herat), Alexandria in Arachosia, and almost certainly Qandahār, on the exciting evidence of a metrical inscription found there by a British excavation team in 1978. There was another major foundation called Alexandria in the Caucasus at an important junction of communications in the Hindu Kush.

How far Alexander intended these places to be permanent pockets of Hellenism is not clear. That Hellenism could survive in these regions is shown by the case of Ai Khanum, which had many of the features of a Greek polis, including gymnasia and an agora with an *oikist* (city-founder) cult. There are even inscribed Delphic religious precepts. Nonetheless, many of Alexander's Greek colonists in Bactria tried to return home to the mainland immediately after his death out of *pothos*, or yearning for their Greek way of life. It must be accepted that the ancient literary tradition exaggerated the extent of, and the Hellenizing intentions behind, Alexander's city foundations. A brilliant reconstruction of that literary tradition suggests convincingly that the exaggerations were in the main the work of tendentious scholars and writers in Ptolemaic Alexandria whose aim was to disparage the urbanizing efforts of the Ptolemies' great rivals the Seleucids by reassigning to Alexander himself many foundations that were actually Seleucid.

Bessus and Satibarzanes were not the last satraps of eastern Iran to offer resistance. It took fully two years (until spring 327) to suppress Spitamenes of Sogdia and other tribal leaders. The period was full of strain, culminating in the disastrous quarrel between Alexander and Cleitus, one of his senior commanders and the newly appointed satrap of Bactria at the end of 328. The quarrel ended in Alexander actually killing Cleitus with his own hands in drunken fury. The issue was a personal one, which, however, merged with a matter of principle: Cleitus had criticized Alexander's leadership (there had admittedly been at least one military reverse due perhaps to inadequate planning), comparing him unfavourably with his father Philip. Before the army moved in the direction of India, there were two more incidents that widened the gap between Alexander's conduct and traditional Macedonian attitudes.

First, Alexander attempted to introduce the Persian court ceremonial involving *proskynesis*, or obeisance. Just what this entailed is disputed. Perhaps it amounted to different things in different contexts, ranging from an exchange of kisses to total prostration before the ruler in the way a Muslim says his prayers. What is not in doubt is that for Greeks this meant adoration of a living human being, something they considered impious as well as ridiculous. It was the court historian Callisthenes who voiced the feeling of the Greeks. The *proskynesis* experiment was not repeated: Alexander did not in the end insist on it. It is difficult, however, not to connect Callisthenes' role in this affair with his downfall not long after, allegedly for encouraging the treason of a group of royal pages. This was the second of the two alarming incidents of the period.

India was the objective in 327, though Alexander did not reach the Indus valley until 326, after passing through Swāt Cas from the district of the Kābul River. In 326, at the great Battle of the Hydaspes (Jhelum), he defeated the Indian king Porus in the first major battle in which he faced a force of elephants. How much farther east Alexander might have gone is a question that has fascinated posterity, but the curiosity and patience of his army was exhausted. At the Hyphasis (Beas) River he was obliged to turn back.

Alexander did not, however, retrace his path but took the route southward through the Indus valley toward the Arabian Sea and the Gulf of Oman. He narrowly avoided death at the so-called "Malli town," where an arrow seems to have entered his lung. The subsequent march westward in 325 through the desert region of Gedrosia (Balochistan) was a death march. Its horrors emerge vividly enough from the literary narratives, but they are certainly understated. Alexander's motive for ordering the march may have been the desire to outdo the mythical queen Semiramis and the legendary Cyrus the Great. But the scale of the catastrophe does suggest that his judgment was by now badly impaired. Meanwhile, Nearchus led the fleet from the mouth of the Indus to that of the Tigris, a voyage recorded by Arrian in his *Indica*, using the account of Nearchus himself.

THE FINAL PHASE

In Carmania, to the west of Gedrosia, Alexander first staged a week-long drunken revel, in which he himself posed as Dionysus, as a release of tension after the preceding nightmare journey. Then he ordered his satraps and generals to disband their mercenary armies, like Artaxerxes III in 359 and perhaps for the same reason, namely, fear of insurrection. This was a period of punitive action against disobedient or negligent satraps. One official who in this atmosphere preferred to abscond rather than brazen out the inquisition was Harpalus, the royal treasurer, who made his way eventually to Athens. The exact fate of the money he took with him was and still is a celebrated mystery. The fact that Harpalus's activities as treasurer had evidently been quite

Marriage of Alexander and Roxane, *fresco by Sodoma,* c. *1511–12; in the Villa Farnesina, Rome.* SCALA/Art Resource, New York

unsupervised was typical of Alexander's short and impatient way with administrative problems. (It is most unlikely that he planned an ambitious financial restructuring of the empire, giving special responsibilities to men with the right expertise. One finds men like Cleomenes in Egypt or Philoxenus in Anatolia combining territorial with financial responsibilities, but no general conclusions can be drawn.)

At Susa in 324 Alexander staged a splendid mass marriage of Persians and Macedonians. He himself had already married a Bactrian princess, Rhoxane (Roxane), in 327, but he now took two more wives, a daughter of Darius III named Barsine (or Stateira) and Parysatis, the daughter of Artaxerxes III. This and other demonstrations of "Orientalizing," including the brigading of Iranian units into the army, overcame a final mutiny at Opis near Babylon. After haranguing the troops, threatening them, and finally sulking, Alexander won back their affections. Following this meretricious and emotional performance, he chose to heal the rift symbolically by a more organized piece of theatre, a great banquet of reconciliation (thus demonstrating for the last time in Archaic and Classical Greek history the usefulness of the banquet, or symposium, as an instrument of social control).

Other actions or schemes in this final phase were of the same megalomaniac type: a request for his own deification, sent to the Greek cities; a demand that they take back their exiles; a monstrous funeral pyre for his dear friend Hephaestion (never completed); and a plan of circumnavigation and conquest of Arabia. So much is well documented. Lists of other spectacular last plans survive, but they are hardly needed. The achievements of the last 13 years were extravagant enough. Alexander died at Babylon, after an illness brought on by heavy drinking, in the early evening of June 10, 323.

GREEK CIVILIZATION IN THE FOURTH CENTURY

The fourth century BC is in many ways the best-documented period of Greek history. There is, admittedly, a greater number of documents from the third century, when inscriptions and papyri abound (there are virtually no documentary papyri before the time of Alexander). The writings of the third-century prose historians, however, are mostly lost. In the fourth century, by contrast, there is an abundance of evidence of all kinds. Inscriptions are much more common than in the fifth century and begin to appear in quantity from states other than Athens.

Historical Writings

Forensic oratory from the fifth century has scarcely survived at all, but from the fourth century there are more than 60 speeches attributed to Demosthenes alone. Most of this corpus of oratory is set in an Athenian context, but one speech of Isocrates deals with business affairs on Aegina. Although there is no fourth-century tragedy and no epinician poetry like that of Pindar, the comedies of Aristophanes from the beginning of the century and those of Menander from toward the end have survived. These are illuminating about social life, as are the prose writings of Aristotle's pupil Theophrastus, especially his *Characters*. The writings of Plato, in their anxiety to define an ideal polis invulnerable to stasis or civil strife, give evidence of the instability of the fourth-century world in which it could be said that in every city there were two cities, that of the rich and that of the poor. Aristotle's *Politics* examines the theoretical conceptions underlying Greek attitudes toward polis life. This is a precious document, although it can be criticized for insufficient awareness of the monarchical and federal developments of the age.

No such criticism can be leveled at the historiography of the age. It is from Xenophon that one learns of the grand plans of Jason of Pherae, and knowledge about Dionysius I is derived, by less direct routes, from the fourth-century historians of the Greek west Ephorus, Philistus, and (toward the end of the century) Timaeus of Tauromenium. In fact, the process of explaining history in terms of personality already begins with Thucydides, who arguably came to see that a dynamic personality like Alcibiades could by sheer charisma and force of character have an impact on events irrespective of the content of his policies. It was surely this aspect of Thucydides' work that Aristotle had in mind when he defined history as "what Alcibiades did and suffered."

Aristotle's nephew Callisthenes began by recording the history of the city-states in a fairly traditional way (which, however, did more justice to the Theban hegemony than had that of Xenophon), but then he joined Alexander's staff in order to write the *Deeds of Alexander*. Evidently, history was now seen as what Alexander did and suffered. Even earlier than that, however, the central role of Philip's personality had been acknowledged by Theopompus of Chios, who (like Callisthenes) moved in the direction of writing history that revolved around the person of a king. He called his history of Greece *Philippica*, "The Affairs of Philip." Meanwhile there were local historians of Attica, such as Androtion, who continued to value Athens's past and even ventured to rewrite (not merely to reinterpret) the facts about it. These men, who are known as Atthidographers, were not simply antiquarians escaping from the monarchic present. On the contrary, the greatest of them, Philochorus, was put to death in the third century by a Macedonian king for his excessive partiality toward King Ptolemy II Philadelphus of Egypt. All these authors were, in different ways, coming to terms with monarchy.

In addition to works of history there are fourth-century treatises that show how Greeks experienced the new military monarchies. Xenophon's *Cyropaedia*, or "Education of Cyrus," is a novel about Cyrus the Great, but it is also a tract on kingship and generalship addressed to the class of educated Greek commanders and would-be leaders. (In comparable fashion Isocrates offered advice on kingship to the semi-Hellenized rulers of Cyprus.) The surviving treatise on siegecraft by Aeneas of Stymphalus in Arcadia (known as Aeneas Tacticus) is valuable not only for the evidence it provides about dissensions (stasis) inside a polis—there is an entire section on "plots"—but also for the awareness both of the ruthless methods of men like Dionysius, who figures prominently, and of the new military technology of the age. (The treatise includes, for example, practical advice on how to defend walls against battering rams.) Aeneas Tacticus's treatise, more than any other surviving prose work of the fourth century, makes the point that this was an age of professionalism.

Many technical monographs are known to have been written in this period but have not survived. For instance, Pythius, who worked on the Mausoleum, also wrote a book about another of his projects, the Temple of Athena Polias at Priene. (There were fifth-century precedents for some of this: Polyclitus of Argos had written a famous treatise on proportion in sculpture and Sophocles a monograph about the chorus.)

Architecture and Sculpture

In the sphere of architecture, the fourth century produced no Parthenon, but it was the great age of military structures. Most of what survives of the elegant fortifications of the northwestern frontier demes of Attica stems from the fourth century. Inscriptions attest refurbishing work on Phyle in particular at about the time of the Battle of Cheronea. Outside Athens there were big projects, such as the temple at Epidaurus and the Mausoleum at Halicarnassus.

Buildings such as the Mausoleum were commissioned by powerful individuals, further proof that the emergence of commanding personalities is a noticeable feature of the fourth century. In some respects it represents a return to Archaic values: a tyrant like Dionysius has much in common with Peisistratus of Athens or Polycrates of Samos, and Philip II of Macedon can be seen as comparable to Pheidon of Argos, a hereditary monarch who transformed his power base into a military autocracy. Revised attitudes toward such individuals are already detectable near the end of the fifth century. It seems that, when Athens founded Amphipolis in 437, its founder Hagnon, father of the oligarch Theramenes, was given some kind of cult in his lifetime. That is the usually neglected implication of a passage of Thucydides, which definitely records the award of cult honours at Amphipolis to the dead Spartan general Brasidas after 422. In the early fourth century another Spartan, Lysander, received cult at Samos, and later in the century Euphron, a tyrant at Sicyon, was buried in the agora "like a founder."

At Athens itself, before the request by Alexander for his own deification, there could be no question of divine cult for a living man (although it is possible that Alexander had already arranged some kind of hero cult at Athens for Hephaestion). Nonetheless, even at Athens there was a marked trend toward more assertive monuments. This is particularly evident in the commemorative choregic monuments built to celebrate victories in the great Athenian festivals. The most famous of these, the Choregic Monument of Lysicrates, which used to be called the "Lantern of Demosthenes," represents a transitional phase. Its inscribed dedication falls between the anonymity (actually more pretended than real) of the corporatist benefactions of Classical Athens and the assertiveness of Hellenistic Greece with its emphasis on individual generosity. On the one hand, the inscription makes clear that what is celebrated is victory by the tribe as a whole. On the other, the great prominence of the man's name stresses individuality, as does the idiosyncratic form of the monument. Clearly, this is an emphatic statement in the first person singular.

Alexander the Great in battle, detail from the so-called Alexander Sarcophagus, marble, c. 310 BC, from Sidon; in the Archaeological Museums of Istanbul. Hirmer Fotoarchiv, Munich

Consistent with these developments is the marked tendency toward portraiture in art. Persian satraps such as Tissaphernes issued coinage with what were obviously meant to be realistic depictions of the satrap's head. Individual rulers were represented by statues in the round, like that of "Mausolus" from the Mausoleum (which may or may not be an attempt to represent Mausolus himself but which incontrovertibly is a portrait of some powerful individual), or by figures on friezes, as those on the "Alexander Sarcophagus" in the Archaeological Museums of Istanbul. Although the workmanship is evidently Greek, the ethos is uncompromisingly royal. Alexander created a new visual image for himself. Unlike the bearded Philip, Alexander is portrayed as clean-shaven, young, and idealized. Lysippus, in particular, is said to have caught Alexander's physical qualities in his royal sculpture portraits.

The Athenian empire had given employment to many artists, architects, and sculptors, both from Athens itself

Mausoleum of Halicarnassus

One of the Seven Wonders of the World, the Mausoleum of Halicarnassus was the tomb of Mausolus, the tyrant of Caria in southwestern Asia Minor. It was built between about 353 and 351 BC by Mausolus's sister and widow, Artemisia. The architect was Pythius (or Pytheos), and the sculptures that adorned the building were the work of four leading Greek artists: Scopas, Bryaxis, Leochares, and Timotheus.

According to the description of the Roman author Pliny the Elder (AD 23–79), the monument was almost square, with a total periphery of 125 metres (411 feet). It was bounded by 36 columns, and the top formed a 24-step pyramid surmounted by a four-horse marble chariot. Fragments of the mausoleum's sculpture that are preserved in the British Museum include a frieze of battling Greeks and Amazons and a statue 3 metres (10 feet) long, probably of Mausolus. The mausoleum was probably destroyed by an earthquake between the 11th and the 15th century AD, and the stones were reused in local buildings.

and from the subject states of the empire. When the empire collapsed in 404, many of these had to seek employment elsewhere. Some went to the courts of satraps like Mausolus or of military rulers like Dionysius: both of these had money to spend on art, building, and fortifications. Another wealthy court was that of Macedon. One remaining recourse in Athens, however, was funerary art. The most famous funerary stelae and sculptured monuments found at Kerameikós, the city's prestigious cemetery, date from this period, before such lavish commissions were outlawed by the Athenian ruler Demetrius of Phaleron after Alexander's death. Some of those buried were foreigners. For instance, there was a precinct for the Messenians, one for some immigrants from Heraclea on the Black Sea, and one for those from Sinope, also in the Black Sea region. (In the Archaeological Museum of Piraeus there is a monument comparable to another one of a Black Sea immigrant, a reminder of Athens's commercial connections with this crucial grain-growing area.) In the Kerameikós there is even a grave of a Persian with a larger-than-life torso of a seated man in Persian dress.

Social and Commercial Exchanges

Whatever the political effects of the King's Peace of 386, it was evidently not a barrier to social and commercial exchanges. Inscriptions in the corpus of Demosthenes' speeches frequently mention trade with ports in Phoenicia and Anatolia and occasionally allude casually to piracy, a classic by-product of such trading activity. There is epigraphic evidence for piracy as well: in the 340s Athens honoured Cleomis, tyrant of Methymna on Lesbos, for ransoming a number of Athenians captured by pirates. Lesbos had always enjoyed trading links with the Black Sea region, and in the fourth century more than ever. One should imagine Athenians and metic Athenian traders (i.e., foreigners resident at Athens) going in numbers via Lesbos and the Sea of Marmara to the rich granaries of southern Russia. Some no doubt settled in these regions, though the inscriptional evidence for Athenians abroad in the fourth century (as opposed to evidence for foreigners settling in Athens or Piraeus) is in need of systematic collation.

Immigration and free movement of individuals between one polis and another are typical features of the fourth century. They are best documented for Athens but hardly confined to it, given the attractiveness of the royal and satrapal courts. At Athens itself, the great magnet for immigrants was naturally Piraeus, the city's densely populated, multilingual, multiracial port. Bilingual inscriptions in the Archaeological Museum of Piraeus, in Greek and Aramaic, testify to the presence of Phoenician traders, who also left more strictly epigraphic traces. (Conversely, Greco-Aramaic stelae in the Archaeological Museums in Istanbul may attest Greek or partially Greek settlements in the Persian empire.) An inscription of the period of Alexander, from the Piraeus, records the response of the Athenian Assembly to the request of some merchants from Cyprus for permission to build a sanctuary to Aphrodite (the goddess, born in the sea, allegedly stepped ashore on Cyprus). The inscription mentions, as a precedent for the request, the Temple of Isis founded by the Egyptian community.

Foreign cults of this kind were not by any means new in the late fifth century. If they seem so, it may be because that period is so much better documented than the early part of the century. But they may have increased in number in Greece as a result of the geographically extensive campaigning of the Peloponnesian War and even the period of the Athenian empire. The cult of Adonis is referred to in Plutarch's *Life of Nicias*, which also mentions the Ammon oracle. Thracian as well as Egyptian cults arrived in Greece in the late fifth century. The cult of the Thracian goddess Bendis at Piraeus features in the first page of Plato's *Republic*. Bendis was perhaps a female counterpart to the Thracian Hero. Cults were both imported and exported: one of the vessels from Rogozen depicts the Greek myth of Heracles and Auge, labeled as such. This is a reminder that the old Olympian cults remained strong. In fact, some of the best evidence for traditional Greek religion comes from this period. It was the century of the highly informative and basically conservative Attic deme calendars (i.e., lists of festivals, chronologically arranged through the year) and the period when inscriptional information about the great Panhellenic sanctuaries entered its richest phase.

Mercenary service, as well as organized campaigning, must have helped to raise consciousness of such foreign cults as those of Isis or Bendis. Greeks often served in Thrace in the late fifth and the fourth centuries. Xenophon, for example, was there at the beginning of the fourth century and heard the so-called "Ballad of Sitalces" (a fifth-century Thracian ruler who is featured in Thucydides) sung at a banquet in Paphlagonia.

Mercenaries constituted one category of Greeks who strayed away from their cities. They were a potentially disruptive force, whether from the point of view of polis-minded Greeks or of autocrats like Artaxerxes III or Alexander the Great. Nobody, however, could dispense with them. The Persian kings used Greek mercenaries in their repeated attempts to recover Egypt in the fourth century—but so did the defending Egyptians.

How far inside the Persian empire these Greek mercenaries penetrated is an intriguing question. An inscription first published during World War II appeared to attest a group of Greek mercenaries on an island in the Persian Gulf in the period before Alexander, but it is possible that the text is actually early Hellenistic. Even Spartans like Agesilaus near the end of his life and Thebans like the general Pammenes in the 350s had to hire themselves out to Persian paymasters, whether loyalist or insurrectionist. (It would be better to speak, in this context, not of mercenaries but of "citizen-mercenaries" because these Thebans and Spartans did not cease to belong to their home cities.) The military monarchies of Dionysius and Philip were to some extent propped up by mercenary forces, whose loyalty was not subject to political but only to financial blandishments. This leads to the conclusion that the mercenary soldier valued his booty (*aposkeue*, literally "baggage") more than he valued his commander. One of the early successors of Alexander the Great, the Greek Eumenes of Cardia, was in effect traded by his troops to a rival for gain. Already under Alexander the elite troops known as "Silver Shields," or *argyraspides*, had taken their name from the conquered Persian treasure of precious metal.

Organized Settlements

Not all interchange between poleis, or all emigration from the polis into nonpolis areas of settlement, however, was of the haphazard kind caused by mercenary service or the peripatetic life-style of artists and craftsmen. Rather, the poleis themselves promoted much organized activity.

First, old ties might be strengthened by renegotiation, or more explicit reaffirmation, of old colonial connections. Inscriptions survive from the fourth century that accord rights of citizenship on a footing of mutuality, for instance, between Miletus and Olbia and between Thera and Cyrene. Some old connections of alliance might be inflated into a pseudo-colonial link. Thus, Hellenistic Plataea, as noted earlier, called itself a "colony" of Athens, which strictly it was not. This claim may well go back to the fourth century, and there is good evidence for other such fabricated claims of kinship in the latter part of this century. An inscription, for example, asserts a colonial connection between Argos and Aspendus in Pamphylia. This is certainly unhistorical but can be explained from the greater prominence enjoyed, in the Hellenistic and Roman periods, by Argos. The reason was that Argos could itself claim a connection with the Macedon of Alexander, and this kind of connection was desirable for obtaining privileges from him or from his successors.

The founding, building, or synoecizing of new cities was another way in which mobility of population was actually encouraged by the poleis themselves. The process is traditionally (and rightly) associated with Alexander the Great himself, but the emphasis is unjust to some innovatory activity in the later fifth and fourth centuries both by individuals (not least Philip) and by cities.

In the late fifth century Olynthus had been synoecized into existence by Perdiccas of Macedon, and the Rhodians had merged the three cities of their island into a new physical and political entity. The same was done in the 360s by the communities of the Dorian island of Cos. Mausolus's new capital of Halicarnassus was the result of a synoecism in which Greeks and native Carians ("Lelegians") were integrated into a new city, which was physically beautified with monumental buildings. Moreover, one can make a case for associating Mausolus with the various refoundations or moving of sites that different kinds of evidence suggest took place at Priene, Erythrae, and Heraclea. Epaminondas's interventions in the Peloponnese led to major urbanization projects at Messene and Arcadian Megalopolis, where the Spartan defeat at Leuctra in 371 may have given an immediate impetus to the new foundation (the alternative date is about 368 and is less likely).

More traditional methods of moving people, such as colonization, were also used. At the beginning of the fourth century Xenophon includes a warm and lyrical description in the *Anabasis* of a site called Kalpe on the Black Sea, praising its situation, fertility, and relative remoteness from rival and established Greek cities in the vicinity. This gives substance to the suspicion that what Xenophon was really trying to do was found a colony of Archaic type—the Euboeans of the eighth century would have jumped at a site with Kalpe's advantages of situation. In the 340s Timoleon of Corinth effected a kind of recolonization of Syracuse from the old mother city. He took with him many refugees and brought prosperity back to an island much battered by internal dissension and endless wars with the Carthaginians—against whom he himself scored some notable successes.

Athens sent a colony to the west in the time of Alexander and the wheat shortage. It was led with symbolic or sentimental appropriateness by a man called Miltiades (the name of the sixth-century founder and dynast ruling in the Chersonese), who went to the Adriatic region. The Adriatic seems to have been a favourite colonizing focus in this period: the scale and even reality of Dionysius's interventions there are controversial, but an inscription gives evidence of a Greek colony on the island of Black Corcyra. The great colonizing surge of the fourth century came, however, in the wake of Alexander. Once again, the Ionian Greeks took the lead, just as, on Thucydides' evidence, they had colonized Ionia itself even before the organized phase of colonizing activity in the eighth century.

Also in the fourth century a great number of citizenships were granted to individuals from whom favours were expected or by whom they had already been conferred, or both. (One standard motive, occasionally made explicit, for the recording of such honours in permanent form was to induce the recipient to continue his generosity.) Most of the evidence is Athenian, but the phenomenon was surely not confined to Athens. Even Persian satraps like Orontes could be enrolled as Athenian citizens, not to mention Macedonians like Menelaus the Pelagonian, a king of the Lyncestians (an independent Macedonian subkingdom until annexed by Philip). This man received citizenship in the 360s because he was reported by the Athenian general Timotheus as helping Athens in its wars in the north. A further and frequent motive for such honours, and one that anticipates the Hellenistic age, is an expression of gratitude for gifts of grain. The Spartocid kings of the Bosporus (southern Russia) were honoured because they had promised to provide Athens with wheat, as their father Leucon had done before them.

This kind of benefaction is called *euergetism* (the word derives from *euergesia*, or "doing good deeds"). Now that Athens no longer had the naval power to direct all grain forcibly toward its own harbours, much had to be done by exploiting benefactors. *Euergetism* of this sort, however, was not entirely new: as early as 444 BC, Egyptian grain in large quantites had been sent by a rebel pharaoh at a time when Athens was certainly not (as it gradually became) a city armed merely with a cultural past and a begging bowl.

CONCLUSION

No treatment of the golden age of Greek civilization should end without emphasizing the continuity both with what went before and with what came after. Continuity is clearest in the sphere of religion, which may be said to have been "embedded" in Greek life. Some of the gods alleged to have been relatively late imports into Greece can in fact be shown to have Mycenaean origins. For instance, one Athenian myth held that Dionysus was a latecomer, having been introduced into Attica from Eleutherae in the sixth century. There is reference to Dionysus (or *di-wo-no-so-jo*), however, on Linear B tablets from the second millennium BC.

Looking forward, Dionysus' statue was to be depicted in a grand procession staged in Alexandria in the third century BC by King Ptolemy II Philadelphus. (The iconographic significance of the king's espousal of Dionysus becomes clear in light of the good evidence that in some sense Alexander the Great had identified himself with Dionysus in Carmania.) Nor was Classical Dionysus confined to royal exploitation: it has been shown that the festivals of the City Dionysia at Athens and the deme festival of the Rural Dionysia were closely woven into the life of the Athenian empire and the Athenian state. Another Athenian, Euripides, represented Dionysus in a less tame and "official" aspect in the *Bacchae*. This Euripidean Dionysus has more in common with the liberating Dionysus of Carmania or with the socially disruptive Dionysus whose worship the Romans in 186 BC were to regulate in a famous edict. The longevity and multifaceted character of Dionysus symbolizes the tenacity of the Greek civilization, which Alexander had taken to the banks of the Oxus but which in many respects still carried the marks of its Archaic and even prehistoric origins.

This is just one manifestation of Greece's prehistoric origins, but there are others as well.

Later the Greeks would fall to the Romans, weakened. But their unforgettable influence lives on. Their ideas percolated through many parts of the world. They were remarkably modern and forward-looking. They made many contributions to modern thought. Even their faults, splashed plainly across the pages of Thucydides, revealed a straightforwardness and willingness to confront problems directly that was perhaps umatched in the ancient world. Unlike some cultures, which had highly formalistic styles of art and communications, ancient Greece was in a constant struggle between tradition and an enduring sense of itself and at the same time an incredible hunger to reinvent and improve. Their art became more and more naturalistic over time.

Why is it that our language is so rich in words and concepts from these ancient people? Words like *philosophy*, *democracy*, *politics*. It is because they gave those words and the concepts behind them force and power.

Appendix: Pre-Greek Aegean Civilizations

To understand the ancient Greek civilization during the Archaic and Classical periods, it is important to understand, at least to some degree, what came before. For thousands of years, listeners and readers have been thrilled by tales of King Minos and the labyrinth, of the fierce battles of the Trojan War, and of the adventures of Odysseus. No one knew what basis these stories had in reality. Some ruins were left behind, some hidden. But the Greeks of the Archaic and Classical periods knew that peoples of earlier times trod on their same ancient lands, grew olives in the dry, unforgiving earth, sailed expertly between its islands on wine-dark seas, and spun unforgettable stories of gods and legendary heroes that helped them to understand the capricious world in which they lived.

Despite the presence of some ruins and ancient artifacts, no one back then knew for sure how much of these stories was real. Even though modern people are farther away in time from these ancient civilizations, including the Minoans, the Achaeans, and the Mycenae, in some ways we now know more about these cultures than people in past eras did. In addition to stories, we have uncovered artifacts and architecture that tell us more about this ancient time.

Some of that mystery has been revealed to us, such as when the Palace of Knossos on Crete was uncovered in excavations in 1900, and even earlier, when the ruins of the once-great city of Troy were uncovered.

This mixture of reality and myth may never be archaeologically complete and may always be a source of some frustrations to those who want to know. Still, the art, architecture, and stories that remain help modern readers to understand the worldview. This appendix will explore these early semi-mythic times before recorded history.

MINOAN CIVILIZATION

The Minoan civilization was a Bronze Age civilization of Crete that flourished from about 3000 BC to about 1100 BC. Its name derives from Minos, either a dynastic title or the name of a particular ruler of Crete who has a place in Greek legend.

Crete became the foremost site of Bronze Age culture in the Aegean Sea, and in fact it was the first centre of high civilization in that area, beginning at the end of the third millennium BC. Reaching its peak about 1600 BC and the later 15th century BC, Minoan civilization was remarkable for its great cities and palaces, its extended trade throughout the Levant (the lands that border the Mediterranean on its eastern side) and beyond, and its use of writing. Its sophisticated art included elaborate seals, pottery (especially the famous Kamáres ware with its light-on-dark style of decoration), and, above all, delicate, vibrant frescoes found on palace walls. These frescoes display both secular and religious scenes, such as magical gardens, monkeys, and wild goats or fancifully dressed goddesses that testify to the Minoans' predominantly matriarchal religion. Among the most familiar motifs of Minoan art are the snake, symbol of the goddess, and the bull. The ritual of bull-leaping, found, for example, on cult vases, seems to have had a religious or magical basis.

By about 1580 BC Minoan civilization began to spread across the Aegean to neighbouring islands and to the mainland of Greece. Minoan cultural influence was reflected in the Mycenean culture of the mainland, which began to spread throughout the Aegean about 1500 BC.

By the middle of the 15th century the palace culture on Crete was destroyed by conquerors from the mainland. They established a new order on Crete, with centres at Knossos and Phaistos. Following the conquest, the island experienced a wonderful fusion of Cretan and mainland skills. The Late Minoan period (*c.* 1400–*c.* 1100 BC), however, was a time of marked decline in both economic power and aesthetic achievement.

Daedalus

The mythical Greek architect and sculptor Daedalus was said to have built, among other things, the paradigmatic Labyrinth for King Minos of Crete. Daedalus, whose name in Greek means "skillfully wrought," fell out of favour with Minos and was imprisoned; he fashioned wings of wax and feathers for himself and for his son Icarus and escaped to Sicily. Icarus, however, flew too near the Sun, and his wings melted; he fell into the sea and drowned. The island on which his body was washed ashore was later named Icaria. Minos pursued Daedalus to Sicily and was killed by the daughters of Cocalus. The story of Daedalus and Icarus has been richly mined by artists throughout the centuries.

The Greeks of the historic age attributed to Daedalus buildings and statues the origins of which were lost in the past. Later critics ascribed to him such innovations as representing humans in statues with their feet apart and their eyes open. A phase of early Greek art, Daedalic sculpture, is named for him.

Knossos

Knossos (Cnossus) was a city in ancient Crete, capital of the legendary King Minos, and the principal centre of the Minoan, the earliest of the Aegean civilizations. The site of Knossos stands on a knoll between the confluence of two streams and is located about 8 kilometres (5 miles) inland from Crete's northern coast. Excavations were begun at Knossos under Sir Arthur Evans in 1900 and revealed a palace and surrounding buildings that were the centre of a sophisticated Bronze Age culture that dominated the Aegean between about 1600 and 1400 BC.

The first human inhabitants of Knossos probably came there from Anatolia in the seventh millennium BC and established an agricultural society based on wheat and livestock raising. At the beginning of the Early Minoan period (3000–2000 BC) they began using bronze and making glazed pottery, engraved seals, and gold jewelry. A hieroglyphic script was invented, and trade with the Egyptians was undertaken. The first palace at Knossos was built at the beginning of the Middle Minoan period (2000–1580 BC). It consisted of isolated structures built around a rectangular court. Knossos produced fine polychrome pottery on a black glazed ground during this period. About 1720 BC a destructive earthquake leveled most of Knossos. The palace was rebuilt, this time with extensive colonnades and flights of stairs connecting the different buildings on the hilly site. The remains of this palace occupy the excavated site in the present day. The administrative and ceremonial quarters of the palace were on the west side of the central court, and the throne room in this area still contains the gypsum chair in which sat the kings of Knossos. This area of the palace also had long narrow basement rooms that served as storage magazines for wheat, oil, and treasure. Workshops were located on the northeast side of the central court, while residences were situated in the southeastern section. An elaborate system of drains, conduits, and pipes provided water and sanitation for the palace, and the whole urban complex was connected to other Cretan towns and ports by paved roads. The art of Minoan fresco painting reached its zenith at this time, with scenes of dancing, sports, and dolphins done in a naturalistic style. The Minoans also replaced their hieroglyphic script with a linear script known as Linear A.

About 1580 BC Minoan culture and influence began to be extended to mainland Greece, where it was further developed and emerged as the culture known as Mycenaean. The Mycenaeans, in turn, achieved control over Knossos sometime in the 15th century BC. The Linear A script was replaced by another script, Linear B, which is identical to that used at Mycenae and is most generally deemed the prototype of Greek. Detailed administrative records in Linear B found at Knossos indicate that at this time the city's Mycenaean rulers controlled much of central and western Crete.

Some time after about 1400 BC, what Evans called the "Last Palace" of Knossos was destroyed by a fire of uncertain origin, and fires destroyed many other Cretan settlements at this time. Knossos was reduced henceforth to the status of a mere town, and the political focus of the Aegean world shifted to Mycenae on the Greek mainland. Knossos continued to be inhabited through the subsequent centuries, though on a much-reduced scale.

Minos

The legendary ruler of Crete, Minos was the son of Zeus, the chief deity of the ancient Greeks, and of Europa, a

Phoenician princess and personification of the continent of Europe. Minos obtained the Cretan throne by the aid of the Greek god Poseidon, and from Knossos (or Gortyn) he gained control over the Aegean islands, colonizing many of them and ridding the sea of pirates. He married Pasiphae, the daughter of Helios, who bore him, among others, Androgeos, Ariadne, and Phaedra, and who was also the mother of the Minotaur.

Minos successfully warred against Athens and Megara to obtain redress after his son Androgeos was killed by the Athenians. In Athenian drama and legend Minos became the tyrannical exactor of the tribute of children to feed the Minotaur.

Having pursued Daedalus to Sicily, Minos was killed by the daughters of King Cocalus, who poured boiling water over him as he was taking a bath. After his death he became a judge in Hades.

Although Athens preserved a hostile tradition, the general account shows Minos as a powerful, just ruler, very closely associated with religion and ritual. In light of excavations in Crete, many scholars consider that Minos was a royal or dynastic title for the priestly rulers of Bronze Age, or Minoan, Knossos.

MYCENAEAN CIVILIZATION

The Mycenaeans were a group of warlike Indo-European peoples who entered Greece from the north starting *c.* 1900 BC and established a Bronze Age culture on the mainland and nearby islands. Their culture was dependent on that of the Minoans of Crete, who for a time politically dominated them. They threw off Minoan control *c.* 1400 BC and were dominant in the Aegean until they themselves were overwhelmed by the next wave of invaders *c.* 1150 BC. Mycenae continued to exist as a city-state into the period of Greek dominance, but by the second century AD it was in ruins. Mycenaean myths and legends lived on through oral transmission into later stages of Greek civilization and form the basis of Homeric epic and Greek tragedy. Their language is believed to be the most ancient form of Greek.

Achaeans

The Achaeans were an ancient Greek people, identified in Homer, who along with the Danaoi and the Argeioi, besieged Troy. Their area as described by Homer—the mainland and western isles of Greece, Crete, Rhodes, and adjacent isles, except the Cyclades—is precisely that covered by the activities of the Mycenaeans in the 14th–13th century BC, as revealed by archaeology. From this and other evidence, some authorities have identified the Achaeans with the Mycenaeans. Other evidence suggests that the Achaeans did not enter Greece until the so-called Dorian invasions of the 12th century BC. It seems at least possible that Homer's Achaean chiefs, with their short genealogies and their renown for infiltrating into Mycenaean kingships by way of military service and dynastic marriages, held power in the Mycenaean world for only a few generations in its last, warlike, and semibarbarous phase, until replaced by the Dorians, their relatively close kindred. The Achaeans of the northern Peloponnese in historic times were reckoned by Herodotus to be descendants of these earlier Achaeans. The name Ahhiyawā, occurring in Hittite documents of the 14th and 13th centuries BC, has sometimes been identified with the Achaeans, but this is disputed.

Agamemnon

Agamemnon, in Greek legend, was king of Mycenae or Argos. He was the son (or grandson) of Atreus, king of Mycenae, and Aërope and was the brother of Menelaus. After Atreus was murdered by his nephew Aegisthus (son of Thyestes), Agamemnon and Menelaus took refuge with Tyndareus, king of Sparta, whose daughters, Clytemnestra and Helen, they respectively married. By Clytemnestra, Agamemnon had a son, Orestes, and three daughters, Iphigeneia (Iphianassa), Electra (Laodice), and Chrysothemis. Menelaus succeeded Tyndareus, and Agamemnon recovered his father's kingdom.

When Paris (Alexandros), son of King Priam of Troy, carried off Helen, Agamemnon called on the princes of the country to unite in a war of revenge against the Trojans. He himself furnished 100 ships and was chosen commander in chief of the combined forces. The fleet assembled at the port of Aulis in Boeotia but was prevented from sailing by calms or contrary winds that were sent by the goddess Artemis because Agamemnon had in some way offended her. To appease the wrath of Artemis, Agamemnon was forced to sacrifice his own daughter Iphigeneia.

After the capture of Troy, Cassandra, Priam's daughter, fell to Agamemnon's lot in the distribution of the prizes of war. On his return he landed in Argolis, where Aegisthus, who in the interval had seduced Agamemnon's wife, treacherously carried out the murders of Agamemnon, his comrades, and Cassandra. In *Agamemnon*, by the Greek poet and dramatist Aeschylus, however, Clytemnestra was made to do the killing. The murder was avenged by Orestes, who returned to slay both his mother and her paramour.

Mycenae

The prehistoric Greek city of Mycenae in the Peloponnese was celebrated by Homer as "broad-streeted" and "golden." According to legend, Mycenae was the capital of Agamemnon, the Achaean king who sacked the city of Troy. It was set, as Homer says, "in a nook of Árgos," with a natural citadel formed by the ravines between the mountains of Hagios Elias and Zara, and furnished with a fine perennial spring named Perseia (after Perseus, the legendary founder of Mycenae). It is the chief Late Bronze Age site in mainland Greece. Systematic excavation of the site began in 1840, but the most celebrated discoveries there were those of Heinrich Schliemann. The term *Mycenaean* is often used in reference to the Late Bronze Age of mainland Greece in general and of the islands except Crete.

There was a settlement at Mycenae in the Early Bronze Age, but all structures of that or of the succeeding Middle Bronze Age have, with insignificant exceptions, been swept away by later buildings. The existing palace must have been reconstructed in the 14th century BC. The whole area is studded with tombs that have yielded many art objects and artifacts.

From the Lion Gate at the entrance to Mycenae's citadel, a graded road 3.6 metres (12 feet) wide leads to a ramp supported by a five-terrace wall and thence to the southwestern entrance of the palace. The latter is composed of two main blocks—one originally covering the top of the hill but largely destroyed on the erection of the Hellenistic temple and the other occupying the lower terrace to the south banked up artificially on its western edge. The two blocks were separated by two parallel east-west corridors with storerooms opening off them. The existence of a palace shrine on the upper terrace seems implied by discoveries of a magnificent ivory group consisting of two goddesses and an infant god with fragments of painted tripod altars and other objects.

At the southwestern corner of the later palace, the west lobby led to the grand staircase of 22 steps, a landing, and another 17 or 18 steps culminating in a small forecourt that afforded entrance to the great court and to a square room immediately to the north. There an oblong area with a raised plaster border has been interpreted by some scholars as the base for a throne where the king sat in audience. Other scholars, however, have regarded it as a hearth and the room as a guest chamber. The throne might then have stood on the right of the megaron (great central hall), a part that has now disappeared. Both the porch and the main portion of the megaron had floors of painted stucco with borders of gypsum slabs and with frescoes on the walls, one apparently representing a battle in front of a citadel. In the centre was a round plaster hearth enclosed by four wooden columns, possibly implying the existence of a clerestory. The 10 plaster layers of the hearth and 4 of the floor suggest that this hall was in use for a considerable time. The roof was probably flat. East of the corridor lay a series of rooms, the most interesting known from its decoration as "the room of the curtain frescoes."

Within the citadel were various houses of retainers. The most imposing, "the house of the columns," rose to three stories in height. South of the grave circle lie the ruins of the "ramp house," the "south house," and the "house of Tsountas." Another building, known as "the granary," from the carbonized barley, wheat, and vetches found in its basement, was erected in the 13th century BC between the Cyclopean citadel wall and one of the grave circles. It continued in use up to the destruction of the city by fire about 1100 BC.

The Late Mycenaean period (1400–1100 BC) was one of great prosperity in the Peloponnese. After the destruction of Knossos, on Minoan Crete, Mycenae became the dominant power in the Aegean, where its fleet must have controlled the nearer seas and colonized the Cyclades, Crete, Cyprus, the Dodecanese, northern Greece and Macedonia, western Asia Minor, Sicily, and some sites in Italy. Mycenaean, rather than Minoan, goods could be found in the markets of Egypt, Syria, and Palestine. Mycenaean raiders harried the coasts of the Egyptians and the Hittites, and at a date traditionally supposed to be 1180, but by some scholars now estimated at about 1250 BC, Agamemnon and his followers sacked the great city of Troy.

In the 16th century BC, Mycenaean art was temporarily dominated by the influences of Minoan art. Cretan artists must have immigrated to the mainland, and local varieties of all the Minoan arts arose at Mycenae. Minoan naturalism and exuberance were tempered by Greek formality and sense of balance, which were already visible in Middle Helladic painted wares and were later to culminate in the splendid Geometric pottery of the Dipylon cemetery at Athens.

Until the mid-20th century, Mycenaean literacy was attested only by a few symbols painted on vases, but in 1952 the excavation of "the house of the oil merchant" and "the house of the wine merchant" outside the walls disclosed a number of tablets in the Linear B script first identified at Knossos and later interpreted by the English architect and cryptographer Michael Ventris to be an earlier form of the Greek language.

Mycenae was burned and destroyed, perhaps by invading Dorians, about 1100 BC, but the outer city was not deserted. Graves of the Protogeometric and Geometric periods have been excavated. Mycenae evidently continued to exist as a small city-state, and the walls were not pulled down. Early in the sixth century BC a temple, from which one fine relief survives, was erected. In 480 Mycenae sent 400 men to fight against the Persians at Thermopylae, and its men were at Plataea in 479. In 470, however, its aggressive neighbour Árgos, which had been neutral in the Persian war, took an ignoble revenge by besieging Mycenae, and in 468 Árgos destroyed it. In the Hellenistic period Mycenae revived, and a new temple was built on the crown of the acropolis. In 235 BC the Argive tyrant Aristippus was killed there, and the city wall was repaired. Nabis of Sparta carried off some of the young men about 195 BC, and an inscription from 194 refers to their detention. A few Roman objects have been found, but when the Greek traveler and geographer Pausanias visited the site about AD 160, he found it in ruins.

The Trojan War

The Trojan War, a legendary conflict between the early Greeks and the people of Troy in western Anatolia, was dated by later Greek authors to the 12th or 13th century BC. The war stirred the imagination of the ancient Greeks more than any other event in their history, and it was celebrated in the *Iliad* and the *Odyssey* of Homer, as well as a number of other early works now lost, and frequently provided material for the great dramatists of the Classical Age. It also figures in the literature of the Romans (e.g., Virgil's *Aeneid*) and of later European peoples down to the 21st century.

In the traditional accounts, Paris, son of the Trojan king, ran off with Helen, wife of Menelaus of Sparta, whose brother Agamemnon then led a Greek expedition against Troy. The ensuing war lasted 10 years, finally ending when the Greeks pretended to withdraw, leaving behind them a large wooden horse with a raiding party concealed inside. When the Trojans brought the horse into their city, the hidden Greeks opened the gates to their comrades, who then sacked Troy, massacred its men, and carried off its women. This version was recorded centuries later. The extent to which it reflects actual historical events is not known.

GLOSSARY

acrimonious Bitter and stinging in nature.

agoge The military education regime for all male Spartan citizens.

alluvial Relating to land with sand, gravel, or clay deposited by flowing water.

amphictyony An association of states in ancient Greece united to protect a common religious centre.

antiquarianism The study of the material culture of ancient societies.

archon Chief officer or magistrate who presided over a city-state.

armistice A cease-fire between opponents so they can discuss peace terms

citadel Fortress built as part of a city's defense, often located in the central town of a polis.

clerestory The upper part of an outside wall that contains windows for letting in natural light, usually in a church or cathedral.

cleruchy Settlement established by the Athenian government outside of Athens wherein settlers retained Athenian citizenship and rights.

demagogue A person who gains power and popularity by manipulating emotions of the people.

deme A village of ancient Greece, with officials at the local level as well as representatives at the state (polis) level.

diaspora A group migration from a country or region.

dithyramb Song honouring or praising a particular subject, often the god Dionysus.

elegiac Expressing sorrow for something in the irrecoverable past.

epinician Ode written in honour of an athlete's victory.

epoch A period of time marked by significant or distinctive features.

eponymous Describing an object, such as a city or institution, that is named after a person.

euphemism The substitution of a mild or agreeable word or expression in place of one that is potentially offensive.

fresco Painting done on wet plaster on a wall or ceiling.

gymnasium Area where male athletes trained for competitive games, socialized, and engaged in intellectual discussion.

gypsum A mineral used in manufacturing cements and plasters.

hegemony Leadership or influence of one nation over others.

hektemorage System in which individuals voluntarily gave a sixth of their produce to richer or more powerful individuals in exchange for protection or other benefits.

helot Serf in ancient Sparta.

hoplite A heavily armed foot soldier of ancient Greece.

inchoate Not yet fully developed, unorganized.

isonomia Equality of rights.

liturgy In ancient Greece, a public service in which an individual financed a state project.

meretricious Pretentious, gawdy.

numismatic Pertaining to money or currency.

onomastic Relating to proper names.

ostracism Banishment from a state of an individual who is considered a threat. The term of banishment was determined by a vote and the individual did not receive a trial.

perioikoi Individuals, often from neighbouring areas, who could obtain only some of the rights and privileges afforded to full citizens.

polis A city-state of ancient Greece.

quiescence Quiet, inactive.

recalcitrant Resisting authority, hard to deal with.

sacrosanct Considered sacred.

satrapal Ruled under the ancient Persian monarchy.

symposia Banquet or feast, intended for males, where ideas on politics and philosophy were often exchanged and poetry was read.

synoecism The merging of smaller town and village units into a single larger city.

timocracy System of governance in which property ownership is required for office.

tripartite Consisting of three parts.

trireme An ancient warship that had three tiers of oars on each side of the boat.

vulgate Text or reading that has gained wide acceptance.

zenith The highest point.

BIBLIOGRAPHY

A wealth of information on ancient Greek civilization is provided by the relevant volumes of *The Cambridge Ancient History* (1923–2005), most of which are in their 2nd edition. Of special note are John Boardman et al. (eds.), *Persia, Greece, and the Western Mediterranean, c. 525–479 B.C.*, vol. 4, 2nd ed. (1988); D.M. Lewis et al. (eds.), *The Fifth Century B.C.*, vol. 5, 2nd ed. (1992); and D.M. Lewis et al. (eds.), *The Fourth Century B.C.*, vol. 6, 2nd ed. (1994). Note also the excellent accompanying *Plates to Volume IV*, new ed. (1988), and *Plates to Volumes V and VI*, new ed. (1994), both ed. by John Boardman. There is a great deal of new and up-to-date material in Simon Hornblower and Antony Spawforth, *The Oxford Classical Dictionary*, 3rd ed. (1996). John Boardman, Jasper Griffin, and Oswyn Murray (eds.), *The Oxford History of the Classical World* (1986), is also worth consulting. Michael Grant and Rachel Kitzinger (eds.), *Civilization of the Ancient Mediterranean: Greece and Rome*, 3 vol. (1988), discusses the geography, inhabitants, arts, language, religion, politics, technology, and economy of the area from the early first millennium BC to the late fifth century AD. Broad coverage of the physical and cultural settings and of archaeological discoveries is also provided by Peter Levi, *Atlas of the Greek World* (1980); and Nicholas G.L. Hammond (ed.), *Atlas of the Greek and Roman World in Antiquity* (1981). Overviews of the histories of Greek civilization include Nicholas G.L. Hammond, *A History of Greece to 322 B.C.*, 3rd ed. (1986); J.B. Bury and Russell Meiggs, *A History of Greece to the Death of Alexander the Great*, 4th ed. (1975), revised to take account of new evidence; Oswyn Murray, *Early Greece*, 2nd ed. (1993); J.K. Davies, *Democracy and Classical Greece*, 2nd ed. (1993); F.W. Walbank, *The Hellenistic World*, rev. ed. (1992); Amélie Kuhrt, *The Ancient Near East, c. 3000–330 BC*, 2 vol. (1995); Robin Osborne, *Greece in the Making, 1200–479 BC* (1996); Simon Hornblower, *The Greek World, 479–323 BC*, 3rd ed. (2002); and Graham Shipley, *The Greek World After Alexander, 323–30 B.C.* (2000). Many ancient historical sources are available in *The Loeb Classical Library* series, with original text and parallel English translation; and in the series *Translated Documents of Greece and Rome*.

INDEX

A

B

C

D

E

F

G

H

N

O

P

R

V

W

X

Z